Rape in Paradise

Rape in Paradise

THEON WRIGHT

Introduction by Glen Grant

MUTUAL PUBLISHING
HONOLULU

Printed and bound in Australia by
The Book Printer, Victoria
Cover design by Tamara Moan, Bechlen/Gonzalez Inc.
Cover photo by Douglas Peebles
ISBN 0-935180-89-3

*This book contains the complete text of the
original hardbound 1966 first edition.*

RAPE IN PARADISE

Introduction by Glen Grant © 1990 by Mutual Publishing

Contents

Illustrations

The Legacy of the Massie Case

Introduction by Glen Grant

It had all the ingredients of a best-selling sordid potboiler: The setting is a lazy Pacific town where Polynesians and Asians live amicably under the patriarchal control of a small, Caucasian sugar oligarchy. A young, good-looking white woman claims that late one night she is abducted from Waikiki and taken to a lonely tropical road where she is raped and beaten by several Hawaiian ''hoodlums.'' A few hours later five island men of Hawaiian, Japanese, and Chinese ancestry are arrested. Circumstantial evidence strongly points to them as the alleged rapists. Because the victim's husband is an officer in the United States Navy, the Admiral of the Pearl Harbor fleet, who has strong racial prejudices, applies political pressure to make an example of the defendants. This is called ''protecting white women.''

As the trial of the alleged rapists bogs down in conflicting evidence, exposing the police force's incompetence, the husband, assisted by two navy buddies and his mother-in-law, takes matters into his own hands. One of the Hawaiian defendants is kidnapped as he stands in front of the courthouse, supposedly makes a "confession" to the husband, and then is murdered in a fit of insane jealousy. The husband and his accomplices attempt to dispose of the corpse, but are arrested following a high-speed automobile chase.

The murder trial of the husband, his naval friends, and the grief-stricken mother-in-law attracts national attention as one of the country's leading criminal lawyers agrees to represent the four defendants. Relying on the "unwritten law" that allows a husband to vindicate his wife's honor, the case for the defense becomes a *cause célèbre* for politicians who doubt that a non-white community in American territory can govern itself. When a measure of justice prevails and the defendants are found guilty and sentenced to ten years in prison, the pressure from Washington, D.C. is irresistible—the sentence is commuted by the governor to one hour spent in his office, sipping tea. The defendants then depart the islands, leaving behind a racial sore that will take decades to heal.

If the sex, racism, political intrigue, and violence of the infamous Massie case were hard-boiled detective fiction, it would be criticized for being too contrived. But as history the series of criminal events that shook Honolulu society beginning on the evening of September 12, 1931, are stark reminders that Hawaii's past has sometimes been shaped by very ugly passions that seem wholly out of place in an island environment so seemingly tranquil. As one wades through the conflicting evidence of the "Ala Moana Rape Case," the heavy-handed involvement of the navy in a civilian criminal matter, the murder of Joseph Kahahawai, Clarence Darrow's "unwritten law" defense, and the perversion of justice represented in the commutation of the sentence, it is hard not to be stunned by the brazen racism that was unleashed less than sixty years ago in a community now noted for its "aloha spirit."

It is most fortunate that *Rape in Paradise* by Theon Wright, one of the better popular histories of the Massie case, should be reprinted soon after *Blood and Orchids,* the widely read fictional account of Hawaii's most famous crime, which was recently made into a television mini-series. With his dramatic hour-by-hour account of the events surrounding the evening of September 12th through the murder of Kahahawai, the legal complexities of the celebrated trials, and the behind-the-scenes political maneuvering, Theon Wright offers an important factual account that is far more compelling than any fictional retelling. As a reporter who covered the Massie trial and a family friend of Clarence Darrow, Wright writes with a direct, first-hand narrative style that teems with the life of Honolulu's streets, places, and people in the 1930s. Rather than the misspelled street names and fabricated characters found in *Blood and Orchids*, Wright's story is a slice of reality from Hawaii's past written with the insight of a *kamaaina*, or long-time resident.

Most importantly, Wright's work strikes at the heart of the injustices represented by the Massie case. Although later criminal investigations would exonerate the so-called "Ala Moana Boys" from their complicity in Mrs. Massie's abduction, beating, and rape, the five men would carry the stigma of the false allegations for the rest of their lives. Former Hawaii Supreme Court Associate Justice Masaji Marumoto has persuasively argued that the stigma of "rape in paradise" was also borne by the Territory of Hawaii—statehood for the islands, he avers, was delayed for three decades in part because of the ugly racial undercurrents exposed in the Massie case. Hawaii's multi-racial population was deemed by national politicians as simply unassimilated and incapable of self-rule.

Perhaps the bitterest legacy left by the Massie case was caused by the commutation of the sentence of the convicted murderers to a mere one hour spent in the governor's office. As many critics claimed in 1932, this was but one more instance of "one law for the *haoles* and one law for the non-whites." That a handful of individuals could be placed above the written law to protect political and racial interests reveals, Wright stresses, the audacious, strong-handed tactics of the territorial authorities. In the fictional *Blood and Orchids* account of the Massie case, the murder defendants receive their just punishment of several years of hard labor at Oahu Prison. Perhaps the truth would have seemed too fantastic or depressing for a modern audience.

Today Honolulu is the eleventh largest city in the United States. The population of the islands is close to one million. Crimes far more violent than those committed in the 1930s are commonplace. Rape in paradise has become a very real, tragic fact of island life. Racial tensions have not disappeared as economic inequalities, growing tourism, and the influx of new immigrants from Southeast Asia and the mainland United States arouse ethnic resentment. One might very well criticize the reprinting of *Rape in Paradise* by asking "Why dredge up this ugly past? Doesn't reliving the Massie case just exacerbate current racial tensions?" As an author of detective stories that attempt to evoke the crimes of pre-World War II Hawaii and a co-author of a three-act play *(Vanishing Shadows)* that depicts the lesser known but equally shocking Three Kings kidnaping and murder case of 1928, I have frequently faced such criticism. One reviewer of *Vanishing Shadows* accused the play of "exposing an open wound" and for what good purpose? The titillation of crime? The compulsion of a good mystery? Isn't there enough present-day violence unleashed in Hawaii without indulging in historic crimes?

I suspect that there is a strong element of voyeurism in the popular interest in fictional and non-fictional crime accounts. The exposed passions of the Massie case have their tabloid allure as does any act of violence that shocks our sensibilities. Yet there is an aspect of the Massie case that warrants particular attention. Among Hawaii's governing elite in the pre-World War II era, there had been a tendency to deny the existence of racial problems in the islands. After all, in the *noblesse oblige* days of Old Hawaii following annexation in 1898, for the white oligarchy to admit racial tensions or conflicts would have been to jeopardize their very tenuous balance of political and economic control. "Hawaii doesn't have the same racial conditions or problems as the mainland" was a truism often repeated for the benefit of outsiders and local "troublemakers."

The Massie case blew the lid off that platitude. And in the effort to deny the social, economic, and racial dimensions of the crisis, the problems were vastly compounded. In modern Hawaii, where news about crime, violence, and racism can have a devastating effect on tourism and our "public image," there seems a similar reluctance to openly address and ameliorate the deep-seated racial and economic injustices that continue to characterize some aspects of island society. As Theon Wright's forthright narrative of the Massie case reveals, the denial of social ills cannot protect our island paradise—it only temporarily shields us from an unexorcised fear to which one day we must surely fall victim.

Foreword

Both crime and justice are parts of civilized society. Crime is inevitable; it is a breakdown or fault in the orderly processes of society and will exist as long as societies are made up of human beings. Justice is the effort of society to repair the fault. Crime is to be expected, since humans are never perfect; but the failure of justice may be more damaging than crime itself. It may indicate a fundamental breakdown in the society that permitted the crime. That, in a sense, is the reason for this book.

On a Saturday night in September, 1931, a crime was committed in Honolulu. A young woman wearing a green evening dress walked out of the lighted doorway of a tavern in the Waikiki Beach section of Honolulu and disappeared into the night. For nearly two hours she was not seen by anyone who knew her, or anyone who at least ever came forward and said he saw her. When she was found, it was on a lonely beach road several miles from the tavern. Her face was badly bruised, her mouth bleeding; later it was found that her jaw was broken. At first she said that she had been beaten up by "some Hawaiian boys"; finally she told police she had been raped.

The young woman was Thalia Massie, the wife of a United States Naval officer; and the story she told, which shocked the people of Hawaii and ultimately a whole nation, was to become known as "the Massie case." This case almost ended self-government in Hawaii. For twenty years it delayed Hawaii's entry into the Federal Union as a state; it almost destroyed the Hawaiian people as a race; and it virtually wrecked Thalia Massie's life.

The tragedy of that Saturday night in Honolulu has never been clearly understood, even by the people of Hawaii—and certainly not

9

RAPE IN PARADISE

by the people on the mainland. Part—but only part—of the story was revealed in two sensational trials. The first trial involved five youths: a Japanese, two Hawaiians and two of mixed blood (Chinese-Hawaiian and Japanese-Hawaiian) who were accused of criminally assaulting Thalia Massie. In the second trial, Clarence Darrow, one of the great criminal lawyers of that era, was called in to defend four white people accused of murdering a Hawaiian boy—one of the five Thalia Massie said had attacked her.

In many ways, the Massie case was the Dreyfus case of the Pacific. Like the Dreyfus case, which changed the course of French history, it had racial overtones, of a different character but no less malignant. It also lay buried for years, as the Dreyfus case did before Emile Zola resurrected it. The record of the Massie case has been allowed to lie moldering in the criminal archives of Hawaii and the dead-files of the United States Navy for thirty-five years. And again like the Dreyfus case, it involved a military caste.

Clarence Darrow came down to Honolulu, as he later said, "hoping to heal racial wounds, but now they are deeper." This was true. The tragedy of the Massie case lay in the fact that while a whole nation of white people believed Thalia Massie's story, two juries in Honolulu refused to believe it. As Darrow prophetically described it, she was left "pursued, shamed and hounded from one end of the country to the other, a living inheritor of Trojan Cassandra's monumental woe."

Darrow was usually on the side of the underdog; but in this case he was in the unusual position of being—as Disraeli put it—"on the side of the angels." He was defending Thalia Massie's husband and her mother, a proud and haughty woman from the blue grass of Kentucky; and two Naval enlisted men. This little group of white people, possessed of an inborn arrogance in a land of dark-skinned people, was charged with the "honor slaying" of the Hawaiian boy.

Darrow called it "the hardest story in human history . . . the fate of a whole family bound up in a criminal act committed by someone else."

The strange mystery of the Massie case seems to lie in that last phrase—"a criminal act committed by someone else." Was it a criminal act committed by someone else? Or did Thalia Massie lie?

Three official investigations—one by the Governor of Hawaii, one by the Navy, and a third by the Public Prosecutor of Honolulu—failed to clear up the mystery, although the first of these, carried out by the Pinkerton Detective Agency, produced at least one startling result. In its official report, the agency expressed the belief that the identification of the five boys accused by Thalia Massie as her attackers was "in error" and that "the kidnaping and rape, as described by Mrs. Massie, could not have been by the accused."

This, of course, raised the specter of a monumental blunder—and tragedy. If this was true, Thalia Massie's husband killed an innocent man; and the "unwritten law" which was quoted freely by the Navy and some of the leading *haoles* (white people) of Honolulu could hardly apply.

In many ways, the Massie case was a complete failure of justice. Under the influence of this "code of honor," imported largely from the tier of Southern states on the mainland, the verdict of the jury was countermanded, and Thalia Massie's husband and mother were allowed to go free. But justice, like nature, abhors a vacuum. The solution to the case seemed convenient at the time; but if the need for justice, that intangible glue which holds civilized people together, is to be overlooked or forgotten depending on whose ox is gored, the fabric of society will eventually disintegrate.

Writing of such matters is a delicate and difficult matter at best; but it is particularly difficult when the events are comparatively recent—within a space of two generations—and many of the principals are still living, some with the bitterness of scarred memories and others with unhealed wounds of conscience. Who is to say that dragging out skeletons and rattling old bones is justified, on any basis? There will always be those who contend that the dead past should bury its dead.

There is no doubt that the events of the Massie case hurt a race of kindly, tolerant people. It may have delivered the *coup de grâce* to this old and graceful remnant of a Polynesian civilization that was already dying out. The circumstances that led up to the Massie case may have been forgotten, but the aftermath, as well as the reasons for these tragic happenings, cannot be wiped away merely by loss of memory.

Perhaps this is the nearest we can come to explaining the purpose of this book. It is not an effort to dredge up things that might better be left buried; nor is it an attempt to justify or condemn anyone. The writer was a newspaperman at the time, covering the Massie case and other events related to it. Later he collaborated, as a reporter, with investigators working on the case, in an effort to uncover facts that lay behind the story told by Thalia Massie.

A good many of these facts—some now part of official records— were known at the time, but were not publicly disclosed. Others were not clearly understood. Still others are parts of court records. By placing these facts and reports end to end, as it were, in the clearer perspective of the three and a half decades that have elapsed since the time of "Hawaii's shame," it may be possible to clarify the mystery, even if it cannot at this late date be entirely solved.

The one overriding reason for reviving the events of the Massie case—more important than the fate of the Hawaiian boy who was killed, or of Thalia Massie and her mother and husband, or even the fate of the Hawaiian people as a race—is the single axiom, or truism, that we must look backward in order to look forward.

The Massie case is not without significance in this decade. In a very direct way, it was a capsule prototype of America today, in the throes of racial disturbances that have marred our concept of human freedom and may have shattered the faith of many people in democratic processes.

Honolulu in the 1930s was not a Selma, Alabama, in the 1960s; yet there are many elements of the Massie case that are not too dissimilar. They indicate what happens to a society of presumably free people under the control and guidance of a small group of self-appointed "elite" or "supremacists"—a situation that is not unfamiliar today.

The inescapable course of events that followed the Massie trials will not seem too dissimilar, either, to a discerning reader. Even in the dissimilar environments of Hawaii and Alabama, we may be able to trace a pattern of what is happening today—and what may happen tomorrow. There is no need to pass judgments or draw conclusions in advance; the events will speak quite plainly for themselves.

12

Rape in Paradise

A Night on the Ala Moana

A narrow road, paved with a thin layer of blacktop that was broken in places so that the coral underlayer showed through like white scars in the moonlight, ran along the beach from the populous Waikiki section into downtown Honolulu, near the waterfront. It was the back road into town, and it was called the Ala Moana, which means "beach road." The road began where John Ena Road turned southward into Fort De Russy and the Waikiki Beach area, curving to the northward through an open stretch of algarroba thickets, scrub lantana, and clusters of *panini* cactus. It continued for nearly three miles along this desolate stretch, unmarked by a single street light or dwelling. It finally came out at Kewalo Basin, where the fishing boats lay along the wharves; and from this point it debouched into downtown Honolulu.

This lonely and largely untraveled road was also a kind of poor man's Lover's Lane. There was a small cleared area, near the town end, where an animal quarantine station had once stood. The station had been abandoned, with only the cement foundations left. Scattered rubbish, cigarette stubs and a few broken bottles marked the presence of those who, for one reason or another, chose to drive out to the seclusion of this unsightly place, possibly to watch the

15

waves crash over the reef and roll toward the city dumps, just beyond Kewalo Basin.

The Ala Moana is an entirely different place today. Tall office buildings, stores and gaudy pastel-colored apartment houses rear their neotropical architecture over the bleak area where algarroba and lantana once thrived; and the huge Aloha Shopping Center lines the *mauka,* or "mountain" side of the road. On the seaward side a spacious public park stretches along the shore, laced with coral pathways and provided with bathhouses which offer free access to the beach. Remnants of the old quarantine station have been obliterated, as have all other traces of what was once known as "Hawaii's shame." The park itself was built to erase painful reminders of a shameful event supposed to have taken place on the old Ala Moana some thirty-five years ago.

Honolulu in the prewar 1930s was a far different city from what it is today. It was a small, bustling port, with a rising tide of seagoing commerce, just out of its nineteenth-century swaddling clothes, beset with growing pains, and not quite adult. A onetime columnist for the *Pacific Commercial Advertiser* (now the *Honolulu Advertiser*) described it as "the smallest big city in the world"—a phrase subsequently expropriated, in a slightly different form, by Reno, Nevada.

In many ways, Honolulu was like Reno. In spite of the National Prohibition Act then in force, locally distilled *okolehao,* the Hawaiian equivalent of "white mule," flowed freely. A rising tide of tourists, known as *malihini haoles,* or "new whites," had begun to pour into the Islands, many settling there to form another major ingredient of the racial and social mixtures in the "melting pot of the Pacific." Had Honolulu been farther south along the trade routes to the Antipodes, like Pago Pago, Souva or Nouméa, it might have gone on living a life of sleepy tropical torpor; or if it had been closer to the Mainland of America, it might have become a small version of San Francisco. Farther to the West, near the Asiatic continent, it could have been a minor Manila or Shanghai.

As it was, it was none of these. Situated squarely on the crossroads of the Pacific, and lying within the tropical belt, it was a mixture of all these places, and yet like none of them. Honolulu had collected, in the course of its adolescence, the best and the worst from both sides of the Pacific. It had the virtues and vices of both the East and the West. In the lower downtown section, for example, shrewd Chinese merchants, some of whom had gotten rich in the opium trade during the reign of King Kalakaua, sat smugly in strange-smelling stores and toted up their wealth on old Chinese abacuses.

Along the foothills, rising behind the tree-matted city, was a different sort of community, representing no visible vices, but on the other hand an austere morality, not unmixed with the rewards that came from early missionary activities, such as spacious mansions lying on broad, well-tended land with magnificent tropical foliage. These were the homes of the *kamaaina haoles*—the "old whites," whose forebears had been tight-fisted Scottish and English merchants, shrewd Yankee traders, and most of all, the founders of the missionary dynasties who had come to Hawaii from New England early in the nineteenth century to spread the Gospel among the natives of the Sandwich Islands.

The descendants of the missionaries were now the great landowners, controlling nearly all the business in the Islands; introducing modern agricultural methods, new political systems, and, to some extent, replacing the old Hawaiian caste system of royalty and subjects with their own more civilized caste system.

There was another part of Honolulu to which tourists were seldom taken, and which old-timers preferred not to see. This was the lowland area north of the waterfront, known as Iwelei and Palama. This section housed the slums of Honolulu, and was filled with strange smells, muddy streets and small frame houses that were little more than shacks. The sweet, sickly odor of the pineapple canneries, mingled with the stench of the salty marshlands below the city, was wafted across the grimy flatland until it became a natural smell to the inhabitants. There were small Chinese stores and many Filipino barber shops in Iwelei. The latter had lady barbers, and were patronized by soldiers from Schofield Barracks and sailors from Pearl Harbor, as part of the residual business inherited from an earlier day when Honolulu was a brawling windjammer port, visited by sailors from all the ports of the world. This part of

17

Honolulu had become a conglomeration of poverty, vice and disease; and it was here that many of the young people of Honolulu grew up.

These were a mixture of many races—Hawaiians, part-Hawaiians, Portuguese, Japanese, Chinese and Filipinos. There were few *haoles* in this neighborhood; and most of the residents of the area learned at an early age to shout at the white boys: *"Haole pilau!"* This, loosely translated, means "the white boy stinks."

In spite of the lack of white people in the community—or possibly because of it—the boys in Palama led a rather cheerful life, growing up largely in isolation from the sons of the white merchants and sugar planters who lived in the foothills. At night they would gather around the open fronts of *saimin* shops, chewing on a "crack-seed" or cheap Chinese candies; and some of the older boys would frequent the windowless "shops" where beer could be obtained. Or they would cluster under street lamps on the muddy, unpaved roads of Palama and Kalihi, farther to the north, playing guitars and singing sweet, plaintive melodies of old Hawaii, such as Queen Liliuokalani's love song, *"Imi au i au oe,"* or even such ribald songs as "Manuela Boy!" and "Spilling Swipes on a Red Holoku." For the most part, they were a happy people, slightly bitter at the loss of land and the easygoing life their forefathers had led; but still not bitter enough to do much about it.

On the night of September 12, 1931, five boys from this area met more or less by accident on the other side of town, at Waikiki Park, a glittering haven of syncopated sound, with shooting galleries, roller coaster, Ferris wheel, and a dance hall. The Order of Eagles had given a dance at the pavilion that night, and two of the boys—one Hawaiian and the other Japanese-Hawaiian—had wanted to "catch the last dance"; so they had left a *luau*—a Hawaiian feast—in their own neighborhood and driven out to Waikiki in a car owned by one of the boys. The two who wanted to dance had gone into the pavilion, and the other three—a Japanese, another Hawaiian and a Chinese-Hawaiian—remained outside beside the car. Finally they decided to drive back to the other side of town, and return later.

Waikiki Park was located at the intersection of Kalakaua Avenue, the broad thoroughfare which ran all the way from Waikiki into town, and John Ena Road. The latter street, as has been noted, forked into two roads a couple of blocks toward the beach, the northern fork being the old Ala Moana road.

There was nothing unusual about this Saturday night; and there was nothing unusual about the five boys from the northern side of town being there. They all had met casually at the *luau*. One of the boys, a powerful Hawaiian called Joe Kalani, was a bit drunker than the others and stayed in the back seat of the car, half asleep. The driver was the Japanese called Shorty, and the third boy in the car was the Chinese-Hawaiian, Henry Chang.

They had decided that before returning to the park they would stop by at the *luau* again, and see if there was any beer left.

Ala Wai Inn, Saturday Night, September 12, 1931

It was Saturday night at the Ala Wai—in other words, "Navy night." This was the night when local people stayed away, leaving the place to the Navy. The dark-skinned doorkeeper stood at the brightly lighted entrance, framed against the subdued light from the dance floor. He smiled and nodded affably as each group of Navy officers and their wives and friends came up, ushering them to their booths or calling to the waitresses inside. He was called Joe, and only a few knew his last name, which was Freitas. He was a short, swarthy man with instinctive friendliness and the manners of a professional floorwalker.

Most of the officers wore mufti—white linen suits; and Joe knew from experience that they were mostly lieutenants. He could always spot Navy people; to begin with, nobody but Navy people would come to the Ala Wai wearing coats. Local *haoles*, or *hapa-haoles* like Joe Freitas (he was half-Hawaiian and half-Portuguese), seldom wore coats anywhere in the evening, unless it was at the Royal Hawaiian or the Moana Hotel *lanai*, where coats were required. They were not required at the Ala Wai; but Navy people came there wearing coats because it seemed more in keeping with their position in the community. For the most part the junior of-

19

The Ala Wai Inn. In the foreround is the Ala Wai Canal.

ficers could not afford the Royal Hawaiian, or even the Moana, so they came to the Ala Wai, which was cheaper without being tawdry.

There was always a good orchestra at the Ala Wai, and the place was lively. It had once been a single-story hotel, facing Kalakaua Avenue, some distance from the beach. Since the beach hotels took most of the tourist trade, it had been remodeled into a night club, the only one of any size or importance in that day in the Waikiki area. It was set back from the road, with bright lights around the door and dim lights inside, giving it a warm, inviting atmosphere. The only competing place that offered music and dancing was Waikiki Park, across the Ala Wai canal at the corner of Kalakaua Avenue and John Ena Road. It had brighter lights, and a dance pavilion that drew a far different class of people.

Joe noticed one particular party that came in this night. There were six in the group, arriving at about nine-thirty. It was identified as the "Branson party" by one of the young officers who asked to be shown to their dining alcove, which was reserved. These alcoves were arranged like booths around the dance floor. They were trimmed with Chinese woodwork along the edges. There were two tiers of booths, one at the floor level and the other on the mezzanine, extending a few feet over the lower tier so the occupants could look down upon the dancers. The floor was circular, with teakwood lattices around the edges, giving the arrangement a kind of pseudo-Oriental decorative effect.

One of the members of the Branson party seemed familiar. He was a rather short, thin-lipped man with small features, who smiled as he came in, nodding at the doorkeeper and clapping him on the shoulder. Joe was used to these slaps on the shoulder and being called by name; it was usually a substitute for a tip.

"Good evening, Commander," he said, smiling with a trace of irony. He was sure the young officer was not a commander, or even a lieutenant commander. They were usually a bit older, and walked with self-conscious dignity as if they were aware of the respectful attention of the junior officers, but did not want to show it. Joe had no reason to recognize any rank above a commander, because captains and admirals never came to the Ala Wai.

The officer stopped an instant, and said, "Haven't I seen you before?"

Joe remembered him. He had often seen him at the Thursday night fights at the submarine base at Pearl Harbor, where the thin-faced officer sometimes served as announcer. Joe was an inveterate patron of the fights at the Navy Yard, since they cost nothing and produced matches that were usually good and bloody. He always arrived early to get a seat as near the ringside as possible, and yelled at the top of his lungs whenever a dark-skinned gladiator from Honolulu drew blood from one of the "white meat" boys of the Army or Navy.

He figured this was why the lieutenant recognized him—because he yelled so loudly. Like most people who lived in Hawaii, Joe had no definite feeling of antagonism toward *haoles;* and yelling at the fights was not, in his judgment, an act of racial feeling, or even rowdyism. It was merely a demonstration of home-town loyalty to the "local boys" from Honolulu—whether Hawaiian, Portuguese or even Filipino did not matter. The bouts usually matched service-men against local fighters, probably because they brought out harder fighting and made for a livelier evening with more cheering on both sides. Since the dark-skinned entries usually won, this was a highly commendable kind of sportsmanship as far as Joe Freitas and his fellow Honoluluans were concerned.

"Yes, sir," he said politely. "I go to the fights a lot. I've seen you there."

"Of course," the young officer said, smiling again in a condescending way, and passed into the dance room. Joe could easily tell the difference between a friendly word and the patronizing air that some of the officers displayed. That was one point he noticed about *malihini haoles*. When a regular *haole* came into the Ala Wai, he would usually say "Hello," or "Good evening," or simply wave his hand. But the young Navy officers would often call him by name, and slap him on the back as if they were old friends. He always smiled and nodded, even when he didn't know who they were. He was friendly by nature, and his job was to make guests feel welcome. He regarded *malihini haoles* as good for buisness, even if they sometimes called Hawaiians "natives" when they talked among themselves.

The incident of the thin-faced lieutenant fixed in Joe's mind a recollection of something else he had noticed when the Branson party came into the inn. A girl in a green dress, with the party, had walked slightly ahead of the others, her head bent forward in a kind of stoop. She seemed to be angry or troubled, or possibly a bit drunk. Joe did not like to see people come into the Ala Wai looking that way, particularly women. It often made for disturbances that were not good for business.

Part of his job was to watch people during the dancing and to see that no trouble occurred. There was always some drinking inside the inn, within the booths, but it was usually fairly quiet and even surreptitious, the drinks being poured from under the tables. For the most part, guests went out to their cars in the parking lot to drink. There was no particular effort to catch anyone with a boottle, but it was considered good taste not to make a public demonstration of drinking in view of the fact that the National Prohibition Act was still on the books. Whenever a United States Deputy Marshal was about to show up, Joe Freitas always knew about it in time to pass the word around so the drinks would disappear from the tables.

Later in the evening Joe heard that the girl in the green dress had slapped one of the Navy officers during an argument, which merely confirmed his convictions.

Waikiki Park, 11:30 P.M.

An eighth of a mile toward Diamond Head, across the Ala Wai Canal, lay the glittering assemblage of Waikiki Park. It was Honolulu's only permanent amusement park. Although the Fernandez Carnival came almost every year and set up business on the waterfront, across from the Navy pier, the carnival lasted only a few weeks each year, and there was no dancing. Waikiki Park was open all year, and it had a popular dance pavilion where young men came in shirts and blue jeans, and the girls wore sweaters and short skirts.

On this particular night the usual noises were achieving a crescendo, preparatory to the closing time just before midnight. Girls waved and screamed at friends from atop the Ferris wheel or from the jerking roller coaster as it roared by. Within the dance hall the crowded floor became more dense, if possible, until it was a single revolving wheel of humanity, with the orchestra drumming out monotonous renditions of "Moonlight and Roses" and "Charlie, My Boy!" Dancing and music were part of the lives of people in Honolulu; the Hawaiians themselves, from a race whose culture was diminishing under the pressure of the *haole* civilization that had descended upon them, still retained an instinctive love for rhythm and dancing. When they sang among themselves, usually the melodies of old Hawaiian chants, converted into songs by the early missionaries; but in places like Waikiki Park the old songs had been replaced by the brassy music of the twenties, played "Hawaiian style."

At the foot of the Ferris wheel several cars were parked, near the entrance that opened on John Ena Road. The three boys had returned from the other side of town and now waited for the other two, who had gone in for the last dance. A friend, John Puaaloa, passed by, and the Japanese youth, "Shorty," stopped him.

"Got a stub?"

Henry Chang said, "Hello, John," and the man nodded.

He fished in his pocket, and finally produced a ticket stub. It was customary, late in the evening, for those coming out of the dance hall with used ticket stubs to pass them on to those who might want to go inside to meet a friend, or catch the last dance. Shorty took the stub, thanked the man, and handed it to the Chinese-Hawaiian, Chang.

"Go get Benny an' Mac," he said. "Tell 'm hurry up. We got to go back Correa's place before everybody go home. Maybe they got some beer left."

Chang was a rather small, chunky youth with a quick, athletic step. He hurried toward the door to the dance pavilion, from which patrons were already beginning to stream out. It was about five minutes before midnight, and at that moment the music stopped in the dance hall.

24

Harold Godfrey told the Chief Inspector of Detectives for Honolulu, John McIntosh, four days later, on September 16:

> On the night of September 12th a dance was given by the Order of Eagles at Waikiki Park, which I control. The dance stopped at 11:55 P.M. It should have stopped at 11:45, as that is my rule.[1]

Ala Wai Inn, 11:35 P.M.

The dining booths at the Ala Wai Inn faced the dance floor in a horseshoe-shaped ring. At the far end of this horseshoe, in a booth on the upper tier, there were several Navy officers and their wives, and some kind of altercation was going on. The lights were always dim in these booths, most of the illumination coming from small lights inside the booths; and it was not possible for those on the dance floor below to know what was going on.

It was well after ten o'clock, and most of the people who had come merely to dine had gone home. However, there were late arrivals who now filled the dance floor so that the place actually was livelier than ever. Since it was "Navy night" most of the patrons were Navy people, many of whom had homes in Honolulu. A few civilians sat by themselves, taking little part in the general exchange that went on among the Navy people passing each other on the dance floor or going to and from the dining alcoves.

In one of the booths on the upper tier a young Navy officer was sitting with a group of civilians—all white people, but strangers to him. He was a slender, strongly built young man, of medium height, quite good-looking; and he was explaining with considerable animation some of the intricacies of submarines. Joe Freitas had noticed him when he arrived with the party of six that was identified as the Branson party. This was Lieutenant Branson. He was wearing a sack coat and dark trousers.

The sudden raising of voices in the next booth attracted the attention of the young lieutenant. He stopped talking and glanced up. Then he said to the civilian party listening to him, "Excuse me, please!" and rose and left the booth.

In the adjoining booth, facing toward the orchestra, Lieutenant Commander Miller had been sitting with his wife and guests, a couple of junior officers and their wives. Two of his guests—

Lieutenant Fish and his wife, Susan—were dancing on the floor below. The other two were Lieutenant Stogsdall and his wife; and one of the chairs across the table from Stogsdall was occupied by the girl in the green dress.

She had apparently just come into the booth, and she was leaning across the table, talking in a fairly loud voice to Lieutenant Stogsdall. She was blondish, with hair that hung almost to her shoulders; and her face, while quite pretty, had a perpetually pouting expression. Her blue eyes, set rather prominently in her face, were directed at Stogsdall.

"You're no gen'l'man, Lieutenant," she said. Her voice was slightly thick, and she moved her fingers awkwardly on the table, as if uncertain what to do with them.

Stogsdall was young and good-looking, in a rugged way. His face contracted in a frown, and he rose as if to leave. Behind the girl in the green dress stood Lieutenant Branson, who had come into the booth. He was holding the back of her chair and leaning foward.

"Take it easy, Thalia—this is a public place."

"Don't care!" the girl said, shrugging away the hand which he put on her shoulder. "You're no gen'l'man, Lieutenant, talking to me that way!"

"You're a louse," Stogsdall said; and the girl in the green dress half rose from her chair, leaned across the table, and slapped him in the face. Stogsdall blinked, and passed his hand across his face. Then he turned quickly to his wife, who was sitting at the other end of the table. She nodded, and he rose and went over and helped her to her feet. Commander Miller also arose, looking uncertainly at the girl and at Stogsdall.

At that moment, Susan Fish came into the booth with her husband. She looked at the girl who had just slapped Stogsdall, and then turned to her husband:

"I think you'd better get Tommy."

Lieutenant Fish nodded and left. A few minutes later Lieutenant (j.g.) Thomas Massie came back with him, and the Miller party left. Branson, who had been standing behind Thalia Massie's chair, returned to the nearby booth and resumed conversation with the party of civilians, to whom he had been explaining the workings of submarines.

In a statement to Inspector McIntosh, in the Detective Bureau, on September 22, Susan Fish gave the following story:

Q. Were Lieutenant Branson and Lieutenant Massie in your booth?
A. Lieutenant Branson was. We were about to leave and my husband didn't want to leave Thalia alone, so my husband went and got Lieutenant Massie to come and look after his wife.
Q. Have you any idea what time it was when you left?
A. It must have been near 11:30. We took the Millers home and when we got home just before I got in bed I looked at the clock and it was a few minutes before 12 o'clock.[2]

The habit of members of Navy parties migrating from booth to booth during an evening was not unusual. No one actually remembered when Thalia Massie came into the booth, or whether Branson was with her, or had followed her into the booth. In a statement to District Attorney Griffith Wight on September 23, Lieutenant Fish gave the following account:

Q. [Where was] Mrs. Massie?
A. I was at the end of the table, she at the other; she was talking with . . . I forget who was sitting across the table from her at the time. I got up to dance two or three minutes after she came in.
Q. Did you hear Mrs. Massie and Stogsdall have an argument?
A. I think I was out of the room at the time—as I remember I wasn't in the room at the time.
Q. You don't remember his calling her a louse?
A. No, because when I came back from the dance Mrs. Fish was outside and ready to go.[3]

Lieutenant Commander Miller also made a statement to Inspector McIntosh, substantially verifying the stories of Lieutenant Fish and his wife. He said Lieutenant Fish went to look for Lieutenant Massie and returned with him. Shortly afterward he and Mrs. Miller left with the Stogsdalls and Lieutenant Fish and his wife, leaving Tommy and Thalia Massie alone in the booth.

Waikiki Park, 11:55 P.M.

As Harold Godfrey said, the music at the dance pavilion stopped at 11:55 P.M. The crowd, which had been trickling through the door for several minutes, poured out as the lights in the dance hall began to dim. It was a happy crowd, good-natured, friends waving farewell to each other. Harold Godfrey was a good manager; he saw to it that the patrons at the park were always in good spirits, but not too exuberant. As he often said, Waikiki Park was a place for fun, not for fighting.

The Japanese called Shorty and the big Hawaiian boy wearing blue jeans and a short-sleeved blue silk shirt stood beside the Ford touring car, waiting for Henry Chang to return with Benny and Mac. Shorty's real name was Shomatsu Ida, but he was called Horace in school and Shorty by his friends. He was lean and strong, with a serious face and dark, intelligent eyes.

Joe Kalani, whose real name was Joseph Kahahawai, was a strapping Hawaiian, older than the others—he was about twenty-eight and Shorty and Chang were in their early twenties. He had achieved some reputation as a boxer in Honolulu under the name of Joe Kalani. His face was long and angular, molded in the rugged contours of the Polynesian people; his powerful frame was built for heavy duty—heavy shoulders and thick, muscular legs. He had come from Kawailoa, on the windward side of Oahu, where he had grown up among the more rustic "old-time" Hawaiians, and was therefore known as a "country *kanaka*." They were not considered as smart as the boys who had lived all their lives in Honolulu. Joe Kahahawai now lived in the Palama district, south of King Street, in the flat-lands between Palama and Iwelei. He had worked as a youth in the pineapple cannery near his home, trucking crates of pineapples. He lived at the home of his mother, Mrs. Esther Anito, while his father, John Kahahawai, still lived across the *Pali* on windward Oahu.

In a few minutes Chang came out. With him were two other boys, both dark-skinned and of medium height, but of different build. The Hawaiian, Ben Ahakuelo, was solidly built and handsome, with a smooth face and dark, lively eyes. He nodded to several people as he walked out; one, Tatsuo Masuda, spoke to him.

"You coming out to practice tomorrow, Ben?"

Ahakuelo nodded. He was well known in Honolulu as a star football player, and also as an amateur boxer. Unlike Joe Kahahawai, he had never boxed for money. But he was also known for something else, an incident involving a Chinese girl. He had served four months in Oahu prison for attempted rape, and had been released when the girl finally told the parole board that the "attempt" was not entirely without her cooperation.

The fifth boy, David Takai, variously known as "Mac" and "Eau" (pronounced "ee-ow"), was the least impressive of the five, swarthy of color, with the sharp, black eyes of an Oriental. He had not distinguished himself either as an athlete or in any other way; but he lived in the Palama neighborhood, and was good-natured and well liked.

These five had gathered more or less by accident at the home of Sylvester P. Correa, a member of the Honolulu Board of Supervisors and a popular politician among Portuguese and Hawaiians. The wedding of one of his daughters had been celebrated that night with a *luau* in the broad tree-covered Correa place, just off School Street, in a neighborhood of middle-class respectability, south of Palama Settlement. There were perhaps fifty or sixty guests at the *luau*, and several who had not been personally invited came "with friends." These included Ida, Chang and Takai. This was a Hawaiian custom; anyone who knew someone at the *luau* was welcome, as long as he behaved himself. Joseph Kahahawai was a friend of Mina Correa, one of the daughters; and Ben Ahakuelo knew Sylvester P. Correa, Jr., a son, who was called Peter. Horace Ida also knew the Correas; he and the other two had not been invited, but came with invited guests whom they knew.

All five lived within a radius of a mile of the Correa place. Ahakuelo lived on Frog Lane, almost across the street from the rambling Correa home; Ida's home was on Cunha Lane, off Vineyard Street, about a block and a half away; and David Takai lived on nearby Liliha Street, near Palama Settlement, a charitable institution which the missionary families had established to provide medical and other help for the less fortunate people of that area. The other two—Kahahawai and Chang—lived in lower Palama.

These five boys were to go down in the annals of Hawaii as "the Ala Moana boys," a phrase that was to become a stigma for all of Hawaii.

Ala Wai Inn, about Midnight

Joe Freitas did not see the girl in the green dress again until toward the end of the evening. It had been a gay, friendly night, except for the incident in the upper booth when the girl had slapped the lieutenant. Joe observed her covertly as she stood in the doorway, looking out at the stream of automobiles passing along Kalakaua Avenue. It was a moonless night, clear and calm, with the scent of tropical flowers in the air.

Joe permitted himself a sidelong glance at the girl. She still stood in a slightly stooped posture, her head forward, and she seemed to be angry. Joe had felt a slight pleasure in the report of the face-slapping incident. Nothing really important had resulted, such as a fight; and it was always a bit pleasant to find these chinks in the smooth surface of the behavior of these *malihini haole* fellows and their women, even though Joe realized it was not good business at the Inn to have a *wahine* slapping a man around.

The girl turned and said, "Hello, Sammy," to a dark-skinned young man who passed her on his way out of the inn. Joe did not hear what they said, but he recognized the boy. It was a fellow that Joe knew, who often hung around with "Tahiti," one of the music boys with Joe Crawford's band. Crawford played on Maui, not at the Ala Wai; but the members of the band often came to the Ala Wai to listen to the music. It was around midnight; Joe remembered the time because the music had just stopped at Waikiki Park across the canal.

At 11:55 the last dance had been announced, but one of the guests—Lieutenant Branson, the host of the party to which the girl in the green dress belonged—had taken off his shoes and was dancing in front of the orchestra. The crowd applauded and yelled "More!" and so the orchestra kept on playing.

Waikiki Park, 12:00 Midnight

Shorty Ida jumped into the front seat of his car, behind the wheel, and the others climbed in after him. Chang, like Kahahawai, was wearing bluejeans and a white silk shirt, which was the fashion among young men of certain social circles in Honolulu; Takai also was wearing a white silk shirt and gray trousers. The two, with Kahahawai, who was still slightly drunk, slid into the back seat. Ben Ahakuelo climbed into the front seat beside Ida. He was wearing a light blue shirt and brown trousers.

As Ida started his car—a Ford touring car, bearing license number 58-895—a girl in another car, parked in the rear of Ida's Ford, called out:

"Hey, Benny!"

Ahakuelo waved at the girl, and also at the driver of the car, whom he recognized as "Tuts" Matsumoto, one of the downtown "sporting set." Matsumoto was facing in the other direction, however, and did not see him. A second girl was sitting in Matsumoto's car, a Ford roadster; and two youths jumped aboard, seating themselves facing backward on the folds of the top, which had been pulled down against the back of the seat.

The girl who had called to Ahakuelo was later identified as Margaret Kanae, a rather shy Hawaiian girl of sixteen, the daughter of Frank Kanae, a former football player of some prominence in Honolulu and at one time a member of the Honolulu Police Department. Margaret had gone to Kamehameha School for Girls, but had left before finishing grade school, and was known to be a girl without any marked powers of observation, as her later statements indicated.

Matsumoto afterward recalled that she had said to him, "Benny I think is over there," but he merely shrugged and gave his attention to backing his car around so he could drive out of the parking area to John Ena Road. Had he looked around he would have known whether Ben Ahakuelo was in the other car, since he had known him personally for several years.

Matsumoto's time of departure from Waikiki Park was definitely established by Harold Godfrey, the manager. In a statement given to detectives later, Godfrey said:

31

About ten minutes of twelve I told the leader of the orchestra to stop, which he did about five minutes later. I remained around until the people left and left for home about fifteen or twenty minutes after twelve o'clock A.M. At that time there were about three cars parked on the lot not counting my own. One of these cars belonged to Tatsumi Matsumoto. This was a Ford touring car with the top down.[4]

Matsumoto's car was the last to leave the parking area. He did not see the Ford touring car in which Ben Ahakuelo was riding until some time later. Thus Margaret Kanae, whose accounts were conflicting and uncertain and could not be relied upon, was the last person to have seen Akahuelo and the other "Ala Moana boys," riding in Shorty Ida's car when it left Waikiki Park on the night of September 12.

Sunday, September 13, 1931

About ten minutes after midnight a neatly dressed young man left the dance pavilion at Waikiki Park with his wife. His name was George Goeas, and he was assistant cashier at the Dillingham Insurance Company in Honolulu. He did not know Kahahawai or any of his friends—although he had once seen Ben Ahakuelo in an amateur boxing match; but he had stopped to chat with some friends, and thought he remembered seeing Ahakuelo. He and his wife left the park and crossed the street to his car, which was parked on John Ena Road, facing toward the beach.

George Goeas was Portuguese, one of the upper level of his nationality who had broken away from the immigrant class originally imported into Hawaii as plantation laborers. He was well educated and ambitious, and had moved up quickly to a position of importance in a Dillingham organization, which was a sure road to success in Honolulu.

As he later told friends: "I wish I had never gone to Waikiki Park that night. I had a good time, but I don't like to get mixed up in things like this. Whatever I say, somebody will be sore. They asked me what time it was, and I remembered because I looked at my wife's wrist watch when they announced the last dance. It was thirteen minutes to twelve; I remembered that, and I had to say so

32

when they asked me. They wanted to know if I could be mistaken, but how could I? It took maybe five minutes for the last dance, and then we stayed around a few minutes talking to people. It had to be after midnight when we left, so I said so. I was in a good mood then, but I feel like hell now."

Mrs. Goeas had turned to her husband as they were walking across John Ena Road and said: "George, let's have some noodles before we go home."

Goeas nodded. He had enjoyed the evening; the dancing was always pleasant at Waikiki Park, and on this night the local Order of Eagles had put on even better entertainment than usual. He was in a good mood.

They entered the car, and he pulled out from the curb, intending to stop at a Japanese *saimin* stand at the corner of a lane about a hundred yards down John Ena Road in the direction of the beach. He parked just short of the *saimin* stand at the corner, ordered the noodles from the man at the stand, and sat in his car with his wife waiting for them to be brought over on a tray.

A girl wearing a long green dress passed alongside the car, walking very slowly, her head bent forward. A few feet behind her a white man, walking at a slightly faster pace, apparently was overtaking her. In a statement on September 17 to Deputy Inspector John Jardine, at Honolulu Police Headquarters, Goeas said:

> I and my wife left the Waikiki Dance Hall about 12:10 A.M. Before going home, she asked me to eat noodles with her. We took the entrance of the John Ena Road when we left the park. I got my car which was parked opposite the entrance on John Ena Road and drove about seventy-five yards down on John Ena Road from the entrance to the park. We ordered some noodles, and while waiting for the noodles, I noticed a white woman walking down with her head bent down, and the way she walked seemed as if she was under the influence of liquor. About a yard and a half from her we saw a white man following directly in the back of her. He kept this place for about twenty-five yards and from there on I could not see as there was a store blocking the view.
>
> Q. Can you give me a description of the woman and how she was dressed?
> A. I believe she was about five feet four or five inches tall, medium build, and she wore a green gown.

33

Q. What about the man, how was he dressed?
A. He was a white man, about five feet nine inches tall, weight about 165 pounds, was bare headed, and wore a dark brown suit. He looked like a soldier to me.[5]

George Goeas' wife remembered a good deal more. She first saw the woman in the green dress as she was walking around the front of the Goeases' car to get in from the side near the sidewalk. The woman was walking toward the beach, only a few yards from the car; and the white man was walking behind her.

"It looked to me," Mrs. Goeas said, "as if she was mumbling, and she had her head hanging over on the right side."

Mrs. Goeas, being a woman, had observed the woman's dress more carefully than her husband. It had sleeves to the elbow, was tight around the waist with a full ankle-length skirt. There was a small bow in the back, and the dress was green. The woman's hair hung at "three-quarter length," almost to her shoulders; and it was tied in the back. Mrs. Goeas was not sure how it was tied, but she knew it was tied. She described the woman's hair as "light brown."

George Goeas also recalled that as he was leaving the vicinity of Waikiki Park, having turned back on John Ena Road toward Kalakaua Avenue, to the east, he saw two cars parked near the Park entrance, one facing Kalakaua Avenue and the other in the opposite direction, facing the beach. The first looked like an Essex touring car, he said; the one facing the beach was a Ford touring car, parked just below the *saimin* stand.

John Ena Road, 12:10 A.M.

Alice Aramaki worked in her father's barber shop, next to the taxi stand on John Ena Road. She usually closed the barber shop sometime after eleven o'clock, and then went over to her sister's store next door, where she lived with her sister in back of the store. The front of the store faced directly on John Ena Road.

Waikiki Park was across the street, farther up on the *mauka*, or mountain, side. It lay at the northwestern corner of the Waikiki area; Kalakaua Avenue, which ran through Waikiki, passed the park just before it curved to the eastward where it joined King Street, perhaps a mile beyond, on the route into town. Ala Wai Inn also lay to the north of the Park, on the same side of Kalakaua, in a corner now occupied by a service station and an apartment hotel. In those days there were only a scattering of Japanese stores until Kalakaua crossed Kapiolani Boulevard, one of three broad thoroughfares extending from downtown Honolulu toward Waikiki and the Diamond Head area.

The place where John Ena Road began, at the corner of Kalakaua Avenue, was always bustling with automobiles and people, particularly around the time the park "let out"; in fact, from early evening until after midnight, there was hardly an hour when the short thoroughfare leading into Fort De Russy was not crowded.

Alice often watched the crowd coming out of Waikiki Park. It used to be known as "Aloha Park" and Alice had gone there a few times, but not often, because she had to keep the barber shop open late to take care of people going into the park. On Saturday nights there were lots of people and cars, and she often stayed up as late as one o'clock watching the crowds.

On the night of September 12 she had closed the barber shop about a quarter to twelve, and gone over to her sister's store. She stood inside, leaning against the icebox, watching the crowd pass by. Alice was a pleasant, plump-faced Japanese girl who worked most of the day and this was one of her important after-work amusements—just watching the crowd.

When the music stopped in the park she knew the dance was over, and the lights would go out. For several minutes she stood beside the icebox in the store, watching people come out. There were seldom many *haoles* at Waikiki Park; the crowd was mostly Japanese, Chinese, Hawaiians and a few Portuguese and Filipinos.

Alice Aramaki noticed a woman walking rather slowly down the sidewalk, passing in front of the store. Her head was bent forward, and she shuffled along without paying much attention to the crowd on the sidewalk. In a statement made in the presence of Inspector McIntosh, on September 16, she described the way the woman was walking.

> Slow, with bowed head. Just had her head down and was walking slow . . . I first notice this woman because she is a *haole*, with brown hair. She wear a long green dress, I think a long evening gown. I didn't see her face. She passed by and I seen her back.

35

Q. Was there any person with her or following her?
A. I don't know if he was following her. I think he is a *haole*. He had on a white shirt. No coat and no tie.[6]

She placed the time at a few minutes after midnight "because it was after the dance." She had not paid much attention to the woman, since she passed out of her range of sight a few steps beyond the store. It was not until she read in the papers about the attack on Mrs. Massie that she decided she ought to come to the police and tell them what she saw.

John Ena Road, 12:15 A.M.

Eugenio Batungbacal and three friends had been driving through Waikiki just before midnight. They turned off Kalakaua Avenue and parked on John Ena Road across from the entrance to Waikiki Park. Two of the men in the car jumped out and walked through the entrance toward the dance pavilion; Eugenio and the other man stayed in the car.

They remained until the music stopped, when their friends came out and joined them. Neither Eugenio nor his friends was exactly sure of the time; they had stopped to talk with some other friends coming out of the park. As soon as they were all in the car, Eugenio said, "Let's go!" and pulled away from the curb, heading down toward the fork in the road. He thought this was about 12:15 A.M.

They had gone only a few yards down John Ena Road when one of Eugenio's friends, James Low, from Hawaii—a minor political figure there—poked him and said, "It looks like they are forcing that woman."

The others in the car looked down the street. A woman in a green dress was walking along, rather slowly; and it appeared that two men were holding her arms and were either helping her to walk or forcing her along. In any event, it was some weeks before any of this group told police what he saw, and their accounts at that time differed substantially.

According to Eugenio Batungbacal, it "looked like four or five men were forcing a woman into the car." He said they held her arms and another man was walking behind. The street was fairly crowded with the celebrants who were leaving Waikiki Park, and there were several autos in the street, so it was not surprising they all had slightly different stories of what happened.

Two of Eugenio Batungbacal's friends were Chinese from Honolulu; and both seemed to recall that the woman appeared to be trying to get away from the two men holding her arms. She made no outcry, however; and it was their general feeling that she was being led from—or to—a party. When Eugenio reported this matter to the police, some weeks later, he was asked if he heard any cries or screams. He said he had not.

"Did any of you in the car say anything when you saw her?" Deputy City and County Attorney Griffith Wight asked. The questioning was in his office at the City Hall.

Eugenio shook his head.

"I didn't," he said. "James Low said to drive the car slowly so we could see what happened. I drove the car slow. I didn't look, but James Low and the other guys, they are the ones that can give you more about it. James Low said, 'It looks like they are forcing the woman.'"

James Low had a slightly different account of what happened. He came in on November 10, 1931, to the Detective Bureau and talked with Deputy Inspector Jardine and Detective Stagbar:

> We first went in the dance pavilion—Waikiki Park—then we came out and turned down John Ena Road towards the sea. After we came out of the gate and passed the stores, I saw a lady who looked like she was drunk—intoxicated—and immediately behind her was a man following her—about two or three feet—and in front of her was a car along the curb, facing the sea. . . . I was attracted by a call from two ladies coming from the opposite direction. After we passed a little way I asked [Eugenio] to stop and turn around.
>
> Q. This automobile—did she appear to you to be going into the automobile, or just walking along?
> A. From the newspaper article I saw the following day I judged that they were going in the car.[7]

It might be noted in passing that these men, although socially friendly, came from different walks of life. Roger Lieu, whose Chinese name was Lieu On Kwok, and Charlie Chang were partners in a Chinese company known as Sun Chong Co., which was in the business of construction and building supplies. One of their good customers was the United States Navy. James Low, on the other hand, was an ambitious politician who had moved from Hilo, Hawaii, to Honolulu and was interested in being elected to the Territorial legislature. In this respect, their personal and economic interests might be regarded as derived from opposite sides of the Hawaiian political fence.

Downtown Honolulu, 12:25 A.M.

Tatsumi Matsumoto—or "Tuts," as he was generally known in the sporting circles of Honolulu—drove his car through the Waikiki Park gate into John Ena Road and turned up toward Kalakaua Avenue. Two girls, Margaret Kanae, the shy Hawaiian girl, and Sybil Davis, a friend of Robert Vierra, sat beside him in the front seat. Perched on the folds of the top, which had been pulled down, and facing backward, were the two young men, Vierra and George Silva.

A sister of George Silva, Matilda, had come to the Park with them but decided to go home with some friends. Meanwhile Matsumoto was held up by Sybil Davis, who was waiting for another girl.

"Wait a little while," she told Matsumoto. "There is another girl. She has my coat."

As Matsumoto explained it:

After the dance was over, we went out to the car and this Matilda Silva left with another party, they did not stay until the dance closed. Then we met two other girls. One was sitting in the car, that is after the dance was over, but we were not sure whether this other girl was going with us, so we waited. She finally came out and sat in the car.[8]

This was Margaret Kanae. Matsumoto then drove through the gate and turned into Kalakaua, driving north and east and crossing King Street, continuing along the new "Kalakaua Extension" to Beretania Street. At this point he turned down Beretania Street toward town. Traffic was light; he estimated that about fifteen minutes after leaving Waikiki Park he was driving past the old McKinley School building—then Lincoln School—which faced northward on Thomas Square.

At this point, Margaret Kanae, the Hawaiian girl, said: "Look—Benny and them is following us!"

Matsumoto did not look back; however, Vierra, facing the rear, saw the car as it drew closer. It seemed to him that Ben Ahakuelo, in the front seat, was waving at him. Vierra called to Matsumoto to slow down, and in a few seconds the second car pulled almost alongside the roadster. Ahakuelo again motioned that he wanted to say something. Vierra first tried to jump from the back of the roadster to the other car; but he was afraid he might fall and be knocked over. When the second car had moved up until it was even with Matsumoto's car, Vierra stepped across to the bumper.

He asked Ahakuelo what he wanted, and the latter yelled: "Where are you going?" Vierra said, "To Judd Street." One of the group in the other car—Vierra was unable to recall who it was—asked him for a match. Vierra pulled a packet of matches from his pocket and handed it to him. The two cars were running side by side, passing in front of the Art Academy across the street from Thomas Square, when Vierra jumped back on Matsumoto's car.

There was an accident or some trouble at Fort and Beretania Streets, near the center of town, and Matsumoto stopped to see what was happening. The other car continued up Fort Street a couple of blocks in the direction of the high Koolau peaks which lie in back of Nuuanu Valley. They turned northward again into School Street. The house of Sylvester Correa was a large, rambling structure set back from School Street among thick clusters of trees; and according to Horace Ida's story, told later, they turned into the yard.

The *luau* was all but over. They could hear singing in the back of the house, where a few boys were playing guitars and ukuleles. The plaintive sounds of the quaint little Hawaiian folk song came through the trees—

Manuela boy, my dear boy,
You too much-a *hila hila* . . .
No mo' fi' cent, no mo' house,
Go *ala paki moi moi!*

the gist of which, loosely translated, is that "Manuela boy" is too

39

shy, and since he doesn't show up with five cents for "crack-seed" for his girl, he may as well go out in the park and sleep.

Ben Ahakuelo and Joseph Kahahawai left the car and walked through the trees toward the house, leaving Ida, Chang and Takai in the car. In a few minutes they came back, and Ahakuelo announced there was no more beer. Ahakuelo had gone to the back of the house and asked one of the boys if there was any beer left. Mina Correa, one of the supervisor's daughters, talked to Kahahawai through the kitchen window. In a statement to Inspector McIntosh, on September 15, Sylvester P. Correa, Jr., one of the sons, gave this story:

> Q. These boys [Ida, Ahakuelo, Kahahawai, Takai and Chang] came back a second time?
> A. Yes.
> Q. When?
> A. After midnight. I came home and they were there.
> Q. They asked you for some more beer?
> A. Yes, and I said there was no more.[9]

After two or three minutes, Ahakuelo left for his home, which was nearby on Frog Lane. The rest piled back into Horace Ida's car and drove off toward Liliha Street, in the Palama district where Takai lived. Just before they reached the intersection of Liliha and King Streets, Ida pulled into the curb and Takai jumped off.

He stood for a minute, and saw what happened immediately afterward. Several cars were passing the big arterial intersection of Liliha Street, from the east, and King Street, running north and south; and Dillingham Boulevard, which curved away to the west and then turned northward toward Pearl Harbor. As Ida started across the intersection, a big Hudson car came down King Street toward town, and Ida swerved to avoid hitting it.

The following day, David Takai gave this account to Inspector McIntosh:

> I was about twenty-five yards away, that time they took me home, and they had an argument. I got off the car and they stay there for a while and had an argument with a woman.[10]

Horace Ida's story was more specific:

I stopped the car where Takai lives. I just made the turn into King Street when a Hudson car came along full speed and almost hit us. I tried to avoid the accident, and I said to them, "What is the matter with you?"

Q. What happened then?
A. Well, when the machine went by, naturally I said, "What is the matter?" He started cussing. He stopped the car about a half a block from us. Naturally we drove by and stopped. This woman came out and started cussing. We all jumped out of the car." [11]

Joseph Kahahawai's story was even more specific:

This car stopped and our car stopped about ten yards from them [in the] rear. Then we drove our car close to them, I went out of the car, and a lady came over, a Hawaiian girl, and she grabbed hold of my throat and said, "What is the matter?" and she grab me and scratch me and I shove her off and she fell down on the running board of her car.[12]

Police Station, Honolulu, 12:45 A.M.

Police Officer Cecil Rickard was walking down Alakea Street, in downtown Honolulu, on his way to the police station in the old Kapiolani Building at King and Alakea Streets. It was about 12:40 A.M. He was due to report for night desk duty at one o'clock, but he always came in a few minutes early. As he neared the doorway into the police station, he heard a screech of tires, then saw a car round the corner from King Street and pull up in front of the police station.

A dark, heavy-set woman bounded out of the car and headed for the doorway. Rickard, knowing he would have to handle the matter—whatever it was—quickened his pace and was behind the woman as she almost ran up the stairway. He nearly collided with a small, wispy little man who was following the woman into the station.

The woman gave her name as Agnes Peeples, and said that the man with her was Mr. Homer Peeples, her husband. She gave a story which was substantially as follows:

While they were driving down King Street toward town just a short time before, approaching the intersection of King Street with

Liliha Street and Dillingham Boulevard, two cars were coming in the opposite direction on King Street, and a third was coming down Liliha Street. Mr. Peeples, a rather self-effacing white man, who seemed to let his part-Hawaiian wife speak for him, was driving the car. Mrs. Peeples' story of what happened is recorded in detail:

> My husband blew his horn when we came to the intersection and a Ford car bearing the license number 58-895 coming from Liliha Street into King Street failed to make a boulevard stop and almost hit our car as they got into King Street. To avoid being hit, my husband stepped on the gas and turned toward the middle of the road; the car 58-895 then went to our right. My husband stopped our car and I sang out, "Why don't you look where you are driving?"
>
> When I said that, my husband started our car to go. One of the fellows in car 58-895 swore at me. They also stopped their car, not abreast of us but a little to the rear of our car. My husband stopped his car again. One of the men, the one sitting beside the driver, said, "Get that damned *haole* off that car and I'll give him what he's looking for."
>
> Instead, I got off the car and pushed him away. He was standing on the right of our car as I pushed him. The driver got off the car, he was a Japanese. As I turned around to see who he was the Hawaiian hit me on the left ear. I staggered back and when I regained my balance I grabbed him by the throat with my left hand and struck him in the face once with my right. I then got into my own car and we went to the police station.[13]

Mrs. Peeples' account of the defense of her person and her rights would probably have remained only an entry in the police records, had it not been for other events that were taking place at about the same time.

Officer Rickard noted the time of her complaint as 12:45 A.M., and the probable time of the altercation as ten minutes earlier—12:35 A.M. At 12:50 A.M. he broadcast a description of the Ford car with license number 58-895 to all radio patrol cars, with instructions to pick it up if they saw it cruising around.

Ala Wai Inn, 1:15 A.M.

It was just after one o'clock when the orchestra, which had played more than an hour overtime, stopped playing. During the hour that followed Lieutenant Branson's shoeless midnight dance the crowd had applauded almost continuously; but finally everyone was tired and the crowd began to drift out.

By one o'clock everyone in the Branson party except Tommy Massie and Branson himself had gone home. Massie was looking around for some trace of his wife.

Branson had been with her earlier in the evening—when she slapped Lieutenant Stogsdall—but he said he had no idea where she was. He had last seen her in the Millers' booth with Massie, after Commander Miller and his party had left.

Tommy Massie, a short, slender young man with a pleasant face, seemed more interested in developing a defense of his own performance of duty as a husband than in searching for his wife.

"She's probably home," he told Branson. "She was mad as hell earlier this evening. I'll call her just to prove I've been looking for her." He looked for a telephone, Branson following him. Later, in the office of Inspector McIntosh, he admitted he had no clear recollection of the time.

"When did you first miss her?" McIntosh asked. He was a kindly man, with a worried look about his eyes. He looked at Massie with a steady, questioning glance.

"Between eleven-thirty and twelve o'clock," Massie said. "That's as near as I can judge—depending on hearsay." He shook his head rather hopelessly. "I went upstairs to the booth where I had seen Mrs. Massie last, and made a complete search."

"You thought she had gone to the toilet, or something?"

"Yes."

"Did you make inquiry among your friends as to whether they had seen her or not?"

"Yes."

"Did you come to any conclusion when you couldn't find her?" McIntosh asked.

"I assumed she had gotten a ride with other friends and gone home."

"What time did you leave?"

"Shortly after one."

"With whom did you leave?"

"Lieutenant Branson."

Massie recalled having spoken to Branson around midnight. The leader of the orchestra had just announced the last dance, and he called out to Branson, who was in the booth upstairs with the civilian party: "Jerry, it's 11:55 and the last dance is announced."

It was then that Branson came down to the dance floor and did his shoeless dance. The crowd was delighted, and applauded until the orchestra agreed to play past the closing period. After that, Massie did not recall much about what happened. He danced several times with Mrs. Branson, but she finally went home, taking the Branson car. By this time the floor was crowded with guests having their last dance; and finally they formed a ring and danced around until the music stopped at one o'clock.

Massie started looking for the rest of his party. He finally found Branson—whom he had not seen since midnight—and asked him if he had seen Thalia. Branson said he had not. It was at this point that Massie decided to call home so his wife would know he had been looking for her.

At the telephone booth, Massie was making the call to his home when two friends, Mr. and Mrs. Pringle, passed by. He explained that he was "calling Thalia so she'll know damned well I've been worried about her."

The Pringles later remembered that this was about 1:15 A.M., as they were then leaving for home. As far as they knew, Massie did not get an answer from his house. A few minutes afterward, Massie and Branson took off in Massie's car, driving up to the home of Lieutenant Rigby, a Navy officer who lived near the Massie home in Manoa Valley, thinking the party might have moved there.

They arrived at the Rigby home at about 1:30 A.M. The maid let them in, and remembered the time; but there was no one else home.

Branson apparently was feeling the effects of a considerable amount of drinking during the evening. He threw himself on a couch on the porch, while Massie again tried to telephone his home. This time Thalia answered.

"Please come home," she said, in a thick voice. "Something awful has happened!"

Ala Moana Road, about 1 A.M.

Eustace Bellinger and his wife lived across the street from Mr. and Mrs. George William Clark. They often played cards; and on the night of September 12 they had played until past midnight. They decided to drive down to Waikiki and have a late snack at the Barbecue Inn.

They drove in the Bellinger car. Mrs. Clark sat in the back seat with her husband and Mrs. Bellinger, and their son, George W. Clark, Jr., sat in front, with Bellinger driving. It was about 12:25 A.M. when they left, but they found the Barbecue Inn too crowded and decided to drive along the beach road to Kewalo Inn, where good fresh fish chowder could be had from the catches of the fishing boats moored in Kewalo Basin.

When they reached John Ena Road, intending to turn off on the Ala Moana, Bellinger found that his gas was low. He drove back to a gasoline station to fill up; and by the time they reached the Ala Moana it was almost one o'clock.

The crowd from Waikiki Park had about disappeared, and the Ala Moana was empty of traffic when they turned into it, heading toward the downtown area. They drove past a coral fill that had been emptied out on the land near the beach from the dredging of the Ala Wai Canal, to make land for future building sites, and then along the empty road. When they had gone for perhaps a mile and a half, Mrs. Bellinger leaned forward and said to her husband, "Look, there's a woman in the road."

Bellinger stopped the car. The woman came to the window on the right side of the car, where young Clark was sitting. Her first words were incomprehensible. Her hair was disheveled, and her face seemed to be badly bruised. Her lips were swollen, and there was a dark mark on her right cheek.

Bellinger reached across the front seat and lowered the window.

"Are you white people?" the woman asked.

Bellinger said they were, and young Clark opened the front door of the car so the woman could move in beside him. Bellinger, in a statement to Inspector McIntosh on September 18, told what happened:

> We asked her what the trouble was. She said she had been picked up by five or six Hawaiian boys who had beaten her up and thrown her out of the car. We questioned her where the boys were and she said they were going to Kalihi.[14]

Kalihi is a residential area on the north end of Honolulu—across the town from Waikiki, about three miles beyond Liliha Street.

Mrs. Clark, sitting in the back seat, was able to observe the woman's dress and her condition. Her hair had tumbled down on her shoulders, and her dress, a green evening gown, was rumpled but in what Mrs. Clark later described as "good condition."

As they drove toward town, Bellinger asked the woman if she did not want to report the matter to the police, and she said, "No, I don't want to go there. Take me home, please. My husband will take care of me."

George Clark, Sr., in a statement to Inspector McIntosh, said:

> We asked her what had happened and she said she had been beaten up by a gang of hoodlums. As to what really happened to her, she told us she had been to a party. She left the party about midnight because someone at the party said something to her that peeved her, so she went for a walk and some fresh air. She said she went along Kalakaua Avenue until she came to a pink store. [There was a pink store at the corner of Kalakaua and John Ena Road.] After she had gone down the road a short distance she said a car drove up behind her and two men jumped off and dragged her into the car. When she cried out for help they punched her on the mouth and held their hands over her face to stifle her cries.

> She said they drove down the Ala Moana until they came to a clump of trees and drove in there. Then the gang beat her up and left her there. We asked if she knew what direction the gang went and she said they went in the direction of Kalihi. We asked if anyone had passed by before we came along, and she said, "no," we were the first ones after she came out of the woods.

> We tried to question her further and get some more information, but she begged us not to ask her too many questions as her jaw

46

hurt very badly. We asked her where she lived and she told us in Manoa. We asked her what part of Manoa and she said Kahawai Street. We took her to Kahawai Street and dropped her off where she said she lived.[15]

As nearly as could be estimated by those in the Bellinger car, it was probably between 1:20 and 1:30 A.M. on Sunday morning when they dropped Thalia Massie off near her home. She was thus back in her home about 1:30 A.M., her mouth bruised and swollen, her cheek discolored, apparently from a blow of a fist, and—as was later discovered in a medical examination—her jaw broken in two places.

Within a few minutes after she got home, according to her story, the telephone rang. It was her husband, Tommy Massie, calling from the Rigby house. She said:

"Please come home—something awful has happened!"

Massie said he drove immediately to his house, leaving Branson on the couch; and from his home, at about 1:45 A.M., he telephoned the Honolulu police to report that his wife had been assaulted by a gang of Hawaiian boys.

Arrest of the Suspects

Police Officer Cecil Rickard was on night duty, sitting on a high stool behind the receiving desk, which was little more than a high counter in the makeshift Honolulu Police Station. He was shuffling papers and making up the night report. The room smelled strongly of creosote, daubed along the baseboards to keep out the cockroaches. There was also the aroma of stale tobacco, characteristic of most police stations. Three desks were set against the wall, with no one sitting at any of them. There were some file cabinets along the walls and a scattering of straight chairs. Otherwise the room had nothing in the way of furnishings. It was a temporary station in the old Kapiolani Building at King and Alakea Streets, used until the new and gaudy Honolulu Police Station could be completed across from the old Post Office Building, where the Honolulu Police Force had been housed since the days of the Revolution in 1892.

Rickard's reports were fairly routine. A few drunks had been picked up at Aala Park and booked. An unsuccessful raid had been made on a Chinese joint near River Street, where gambling was suspected but never quite proved. There was also the report of the affair involving Mr. and Mrs. Homer Peeples, at King and Liliha

48

Streets. Except for these trivia nothing much had happened during the night, or was likely to happen. There might be a few late drunks, to be put in the improvised "tank" on the second floor to sleep it off. These were chiefly bums who had somehow gotten hold of some *okolehao*, or *ng ka pi*, a potent Korean drink, and were merely inoperative for the evening.

Rickard was an experienced and methodical officer, with a reputation for not getting excited, no matter what happened. He usually thought in a straight line, and his ability to keep things under control won him the night duty assignment on Saturdays, which by and large was the most disorderly night of the week. Rickard had already made a routine check on the driver of the car bearing license number 58-895, reported by Agnes Peeples; and he found that it was a Ford Phaeton belonging to Horace Ida, who lived on Cunha Lane. He had jotted this down for future reference, although he doubted if the information would be needed. The case looked like one of those routine altercations between drivers who were probably both drunk and equally irate, with completely different points of view as to how the thing happened and what should be done about it. Since neither car had been damaged, and the only injury seemed to be to Mrs. Peeples' pride, and possibly to the Hawaiian youth she had slapped in the face, Rickard saw no reason to bother any more about it. If the matter wound up in court, it would be the county court, not the police court; and this was more or less out of his range of interest.

At 1:47 A.M. Rickard received a telephone call from a man in Manoa Valley, asking that a police patrol car be sent to 2850 Kahawai Street. A white woman had been assaulted by a bunch of Hawaiian boys.

Rickard's mental processes were not complicated; in fact, they were quite direct. He immediately associated this matter with the incident reported by Agnes Peeples. Before broadcasting instructions to Patrol Car No. 2, which was then on its way to Jack Lane to investigate a reported burglary, he called the Detective Bureau. Deputy Inspector John Jardine, on night duty, answered. Jardine's voice was little more than a mumble, and Rickard surmised that he had been sleeping on his desk. This was a habit in the Detective

Bureau at night, since very little happened after midnight and the man on duty could often catch a catnap.

"Something's up, John," he said. "You might want to stand by. I've got a report that a lady in Manoa—*haole wahine*—has been assaulted by a bunch of night fighters. Probably the same crowd that got in trouble at King and Liliha an hour ago."

Jardine's tone became sharper.

"Assaulted? You say it was a white woman?"

"That's all I've got so far. She was beaten up by some Hawaiian boys. I'm sending Bill Furtado and George Harbottle to check on it. I'll let you know."

Rickard broadcast instructions to Patrol Car No. 2 to go to the address in Manoa Valley and report immediately. He then called Patrol Car No. 1, Detectives John Cluney and Thurman Black, and told them to go to Cunha Lane, pick up Horace Ida, and bring him in for questioning. In Rickard's methodical mind, it seemed quite apparent that two events connected in time must also be connected in fact.

Downtown Honolulu, 1:50 A.M.

Detective Bill Furtado was driving at a moderate speed at Lunalilo Street, on his way to Jack Lane to investigate a reported burglary. George Harbottle, his patrol mate, was slumped in the seat beside him, dividing his attention between things that might be expected to happen on the streets of Honolulu at two o'clock Sunday morning, and the radio, which gave out intermittent messages.

Officer Rickard's voice came in, with its crackling, nasal sound: "Patrol Car Number Two . . . Patrol Car Number Two . . ."

Harbottle flipped the switch and picked the microphone off the hook on the dashboard.

"Patrol Car Number Two, Detective Harbottle."

"Proceed to 2850 Kahawai Street immediately, George. A *haole wahine* says she was attacked by some Hawaiian boys. I've got an earlier report that seems to tie in with it. Report in as soon as you find anything, so I can advise John Jardine. He's standing by. Forget the job at Jack Lane for the present."

Harbottle had turned up the radio receiver, and Furtado listened to the conversation. He quickly turned the car southward and headed for Manoa Valley. His report on this aspect of the investigation follows:

On September 13, 1931, I was on duty on patrol car with Detective George Harbottle. We received a call at 1:50 A.M. while we were on our way to Jack Lane, where a burglary had been committed, to disregard our Jack Lane call and go to 2850 Kahawai Street, Manoa, as a woman had been assaulted. I believe I confirmed the call before leaving, stating that I had received the call and was on my way.

I drove at a high rate of speed headed for Manoa Valley. I met Lieutenant Massie at the door and explained my mission. He told me his wife had been beaten up and assaulted. Mrs. Massie was lying on a couch near the front door. I asked her what happened. She told me that while walking along John Ena Road about 200 or 300 feet from Kalakaua Avenue a bunch of boys who appeared to be Hawaiians, in an old-model Ford or Dodge touring car, stopped alongside of her, jumped out and grabbed her and pushed her into the car, striking her as they pushed her in and drove down the Ala Moana Road and drove a little way off the road and that they assaulted her. She said while they were taking her to the Ala Moana Road they were beating her up on the way.

I asked her if she knew the number of the car in which she had been abducted and she told me she did not. I asked her if she could recognize the boys and she replied she could not recognize them, only by their voices.

I then asked her if she was unconscious at any time from the time they picked her up and the time they finished assaulting her, and she said she was never unconscious at the time. She then told me that after these boys had finished assaulting her they drove off and left her there. She said she then walked out to the main road and an automobile with some white people in it picked her up. She said they wanted to take her to a hospital but she insisted she be taken home and that they took her home.

When I saw Mrs. Massie there was blood dripping from her top lip. The only thing I noticed about Mrs. Massie's face was the busted lip, her hair was all mussed up, and she was crying.[1]

George Harbottle was standing beside Furtado, taking notes. Massie had met them at the door, his thin lips set in a straight line.

He now stood beside the couch while the detectives questioned his wife. As Harbottle later described it, "He was grim and pretty damned mad."

Mrs. Massie lay on the couch, wearing pajamas with a wrapper drawn around her. She was able to speak, but it was obvious to Harbottle that she was suffering great pain when she talked. Her hair was disheveled and her face streaked with tears. As Harbottle later said, "She looked scared—awful damned scared."

Furtado was doing most of the questioning. He asked her if she could recognize the car if she saw it again.

"It was a Ford car," she said. "The back was flapping, and it might have been an old car."

She explained that she had been thrown into the car, and held down in the rear seat, and got only glimpses of the car as her attackers were leaving. She was asked if she had been able to see the license number, and she said she had not.

"Would you be able to identify the boys who attacked you, Mrs. Massie?" Furtado asked.

She shook her head.

Furtado spoke in a low voice and his tone was sympathetic, yet with that relentlessness that has to be a part of the police officer's trade.

"Did you hear any of their names?"

"No . . . except one was called 'Bull.' I remember that name." Harbottle jotted this down in his notes.

"And you can't give us anything about the license number, Mrs. Massie?" Furtado watched her closely. He realized she was in great pain; yet the only real hope of tracking down the assailants was to have some definite information that would identify them, or at least lead to an identification of the car. "I realize this is painful, Mrs. Massie," he said kindly. "But you must try to help us. The only way we can trace them is from what you can remember."

"I'm sorry," she said. Her voice was muffled by her swollen lips. "It was dark . . . I didn't see very much. I don't remember the number of the license."

Harbottle wrote this down.

Lieutenant Massie suddenly broke into the questioning.

"Look here, don't you think you've talked to my wife enough? Your job is to find the car and the people that beat her up—attacked her."

Furtado explained patiently that it was necessary to get all the information possible from Mrs. Massie, if they wanted to track down the boys who attacked her and bring them to justice.

"You said they were Hawaiians," he said to Mrs. Massie. "Are you sure of that?"

She nodded, holding her hand to her mouth. "I'm sure they were Hawaiians. There were four or five—I'm not sure how many."

Furtado went to the telephone and called headquarters. Rickard said a car was already on its way to Manoa with Detectives George Nakea and Frank Bettencourt, dispatched by Jardine to assist them.

Manoa Valley, 1:50 A.M.

Officer William K. Simerson was patrolling Manoa Valley during the early hours of September 13. The valley, scooped out of the western rim of an ancient volcano that formed the backbone of the island of Oahu, was east and south of the downtown area, sloping back toward the mountains that rose like a backdrop of dark blue drapery behind the city. The lower level of the valley was sprinkled with homes of *kaimaaina haoles*—the older generation of white people, who had come to Hawaii as either traders or missionaries, or in their wake, and established a solid economic position in the islands. Many of the homes were spacious, with beautiful gardens cultivated in a combination of English and tropical styles of landscaping that sometimes created bizarre effects.

These were the second- and third-generation executives of the big agencies, such as Castle & Cook, C. Brewer & Co., American Factors, Alexander & Baldwin and so on. A newer and more unruly element had intruded into the upper levels of Manoa Valley in recent years, and it was always advisable to have a police patrol on Saturday nights, just to be sure the new and unruly element did not disturb the sleep of established old-timers with playful parties and other goings-on. Officer Simerson had this assignment on September 12.

Simerson was a bulky man, of Hawaiian blood, who had been an athlete of some fame a few years earlier when he held the world record for the plunge-for-distance. His weight alone carried him almost the length of the swimming course at the Waikiki Natatorium, where the national championships had been held in 1927.

Simerson was walking slowly along Kahawai Street when he saw the figure of a man under the shadow of some trees, apparently shambling along with his coat under his arm. A night watchman named Gomes, who patrolled one of the larger mansions nearby, came out and spoke to Simerson. He had been watching the man, also.

Simerson stopped the man and asked his name and also asked what he was doing in Manoa Valley late at night.

The man said his name was Branson—Lieutenant Jerome J. Branson, USN; and he was going to the house of his friends, the Massies. If Officer Simerson wanted to know anything else, he could go to hell.

The police car dispatched by Jardine passed by at that moment on its way to the Massie house. Simerson flagged it, and the car pulled up at the curb. Detective Nakea got out. Simerson explained the situation, as well as he could.

Branson had been picked up about two hundred yards from the Massie house. He seemed to be in a state of considerable disarray; his shirt was open, his necktie pulled to one side, and as Simerson later reported, the fly of his pants was open. He looked as if he had either been on a party or slept in his clothes.

His manner, as Simerson described it, was "insulting and suspicious." Nakea and Bettencourt decided, in view of the events at the Massie house, that Branson should be questioned further, and he was taken into the patrol car, driven to the Massie place, where he was left sitting in the patrol car while the others went inside.

Massie, inside the house, apparently knew nothing at the time of Branson's arrest. According to the latter's version of his activities, given later at the police station, he had gone to sleep at the Rigby house, on the couch where he had flung himself when he came in

54

with Massie; and he had awakened when he heard the sound of Massie's car starting up.

He decided to go to the Massie home, and started walking the few blocks that separated the two houses. It was at this point that Simerson stopped him and asked him what he was doing on the street at that time of night.

Police Station, 2:30 A.M.

Detectives Cluney and Black, in Patrol Car No. 1, had driven to Cunha Lane as instructed, and found Horace Ida at home, asleep. He was told to put on his clothes and come to the police station for questioning in "an assault case."

As Cluney walked through the yard to the small frame cottage where Horace Ida lived with his mother and two sisters, he saw a Ford car standing in the driveway and stopped to feel the radiator. It was warm.

After he had aroused Horace Ida from his bed, he asked: "Where did you go tonight, Shorty—in your car?"

Ida shook his head.

"I don't go no place," he said. "I lent my junk to a Hawaiian boy. I don't know where he went."

"What Hawaiian boy? What's his name?"

Ida shrugged.

"I don't know his name. Some Hawaiian fellow—I know him, that's all."

Cluney stood for a minute, looking at the Japanese boy. He knew that Horace Ida's car had been at King and Liliha Streets, but as he said later, it did not occur to him that Ida was lying to avoid being involved in the affair with Homer Peeples and his wife. "I knew he was lying to me," Cluney said, "and that's all there was to it."

The reason *why* Horace Ida lied about taking his car out that night became a matter of considerable significance later in the case. His sisters, who had been to a party near Waipahu, about twenty miles from Honolulu, and had just gotten back, both supported his story that he was in bed when they arrived. Nevertheless, Cluney took Ida down to the police station convinced in his own mind that the Japanese boy was lying to conceal something.

At about a quarter to three Cluney and Black brought Horace Ida into the police station and booked him. Chief Inspector McIntosh was not in his office, so Cluney told Ida to wait in the assembly room. Detective Black was in the room, and so was the night duty officer, Cecil Rickard. Cluney went to look for McIntosh.

The actual sequence of the events during this period was never quite cleared up; yet it became a matter of the utmost significance later in the case because of a remark Horace Ida was reported to have made on the way to the police station. A local newspaper, on the Tuesday following the assault, printed a story quoting the Japanese boy as having said on the way to the station:

"I admit one of the boys hit the Hawaiian woman, but we do not know nothing about the white woman." [2]

The two radio patrol officers, Cluney and Black, knew about the attack on "a white woman" because they had been instructed to say nothing about it to Ida when they drove up to Cunha Lane to pick him up. However, Ida could have had no such knowledge—unless he participated in the attack; and for this reason his reported statement was quite significant.

In the official police records, and the verbal reports made later, Cluney stated that he had walked over to the Japanese boy while he was sitting in the assembly room, and said, "It looks tough for you, Shorty."

According to the report written much later, Ida had replied:

I was driving my car. I'll tell you the truth. I was driving my car when the Hawaiian boy who was with me struck the *kanaka* woman in the face. But I don't know nothing about the white woman. [3]

Cluney said that he had not mentioned an assault on a white woman at any time, although he did recall telling Ida he was wanted at the police station for questioning on "an assault case," referring to the incident at King and Liliha Streets with the Peeples' car. However, Cecil Rickard, who was in the room with Black and Ida at the time Cluney was out of the room, said later that he had talked with Ida about the Massie assault.

I asked him [Ida] if he had assaulted a white woman and he told me he had not assaulted any white woman. I asked him if he was positive and he said they did not assault any white woman, but one of them struck this Hawaiian woman.

At the time I asked Ida these questions I believe Officer Cluney and Officer Black were in the room asking questions also. I do not know if Cluney and Black asked Ida if Ida had assaulted a white woman, unless they asked him when they were bringing him in.[4]

Cluney also said he had not discussed the report of the attack on Mrs. Peeples on the way into the station, except to advise Horace Ida that he was being picked up on "an assault case."

After Cluney arrived at the station, he walked into the office of Deputy Sheriff David Hao and then into the office of the Chief Inspector of Detectives. No one was in either room at the time. It was several minutes before he returned to the assembly room, where Ida was sitting with Black and Rickard.

Whether Horace Ida mentioned an attack on "a white woman" before he had an opportunity to know that such an attack had occurred was not mentioned in any of the official reports, written or oral. However, it was definitely implied in the report published two days later in the local newspapers, after the suspects in the case had been rounded up and identified.

This suggestion that Horace Ida had sought to deny any involvement in the attack on "the white woman" before he could have been aware that such an attack occurred was one of the principal grounds for the initial belief in the minds of most of the people of Honolulu, as well as officials of the United States Navy, that the five "Ala Moana boys" were perpetrators of the assault.

It was never clearly determined when, or how, Cluney conveyed this information to Inspector McIntosh. Neither could remember exactly when this happened, because Cluney had not made a written report. According to Cluney's own recollection, he told the Chief Inspector of Ida's statement when he first went into McIntosh's office at about three o'clock. McIntosh himself did not remember when Cluney made the report, or precisely when Ida had denied having attacked "the white woman." His original impression was that it happened en route to the police station from Ida's home; but this was later denied by Cluney himself.

Emergency Hospital, Honolulu, 2:35 A.M.

Detectives Furtado and Harbottle arrived at the Emergency Hospital with Thalia Massie and her husband shortly after 2:30 A.M. Deputy Inspector Jardine met them. He was a small man, with a curious habit of pulling his hat down over his eyes; and when he asked even simple questions they imparted an air of a confidential conspiracy.

He took Thalia Massie into the office of Dr. David Liu, an experienced and capable physician who was on duty. Then he went out on the *lanai*, or verandah, and talked with Lieutenant Massie.

Dr. Liu's report of his examination follows:

Q. What statement did she [Mrs. Massie] make to you?
A. She stated that a car with four to six men drove up to her and two men jumped out of the car and dragged her into the car and soon afterward took her into the brush and each took turn and raped her. She also stated she was of the impression that these men had done it before. She could not recognize the men because it was too dark.
Q. Did you examine her whole body carefully or not?
A. No, I didn't examine her whole body.
Q. Did you make a pelvic examination?
A. Yes, but the patient was raped two hours ago [earlier] and she douched herself before she came to the Emergency Hospital.
Q. Could this woman have had five men rape her and not show any marks?
A. Yes. One reason is because she is a married woman. I had a talk with Doctor Faus [Dr. Robert Faus, chief City and County physician] and he says it is possible.
Q. Was she under the influence of liquor?
A. When I examined her I detected alcohol and she was under the influence of liquor.
Q. Was any car number mentioned in your office?
A. No, not in the office, but they were talking about some number on the porch outside. I heard talking but I did not pay attention to that part. Several people and officers were there. I stayed inside so nobody could talk to me.
Q. Did you know her jaw was broken at that time?
A. No. I examined it and it was tender. A fracture of the jaw is hard to find.[5]

Jardine meanwhile had taken Massie to one side, during the time his wife was in the emergency room, and they stood on the porch, just outside the room where Mrs. Massie was being examined. According to Police Officer George Seymour, who had accompanied Jardine to the hospital, Jardine brought up the matter of Lieutenant Branson and his activities in the neighborhood of the Massie house.

"Could he have had anything to do with this?" Jardine asked.

Massie looked at him in amazement. "That's absurd," he said. "He was with me."

"All evening?" Jardine asked.

"Most of the evening," Massie replied shortly.

At that moment a radio car from police headquarters drew up outside the Emergency Hospital building, on Lunalilo Street, just below the Queen's Hospital. A radio broadcast from Rickard at Police Headquarters, picked up by the patrol car's loudspeaker, advised them that the Ida car, bearing license number 58-895, had been picked up on Cunha Lane, and Ida was being brought to the police station.

The license number was broadcast several times over the patrol car radio receiver, which was within fifty feet of the porch where Jardine and Massie were discussing the case. Seymour, in a statement later, said he heard the number, and he thought it could easily have been heard by Massie. A Navy patrol officer, A. W. McKecknie, was also at the hospital at the time. He was later questioned on the matter of the license number, and he said:

> I tried to get information from the doctor, but he told me the case could not be discussed. Then Mr. Massie came out and told us what had happened and one of the detectives standing there said they had the number of the car they were looking for that had assaulted another woman.
>
> Q. Did he say what the number was?
> A. I thought he did. He said they had a Ford or Chevrolet touring car.
> Q. Did he mention the actual number?
> A. I think he did.[6]

At the time Thalia Massie was taken from the emergency hospital to the police station, shortly after 3 A.M., there appeared to be considerable possibility that the license number of the Ida car had been repeated several times in the presence of Lieutenant Massie and other Navy personnel at the hospital.

Police Station, 3:30 A.M.

Thalia Massie, still in a state of semishock and visibly shaken by her experience, was asked to come down to the detective bureau and give a statement to Inspector McIntosh. At first her husband was uncertain as to the wisdom of this, in view of her physical condition; but Jardine persuaded him that it was essential in the interest of finding her attackers.

Inspector John McIntosh was already at the police station when Thalia Massie arrived shortly before 3:30 A.M. and was escorted into his office. Horace Ida sat in the assembly room outside the door as she passed into the inner office. According to Detective John Cluney, who was standing beside Ida, McIntosh and Mrs. Massie were in the office alone for several minutes. McIntosh finally opened the door and called to Cluney to come in.

Cluney's statement follows:

As I entered the office Mrs. Massie was still seated at the desk and Captain McIntosh was sitting a little to the right of Mrs. Massie. Captain McIntosh asked me the number of the car I had brought in. I had this number written down on a card and I held it before me where Captain McIntosh could read the number himself without telling him and without Mrs. Massie being able to see it.

I had the number 58-895 written in black lead pencil and after Captain McIntosh glanced at the number which I had on this card he called my attention to a number that was written on the blotter on his desk. I glanced at this number and noticed that the number was off one cipher. I would not be able to state at this time whether the number Captain McIntosh had was off more than one number but it was close to the number and I believe it lacked—that is, the number he had—just one cipher from being or corresponding to the number I had.[7]

Later it was disclosed in the record of Inspector McIntosh's interview that night with Mrs. Massie that he had asked her: "What was the license number? Do you know?"

Mrs. Massie replied, according to the record of the interview: "I think it was 58-805. I would not swear to that being correct. I just caught a fleeting glimpse of it as they drove away."

The statement that Mrs. Massie made in the early hours of Sunday morning, to Inspector McIntosh, was fairly lengthy, covering almost every aspect of her story. John McIntosh was a thorough, competent officer who had spent many years in Hawaii and was a veteran on the police force. A lean, angular man of Scottish descent, he had a reputation for a deep sense of justice and fairness. As senior officer in the Detective Bureau he was responsible for the conduct of all criminal investigations; and in this case he took the precaution of taking down Mrs. Massie's statement himself—in his own handwriting.

Following are certain parts of that statement, which later was issued publicly:

Q. Will you relate to me what happened to you tonight?
A. I left home about 9 P.M. with my husband to go to the Ala Wai Inn. In our party were Lieutenant Branson, Lieutenant Brown and their wives. They had been to our house and followed Mr. Massie and I to the Ala Wai in their own cars. When we got to the inn the six of us took a table together.

Around 12 midnight I decided to go for a walk and some air. I walked along Kalakaua Avenue and crossed the bridge over the canal and turned down John Ena Road and walked a block or so down John Ena Road.

A car drove up behind me and stopped. Two men got off the car and grabbed me and dragged me into their car. One of them placed a hand over my mouth. When they got me into the back seat of the car they held me down between them. They were Hawaiians. I begged and pleaded with them to let me go. I struggled to get off the car and away from them and they kept punching me on the face. I offered them money if they would take me back to the Ala Wai Inn. They asked me where the money was. I told them it was in my pocketbook. They grabbed my pocketbook and found there was no money in it. They were driving along the Ala Moana Road all this time heading toward town. I really don't know how far they drove me—perhaps two or three blocks. They drove the car into the undergrowth on the right-hand side of the road, dragged me out and away from the car into the bushes and assaulted me. I was assaulted six or seven times.[8]

Mrs. Massie's account indicated that there were "at least four" in the car—two in front and two in the back seat. She was asked if she knew the make, or model, of the car, and she said: "It was a touring car. I can't say what make it was, but I think it was a Ford."

She was asked if she remembered the license number and she gave the number: 58-805. The number of Ida's Ford Phaeton, it will be recalled, was 58-895.

According to her account, the assailants held her in the little clearing in the bushes—later identified as the site of the old animal quarantine station—for about twenty minutes. As they started for their car, leaving her alone, she said she asked the way into town. One of the boys turned and pointed to the direction of the road. Then they ran for their car and drove off.

Her story continued:

> I managed to get back on the road and stopped a car coming from Waikiki and heading towards town. I told the occupants of the car what happened to me—that I had been assaulted by some Hawaiians—and asked them to take me home. They wanted to bring me to the police station but I asked them to take me home, which they did.
>
> Q. Who were these people?
> A. I don't know. They were white people. There were two men in the front seat and two women and a man in the back seat. I sat in the front seat and they took me home in Manoa. After I got home Lieutenant Massie called me on the phone from a friend's house. I told him to come home at once, which he did, and I told him what had happened to me. He immediately called for the police.
> Q. Would you know the car in which they were if you saw it again, I mean the car in which your assailants rode?
> A. I think I would if I saw a rear view of it and saw the back seat.
> Q. Did you hear any names mentioned?
> A. I heard the name "Bull" used several times and some common name like "Joe" or likened to that.
> Q. Do you think you could identify these men, Mrs. Massie?
> A. I don't know.
> Q. What color dress or gown did you wear tonight at the Ala Wai Inn?
> A. A green dress.

Q. Where is that dress now?
A. At home.
Q. Was it torn at all?
A. I don't think it was.[9]

After Inspector McIntosh had taken the full statement, which was several pages long, he went to the door and called to Cluney.

"Bring the man in."

Cluney called to Horace Ida, who was sitting alone in a chair at the end of the assembly room. The Japanese arose and followed Cluney into the Inspector's office. Cluney stood at one side, and McIntosh looked at Ida a moment, and then said:

"Now look at your beautiful work!"

Thalia said nothing at first, merely looking at Ida. As Cluney later described the scene: "She nodded her head once or twice, and looked at Captain McIntosh as if to imply that this was one of the men who had assaulted her."

Ida stared at the woman, and then shook his head. "I didn't see this woman," he said. "I didn't do nothing to her."

Thalia looked at the Japanese boy very carefully, and then asked:

"Do you know a boy by the name of 'Bull'?"

Ida shook his head, but said nothing. It was Cluney's impression that she was trying to get Ida to answer questions so she could listen to his voice. However, before Ida said anything, McIntosh motioned for Cluney to leave the room.

Cluney noted at the time that Ida was wearing his dark leather jacket when he came into Inspector McIntosh's office.

A few minutes later Thalia Massie left the Inspector's office and was taken to her husband, who was waiting outside. Horace Ida was placed under arrest immediately afterward; and the following morning police picked up Joseph Kahahawai, David Takai and Henry Chang at their homes. Ben Ahakuelo was arrested at Kauluwela School, where he was working out in football practice later in the afternoon. All five were charged with criminally assaulting Thalia Massie.

The Investigation

The decision to arrest the five boys who were in Horace Ida's car on the night of September 12, 1931, was made by Chief Inspector McIntosh. The normal procedure in a criminal investigation requires that some preliminary inquiry into the facts be undertaken before an arrest is made. This may not always be necessary; in cases where the culprit is caught red-handed at the scene of the crime, he may be arrested and the investigation undertaken afterward. But that would not be the usual order of things for an obvious reason: the police have to dig up some information pointing to the suspect before they know whom to arrest.

In the Ala Moana case, the Honolulu police proceeded almost in the reverse of the usual order. They arrested the suspects and then began an investigation. The reason for this could hardly have been fear that the suspects would escape. Getting away from the police in Honolulu at that time was almost an impossibility. The only means of leaving the Islands was by steamer, and police surveillance of steamer departures was so routine that major crimes seldom occurred in the Islands.

There were actually two reasons for making the arrests before any real investigation. The first was the simple assumption that Thalia

Massie's story, linked with the fact that the five accused were already involved in another assault that night and therefore were readily available as suspects, seemed to offer a quick and easy solution to the case. The second reason was more complex, and will be dealt with later because it pervaded not only the investigation, but the murder of one of the boys, the two trials and the tragic aftermath of the Massie case.

John McIntosh was known as "an honest cop." He had been on the Honolulu force for many years, having served under former Chief of Detectives Arthur McDuffie, who had been relieved of his duties after a graft scandal known as the Trask-McDuffie hearings, some years before. Like most "honest cops," McIntosh was first and last a policeman; it was his job to bring malefactors to the bar of justice, leaving it to the County Attorney to handle the business of convicting them.

When Thalia Massie left the Detective Bureau early that Sunday morning with her husband, McIntosh sat for several minutes, rubbing his forefinger against his temple—a characteristic gesture that indicated he was putting things together in his mind. Finally he snapped his fingers and pressed the button that signaled the desk outside.

"Ask Cluney to come in," he said.

John Cluney came in. His hat was pulled over his forehead, and he sat down across from McIntosh without taking it off. It was almost four o'clock, and both were tired.

"We've got the right boys, John," the chief inspector said. "Horace Ida lied when he told you he hadn't driven his car last night. When did he tell you the truth—about the assault on Mrs. Peeples?"

"After we got to the station. He admitted he was driving his car and that one of the boys hit the *kanaka* woman. He said he lied because he didn't want to get in trouble."

McIntosh nodded.

"Well, he's in trouble. A hell of a lot of it! When did he tell you they didn't have anything to do with the *haole* woman? Was that on the way in?"

Cluney shook his head. It was in the police station. McIntosh nodded slowly, and wrote down a few notes on a scratch pad.

65

Horace Ida had said: "Sure I lie! I don't want no trouble with
that Hawaiian woman. Joe Kalani hit her and that's his business.
I only drive the car and I don't want no trouble. That's why I say
I don't drive the car tonight. Cluney say there is an assault on a
woman. I think it is the *kanaka* woman, so I say I wasn't there. I
don't want no trouble, that's all!"

Years later, John McIntosh recalled the way he reached the decision to arrest the five boys. "Look at it this way. When Johnny
Cluney went out to pick up the Japanese boy, the boy lied about
the car. He said he hadn't driven it when he had been out all night
in it. Then Cluney told me what Ida said about not attacking the
white woman. How in hell did he know there was a white woman?
All he was supposed to know about was the Hawaiian woman—and
he had lied about that. When a man lies to me twice, I don't think
I have to take his word for anything. Then Mrs. Massie gave me
the license number of the car she said picked her up. It was only
one figure off the license number of Ida's car. What in hell was I
to think? I called Cluney in and showed him the number she gave
me, and he showed me the number of Ida's car. As far as I was
concerned, that cinched it. These were the guilty boys—and all we
had to do was build a case."

Having decided at this point that Ida and the other four boys
whom Ida had identified as being with him that night were "the
guilty boys," the problem of "building a case" became McIntosh's
chief concern. He called in Officer Claude Benton, who was on
night duty. Benton formerly worked for a tire-distributing firm in
Honolulu, and McIntosh knew he was an expert on tires.

"Take a run out to the old animal quarantine station," he said.
"Look around and see if you can find any good tire tracks. If you
can, we'll get pictures of them and compare them with the tires on
Ida's car." He hesitated a moment, and then added: "Better check
the tires on Ida's car first—so you'll know what to look for."

Benton left; and in order to follow instructions to the letter, he
drove out in Ida's car. McIntosh sat at his desk in the small office he occupied at the temporary Police Headquarters, juggling a
pencil in his big freckled fist. He wrote on a pad: "1. Identification.
2. Time factor." Then he erased the words and reversed the order.

The time factor was the most critical, since it was factual and could be verified. Where had the boys been during the evening? He needed to trace every movement, and if possible find witnesses who saw them.

The Time Factor

One end of the time period for the kidnaping and assault was fixed by the Peeples incident at King and Liliha Streets. The car driven by Horace Ida, with Joe Kalani, the big Hawaiian boy, was known to have been there about 12:35 A.M., Sunday morning. This was established by Mrs. Peeples' statement, and also by Horace Ida's own story.

With the time element anchored at the end, McIntosh had only to work backward, accounting for necessary intervals of time, to establish the time at the beginning. There was one point in Mrs. Massie's statement, which he had written down himself, that had caught McIntosh's attention, and troubled him a bit.

He called in John Cluney, who had been in the office part of the time that Mrs. Massie was with McIntosh, giving her account of the affair. He asked Cluney:

"John, were you in the office when Mrs. Massie made her statement?"

Cluney shook his head.

"Only when I brought Ida in. I left after she talked with him. You asked me to leave."

McIntosh nodded. His forehead was pinched in a frown, and his brown, steady eyes seemed to be veiled in thought. Finally he nodded again.

"Okay, John . . . There are some angles we've got to check right away. How long would it take to drive from the old animal quarantine station on the Ala Moana to King and Liliha?"

Cluney thought a minute.

"About six or seven minutes," he said. "You could make it in that time if you drove by Ward Avenue and there wasn't much traffic."

McIntosh jotted down some figures on a pad.

"I'd like to have you get someone out to the quarantine station as soon as possible. Before sunup. I want the place looked over, and the driving time checked from there to King and Liliha. Better send George Cypher out to handle it."

After Cluney left, McIntosh began to write some more notes on the pad. Since Mrs. Peeples had arrived at the police station at King and Alakea Streets just before 12:45 A.M. to register her complaint against Joseph Kahahawai for hitting her, it was safe to assume the incident at King and Liliha could have occurred less than ten minutes earlier. He wrote down: 12:37 A.M.

Then he drew a time chart, working backward from that time, to establish a probable chronology in reverse. This is what he wrote:

Time schedule

Peeples incident—King and Liliha	12:37 A.M.
Time needed to drive from quarantine to King-Liliha	:06 minutes
Departure from quarantine station	12:31 A.M.
Time needed for assault (Mrs. Massie estimate)	:20 minutes
Arrival at quarantine station	12:11 A.M.
Time needed to drive from John Ena to quarantine	:04 minutes
Time needed for kidnaping	:01 minute
Time of kidnaping	12:06 A.M.

Assuming that it would have taken Thalia Massie ten minutes to walk from the Ala Wai Inn to the place on John Ena Road where she was picked up by the boys who assaulted her, this would establish her departure from the Inn at about five minutes to twelve. It still might have been earlier, but it could not have been later than 11:55 P.M., or thereabouts, for everything to have happened that she said happened.

McIntosh pulled out of a drawer the stenographer's notebook, on which he had written down her statement, and looked at it. He flipped the paper and read several lines; then he shook his head a couple of times, and put the notebook back in the drawer and locked it. He called Cluney in again.

"I want everyone checked that could possibly have talked with Mrs. Massie or seen her at the inn after eleven o'clock," he said. "We'll get statements from them and from Lieutenant Massie as to when he saw her last. Check all the members of her party."

"When did she say she left the inn?" Cluney asked.

McIntosh looked up, his eyes again veiled in thought.

"Around twelve o'clock," he said. "As near as she can remember. She probably wasn't looking at her watch. Anyway, this checks out with the rest of the things we know. Ida says they were at Waikiki Park until the dance ended, but that's just his word. It could have been a few minutes earlier. Anyway, if they left at midnight there was time to pick up Mrs. Massie across the street a few minutes later and do the whole job, the way I've got it figured."

This discussion with Cluney took place about 4:30 A.M. Sunday. At that time the statements of Tatsumi Matsumoto and Robert Vierra, who later said they had seen Horace Ida and Ben Ahakuelo in the car with the other three boys at 12:25 A.M. driving along Beretania Street—about two miles from King and Liliha—were not on record; and there was no indication that any time factors were involved other than those set down by McIntosh.

It was not until the following day that McIntosh learned from Sam Kahanamoku, a brother of the one-time world champion swimmer, Duke Kahanamoku, that Matsumoto and his friends had seen the car driven by Horace Ida on Beretania Street at about half past twelve. It appeared from the information McIntosh had early Sunday morning that Mrs. Massie could have left the Ala Wai Inn "around midnight"; it might have been earlier, but it could be no later than that and still allow time for the other events on the schedule he had drawn up.

Had McIntosh known of the information supplied by Matsumoto the following day, it is quite possible the investigation would have taken a different turn. If the five boys were observed on Beretania Street at 12:25 A.M., it would mean considerable tightening of the time schedule, since they could not have left the old quarantine station at 12:31 A.M., as he had estimated.

Bits of Evidence

When Claude Benton returned from his predawn visit to the old quarantine station, he went into the Chief Inspector's office. He pulled out a pad of paper and drew a picture of the area. The roadway leading off the Ala Moana to the clearing where the quarantine station had once stood was about 150 feet in length, and Benton drew lines on the paper to show the marks of tires that he said would show that a car had skidded around the turn into the road, going perhaps thirty miles an hour, and had been driven into the area of rubble and broken bottles.

"What kind of tire tracks?" McIntosh asked.

"One Goodyear All-Weather and three Silvertown cords—the same as on Ida's car."

"You can testify to that?"

Benton nodded.

"We'll take pictures to be sure," he said.

Benton produced two boxes of matches and a package of cigarettes which he said he had found in the clearing. He also had a ginger ale bottle and a small pocketbook mirror. McIntosh put these in a box in his desk.

Shortly after dawn, which was merely a lightening of the sky since the sun rose from the windward side of the four-thousand-foot-high Koolau mountains that rimmed Honolulu on the east, two other emissaries of the Police Department drove out to the old quarantine station—Officer George Cypher and Bill Hoopai, the Assistant Chief of Police. Bill Hoopai was a heavy-set Hawaiian who had been a member of the department for many years, a genial, round-faced man with a good-humored expression and friendly black eyes. He was of the old school of Hawaiian police-politicos, a friend of former Mayor Johnny Wilson, the Democratic leader on Oahu, and a friend of all Hawaiians. He went out, as he later said, "to keep an eye on things."

It was six o'clock when they reached the clearing at the site of the quarantine station. They noticed tire tracks in the area, which Cypher recognized as having been made by Goodyear All-Weather tires and Goodrich Silvertown cords. What Bill Hoopai did not know at the time was that Claude Benton had driven Horace Ida's car out in his predawn reconnaissance trip a couple of hours earlier.

Cypher and Hoopai reported finding several items of interest: a string of jade-colored beads later identified by Thalia Massie as hers; a brown celluloid barrette, which she also recognized; and later it was said he found a leather purse, which Thalia Massie like-

70

wise was able to identify. The report of finding these items was circulated in the Police Department, and finally found its way into the two English newspapers, the *Advertiser* and the *Star-Bulletin*. The significance of these reports did not develop until a later date.

Later on Monday morning Claude Benton was sent back to the scene—again in Horace Ida's car—accompanied by the Police Identification Officer, Samuel K. Lau, to take pictures of the tire tracks. Lau looked over the area, and shook his head. There were no identifiable tire marks, except the one short track that had been made by Ida's car when they drove into the clearing.

Benton suggested they drive Ida's car alongside the track that was visible—about three feet long—and take a picture of the two side by side.

"Why?" Lau asked. "You just made the first track, and you want me to take a picture of the second one, too?"

Benton looked at the smaller Chinese officer.

"Mac wants the pictures—that's why," he said.

Lau shook his head.

"I would have to testify," he said. "I would have to say both tracks were made by you."

Benton shrugged. They returned to the police station and reported the matter to the Chief Inspector. McIntosh scowled a minute, and finally said:

"I guess it may have been my fault. I drove out there this morning, to check on those tracks myself. I may have rubbed out some of them, and that's why you didn't find them."

The reasons for this curious series of misadventures was not particularly clear at the time—in fact, not until the trial itself. It was not certain whether the unusual mixup was due to carelessness, whether Cypher and Hoopai had deliberately or accidentally driven over the tracks made earlier; nor was it ever made clear in the police reports whether these investigative maneuvers were designed to cover up evidence—or even manufacture it. But in a sense, it set the tone of the investigation. The reported finding of Thalia Massie's purse in Horace Ida's car, for example, lost its significance when it was learned that young George Clark, who had been in the car that picked up Thalia Massie on the Ala Moana, actually brought the purse into Police Headquarters on Tuesday morning following the assault.

Clark explained that the Bellingers and his parents had gone back to Kewalo Inn that night to enjoy their delayed midnight snack, and out of curiosity had driven past the place where they picked up Thalia Massie. They had found her purse, a lipstick and the pocket mirror on the ground beside the road, and had brought it to the police thinking it might be of importance!

The Interrogation of the Suspects

On Sunday night all five boys were in custody, at Police Headquarters. Jardine was running them in and out of McIntosh's office, where the grim-faced Chief Inspector was sitting with Griffith Wight, the Deputy County Attorney, pumping questions at them. A man of medium height, well dressed, with dark eyes and a brown, rather handsome face, walked into the station.

"Hello, Judge," Officer Rickard called from the receiving desk. "Anything we can do for you?"

The man shook his head.

"Just looking up information," he said.

This was Judge William H. Heen, former City Magistrate and one of the most respected lawyers in the community. He was Hawaiian, and next to Johnny Wilson, the former mayor who had been deposed by a Republican-Reformist coalition, was probably the most popular Hawaiian in Honolulu.

Many years later Judge Heen sat in his office, on the sixth floor of the new Hawaiian Trust building in Honolulu, looking out at the changed city of his youth. "I listened to the boys talking that night," he said. "They were sitting on the chairs along the wall— it was the old Kapiolani Building, you know. I'd come down for something—I forget what it was. I knew about this case, but I wasn't involved in it at the time. But I overheard them talking. The boys didn't know I was listening, and I don't suppose they would have cared if they had known. They didn't seem worried. Every time one of them would come out of McIntosh's office and another go in, they would exchange information in whispers. There was a mixup about the way they had come back into town. Ida was the Japanese fellow. I remember him because he was the most serious, and I guess he was the smartest of the lot. He'd been on the Mainland and hadn't remembered that the Kalakaua extension was put through to Beretania Street. It was built while he was in Los Angeles. So he though they had turned down King to Keaumoku Street. They talked in whispers, of course, like any young fellows would do who were picked up by the police. In a police station you don't yell out everything you think.

"Anyway, I asked John Jardine, when he came out of Mac's office, what it was all about. He said, 'These are the guys, all right, Judge—in that rape case.' I thought, 'How in hell does he know—so quick?' You have to know people when you are a lawyer and judge. I'd been a magistrate, you know . . . city judge. You get to know all kinds of people and I could pretty well tell whether a young fellow was lying, or trying to fix up a story. These fellows weren't doing that. They weren't even scared. They were just telling each other what happened, and trying to get their stories together. That's when I decided I'd take the case if they asked me to. I was damned sure they weren't guilty."

The next day Judge Heen had received a telephone call from Ben Ahakuelo's mother. She had talked to Princess Abbey Kawananakoa, the last of the royal dynasty of Hawaii; and the Princess had said, "Call Bill Heen. He'll defend your boy."

Judge Heen laughed. "You know, everybody said the Princess was putting up money to defend the boys. Hell, I never got paid a cent for the case. Neither did Bill Pittman." William A. Pittman, a brother of the late Senator Key Pittman of Nevada, was one of the other lawyers in the case; he defended two of the Ala Moana boys—Joseph Kahahawai and Horace Ida. Judge Heen defended Ben Ahakuelo and Henry Chang. The fifth suspect, David Takai, was represented by a Japanese lawyer, Robert Murakami.

Judge Heen pressed a button and his secretary, Eva Hart, came into the office. She was a *haole*, a pleasant-faced middle-aged woman who had been Judge Heen's secretary for many years.

"Eva, did we ever get paid for that Ala Moana trial?"

73

The Ala Moana suspects. Top left, Horace Ida; right, David Takai; middle left, Henry Chang; right, Ben Ahakuelo; lower left, Joseph Kahahawai.

Eva Hart laughed and shook her head.

"Not a cent. There were stories that the Princess paid you, you know. She called you and thanked you for taking the case. The boy's mother—Mrs. Ahakuelo—had called her and she talked to you."

Judge Heen nodded, and rubbed his hand across his face. He was well into his seventies, and he had seen Hawaii through the storms and troubles of a half century. His old eyes glinted, and he laughed.

"That's right. She told me I wouldn't get a cent for it—and I didn't. But she said, 'Bill, somebody's got to represent these Hawaiian boys and see they get a fair trial.' So I took the case."

He rubbed his fingers across his eyes again, and then put his hands on the polished desk. "I'll tell you one thing—I'd never have taken the case if I thought those boys were guilty! I got all of them in my office, with Bill Pittman—it was a small office then, not like this one. I cross-examined those boys as if I'd been the prosecutor. I told them if they lied, I'd know it—and I'd never take the case. When I got through I was absolutely sure they weren't guilty!"

Meanwhile, McIntosh and Griffith Wight continued to interrogate the five boys. Horace Ida had been the first one taken in, while the others sat in chairs in the assembly room. It was 6:55 P.M. on Sunday, September 13, when Ida was taken into the Chief Inspector's office. Sitting with McIntosh were two Deputy County Attorneys, Griffith Wight and Eddie Sylva. McIntosh was asking the questions.

"How many people were in your car when you rode out to Waikiki Park—the last time?"

"Myself, Chang and Kalani. Three of us."

"When you got inside, what did you do?"

"We could not go inside the dance pavilion so we stayed outside. Mac and Ahakuelo were dancing. We waited and when it was through, we all went home."

"How long before the last dance did you wait?"

"About five minutes."

McIntosh jotted this down on a pad.

"Then you drove down John Ena Road, down to Ala Moana?"

"No, we went to Kalakaua Avenue, drove down Kalakaua Avenue and crossed King Street to Beretania."

"You crossed King Street to Beretania?"

Ida seemed to hesitate; then he said:

"No, we drove down King Street to Keaumoku Street."

"Why didn't you drive straight across?"

Ida's face was puzzled; he shook his head.

"I don't know," he finally said. "We followed a car. Ben knew the boys on the car. We went down Beretania Street, up Fort Street, to School Street, back to the *luau*."

McIntosh asked him about the *luau*—who was there and what they did. But Ida shook his head again. They stayed ten minutes or so in the car, he said, but only Ben Ahakuelo and "Kalani" had gone inside.

"Why didn't you go in?"

"Because we were not invited."

"If you were not invited why did you go back to the *luau?*"

"Ben Ahakuelo knew the people."

They filed into McIntosh's office, one by one. The Chief Inspector covered the events of the previous evening thoroughly, asking questions without raising his voice, seeking little points of difference with which to confuse them. As he said later, "We didn't get much, except the differences in their stories about the route they took and how they sat in the car. Ida said they had gone down King Street to Keaumoku, and then turned over to Beretania. This wasn't important in itself; but it showed they hadn't gotten their story together."

However, there was one point of importance that seems to have been overlooked during the Sunday evening interrogation. That was Ida's remark that they had "followed a car" and that "Ben knew the boys in the car." It was not until Monday afternoon that the significance of this was known to McIntosh.

At one point, McIntosh pulled a string of jade-colored beads out of the box in his desk drawer and tossed it in front of Ida.

"These beads were picked up in your car," he said. "Recognize them?"

Ida looked at the beads and shook his head.

"Maybe my sister's beads," he said.

When Joseph Kahahawai was asked what route they took returning to town, he said he thought they went down King Street from the Kalakaua intersection, "right into town."

When McIntosh pressed this point again, the big Hawaiian said: "I don't remember. I was asleep."

"The other boys say no one was asleep. What street did you take?"

"I was groggy. I don't know."

Later he said, "I remember we turned up, I do not know what place. All I know is we came School Street way . . . We went straight to Correa's place."

"Who went in the house with you?"

"There was some bunch singing . . . I went in with Ben."

"How long did you stay?"

"Two or three minutes . . . We went over and we could not get any beer, so we stood there and see how the boys were singing. We did not go in the house. We stayed by the window looking in."

"Did you talk to people inside?"

"I talked to Mina Correa . . . I asked if they had any beer, and she said, 'No,' so I saw the brother in the back of the yard and I went over and talk to him and he told me, 'You came too late.'"

There were other small discrepancies in their stories, such as Ahakuelo's recollection that he sat in back while the others said he sat in the front seat of the car. Kahahawai also thought they had all gone into the Waikiki Park dance pavilion when they returned for Ahakuelo and Takai; but Henry Chang said he had gone in first alone, and he thought Shorty and Joe stayed outside.

"How long were you inside?" McIntosh asked.

"About fifteen minutes. We stood by the small house (at the Ferris wheel) and a friend of mine came out with a stub and Shorty said, 'Go in and look for the boys.'"

There was also some discrepancy as to the time of departure from the park. Ida thought it was just before the last dance; but Chang, Ahakuelo and Takai all said it was after the last dance ended.

77

Joseph Kahahawai was the last to be questioned; and when he was taken back with the others to the jail cell, McIntosh looked thoughtfully at the two attorneys, Wight and Sylva.

"They haven't quite got their stories together," he remarked. "They've done a good job, but not good enough."

Griffith Wight was a one-time U. S. Army captain, who had married into the family of "Sonny" Cunha, a well-known Portuguese-Hawaiian of Honolulu. Wight was a protégé of Jimmy Gilliland, the County Attorney, and in all probability would present the case for the Territory. He rubbed his hands together with satisfaction.

"I'll tear their story apart when I get them on the stand, Mac," he promised.

McIntosh's expression was thoughtful, and a bit troubled.

"We aren't ready to go to trial yet, Griff—not by a damned sight! These boys have a story that generally hangs together. I know they're lying, and so do you. But we've got to prove it. We've got to dig up witnesses who saw them."

Wight and McIntosh were both *haoles;* and although both had lived in Hawaii for many years it is doubtful that they understood the nature of Hawaiians as Bill Heen did. During the evening, as the boys sat in chairs in the assembly room—one by one going into the Chief Inspector's office, each returning to discuss in low voices what had been said—they talked and laughed among themselves. As Heen watched them, it was evident, as he said, that "they weren't even scared."

"I know *kanakas*," he explained. "If those boys had been lying, they would have looked scared. And they weren't. They were talking to each other, and I was sure they weren't guilty of anything, except maybe raising hell with that Hawaiian woman."

They sat in chairs along the wall, when they weren't being questioned. Kahahawai was the biggest; and he said very little. He was slower than the others. Horace Ida was the smallest and the most alert. He was worried about some of his answers to questions, and when each of the others came out of McIntosh's office he talked with them in whispers. Chang and Takai seemed unconcerned; they sat back against the wall and listened, and nodded now and then; but they also said very little.

Judge Heen's impression was that "they just didn't know what in hell it was all about, and nobody tried to tell them."

Identification of the Suspects

Earlier that Sunday afternoon, Thalia Massie sat in a rocking chair, in the darkened sitting room of the Massie bungalow in Manoa Valley. Four boys stood against the wall, facing her. Her face was partly swathed in a bandage, and the ugly marks of violence still showed in the dark blotches on her cheek and her swollen upper lip, which had been badly cut.

Her prominent grayish blue eyes looked tired and angry. Her husband stood beside her, and behind Lieutenant Massie was another woman, the wife of Lieutenant L. L. Pace of the U. S. Navy. Mrs. Pace and her husband were close friends of the Massies, and she had come over that Sunday afternoon to lend what help she could.

Thalia Massie was a pretty girl, of medium height and slightly given to plumpness. Her expression of petulance, or pouting, was partly obscured by the injuries to her face. Both Massies had come from Kentucky, although Thalia had lived on Long Island near the village of Sayville for several years before she married young Tommy Massie when she was sixteen years old, on the day he was graduated from the Naval Academy at Annapolis.

She was a Hubbard and a Fortescue—two families that had collected the aura of the Army and the blue grass country. Her mother, Grace Hubbard Bell Fortescue, was a niece of Alexander Graham Bell and a daughter of Charles Bell, who had married Mabel Hubbard.

Grace Fortescue's husband, Major Granville Fortescue, had retired from the Army after a career that included duty with Colonel Roosevelt's Rough Riders and later service as an aide to Theodore Roosevelt when he was President. He was widely known in Washington social circles as "Rolly" Fortescue, a name he acquired when he first served in the Fourth Cavalry shortly after being graduated from West Point.

Thalia Fortescue had grown up in an Army atmosphere, with a certain type of reputation to live up to. Her father had been involved in a hazing party during his undergraduate days at Yale University, for example, and had punctuated the affair by firing a pistol shot through the headboard of the bed in which one of the terrified "hazees" was sleeping. For this slight prank, he was permitted to leave Yale. He served in the Philippines and at one time with Cuban rebel forces when he was still in his teens. In 1910 he married Grace Hubbard Bell and Thalia was one of three daughters.

Young Massie had been assigned to the Aircraft Carrier *Lexington* shortly after their marriage, and was later transferred to New London, where the submarine *S-34* was stationed. He was then moved to Pearl Harbor. It is quite possible that after the first glamour of Hawaii paled, Thalia Massie became somewhat bored with the social pursuits of young Navy officers and their wives in Hawaii.

On this Sunday afternoon in Honolulu she looked sullen and hurt. Detective Tom Finnegan, of the Police Department, and Arthur Stagbar, assigned to the County Attorney's office, had arrived with the four suspects. Finnegan went into the house first, and found Thalia Massie with her husband and Mrs. Pace in the rear bedroom. Commander Bates, of the Navy, was also there.

"We've got four of the boys here," Finnegan said. "We'd like to have you identify them." He asked her to talk with them, but to say nothing about being able to identify them until they left the house. When Thalia Massie came into the front room, the four boys were lined up, facing her. They were Joseph Kahahawai, the big Hawaiian who was the tallest of the four suspects; Henry Chang, the Chinese-Hawaiian, shorter and solidly built; the Japanese youth, David Takai, who was called "Mac"; and Horace Ida, smallest of the four, wiry and quite alert. The four boys stared silently, shifting from one foot to the other.

"We told her just to have a conversation with these boys," Finnegan later reported. "We didn't want her to make any comment at the time—as to whether she could tell that they were the boys."

Mrs. Massie's head was propped on a pillow. After looking at them for a moment she turned to Horace Ida, who had been in the office with her when she was giving a statement to McIntosh earlier that morning, and asked him where he had been the night before.

"Waikiki Park," Ida said. "Later we go to Correa's place. Then we go home. That's all." His voice was jerky, but his manner was firm.

One by one she asked each of the other three—Chang, Takai and Kahahawai—the same question. What had they been doing the night before? The answers were short and simple, and much the same. When she came to Joseph Kahahawai, she asked: "Don't they call you Benny?"

The Hawaiian shook his head. "That's Ahakuelo," he said, gruffly. Ida looked at him sharply. Ahakuelo had not been with them at any time during the investigation thus far; as a matter of fact, he was not picked up until Sunday afternoon at the Kauluwela School grounds.

Thalia nodded. Finally she turned to Finnegan and said, "That's all." Finnegan nodded to Stagbar, and the four boys were led outside to the police car. He remained, with Commander Bates, and asked Thalia if she could identify any of them. She nodded.

"Two I know," she said. These, she said, were Chang and Kahahawai. She had been with Ida earlier in McIntosh's office, and presumably had seen him; but she did not indicate to Finnegan that she remembered him.

Earlier, when Detective Bill Furtado had first questioned her at her home in Manoa, within a couple of hours of the time of the assault, he asked whether she recognized any of her attackers, and according to Furtado, "she replied that she could not recognize them, only by their voices."

This version was supported by the statement of Detective George Harbottle, who was with Furtado at the time and took notes. He said:

"He [Furtado] asked her whether she could identify the boys if she saw them and she said she could not at that time. Then he questioned her further and said if she really could identify the boys and she stated she could not, and he asked if she could tell them by their voices, and she said 'Yes,' that is the only way she could identify them, by their voices."

Later in his report in the office of Deputy City Attorney Griffith Wight, Finnegan gave this version of the identification at the Massie home on Sunday:

Q. Who did she speak to first?
A. Henry Chang and the small fellow [Ida]. She held this conversation with them about where they were last night, then she said she was all through.
Q. Did she say, "And they call you Benny?"
A. I don't remember.
Q. These boys were the only ones you held in custody at the time?
A. Yes.
Q. What did she say?
A. Mrs. Massie said she was positive Henry Chang was one of the boys, and the Hawaiian boy—Joe Kahahawai. The other two she wasn't sure.
Q. Was her identification of these boys spontaneous?
A. She talked to them, then she got up and went up to talk to them. There was nothing excitable about her condition at any time; she was normal.
Q. As she told you Henry Chang and Joe Kalani [Kahahawai] were two of the boys, was there any hesitation?
A. No.[1]

Finnegan was quite sure that Ben Ahakuelo was not among the four who were in the room at the Massie home when Mrs. Massie identified her assailants. Nevertheless, this curious contradiction was offered by Lieutenant Massie in a statement on September 21 to Inspector McIntosh:

Q. [*By McIntosh*] On Sunday afternoon were any of these boys brought up for identification by Mrs. Massie?
A. Yes.
Q. How many?
A. Three.
Q. What happened when they walked in, that you saw?
A. The boys were lined up in front of Mrs. Massie.
Q. Before you went into the room?
A. No, when I was in the room. She questioned them—asked the first on her right what his name was. He gave his name. She asked the middle one what his name was and he told her; then she said to the third one, "Don't they call you Benny?" He said, "Yes, that's my name."[2]

The fact that on two occasions the presumption was raised that Ben Ahakuelo was among those questioned—when he had not been arrested at the time—was never explained, even in the subsequent trial testimony.

Later in the day, Ben Ahakuelo was arrested and charged with being a party to the assault. Detectives Jardine and Stagbar took him to the Queen's Hospital, where Thalia Massie had been taken Sunday afternoon for further examination of her injuries. There was a nurse in the room with her when she arrived, but she left immediately. Lieutenant Massie was not in the room at the time.

Two of the boys she had seen earlier—Chang and Takai—were also with Ben Ahakuelo. She asked each of the boys to give his name, and when she came to Ahakuelo, she asked: "Don't they call you Benny?"

Ahakuelo replied that they did.

Stagbar's late report on this follows:

Later in the afternoon [of September 13th] I accompanied John Jardine to the Queen's Hospital. Lieutenant Jardine and the defendant Benny Ahakuelo and two other boys, suspects at the time, to be identified by Mrs. Massie. I do not recall the room she was in at the time or the number of it. At that time she asked each one their names and asked Benny as to whether he was called Benny. I believe his answer was that he was called Benny. There was some conversation between Benny and Mrs. Massie but I do not recall just what it was. She did not identify Benny in my presence, it having been prearranged that she was not to identify Benny in his presence and I believe Lieutenant Jardine later returned to the Massie home, but what she told him I do not know.[3]

Up to this point the record is very clear that no one except the suspects in the Ala Moana assault had been exposed to Thalia Massie for identification. This acquired some significance later for two reasons: First, there were subsequent interviews in which Thalia Massie was able to provide further identifying evidence, and —as will be seen—the police method of identification, exposing only those suspected of being her assailants, assumed paramount importance in the trial of the five youths.

A third identification session was held the following day, Monday, September 14, at Thalia Massie's room at the Queen's Hospital.

On this occasion there were present for the first time representatives of the City Attorney's office. Stagbar's report on this session follows:

I accompanied Captain McIntosh, Mr. Wight of the City Attorney's office, Ed Sylva, of the same office, Detective Machado and someone else to Mrs. Massie's room at the Queen's Hospital, together with the defendants Benny Ahakuelo, Horace Ida and Joseph Kahahawai, for further identification.

At this time Ida wore a leather jacket, a sort of chamois skin texture. Ida was asked to stand alongside Mrs. Massie's bed, whereupon Mrs. Massie felt the jacket. After touching it, she quickly withdrew her hand and stated that it was the sort of jacket that the driver of the car that had abducted her wore.

There was some conversation as to Ida's movements on the night before between Mrs. Massie and Ida, and he was also placed in a sitting position at the foot of Mrs. Massie's bed with his back toward her, in order for Mrs. Massie to get a good look at the back of his head just as she had seen the driver of the car that night.

Ida was then taken into the corridor and set on his haunches, as the catcher of a ball team stands directly behind home plate, directly across from Ben Ahakuelo. At this time Ida made a motion to Ben Ahakuelo which I interpreted as a motion to designate the route they had driven from Waikiki Park to the *luau* on School Street, as some of the defendants' stories differed as to the route they had taken.

After leaving the hospital I asked Ida what he meant by the signal and he told me some of the boys were mixed up as to which way they turned on the route we took back from the Park that night.[4]

The "mix-up" with reference to the route was in the different versions they had given in the interrogation the previous evening in McIntosh's office. This conflict might have been regarded as natural, due to Horace Ida's unfamiliarity with the Kalakaua "extension" past King Street, and Kahawai's apparent "grogginess"; but it was seized upon by the County Attorney's office as a point of great significance.

At that time the police did not have the report of Tatsumi Matsumoto, in which Ida's car was definitely identified by Robert Vierra as having been on Beretania Street, near Thomas Square, when he jumped from one moving car to the other to talk with Ben Ahakuelo.

Identification of the Car

Inspector McIntosh had assembled sufficient information by Tuesday afternoon to recognize some major complexities in the case, which at first had appeared a rather simple matter of identifying the suspects and checking out the time element.

The first complication occurred Monday morning. McIntosh was told by John Cluney, who got the report through the police "grapevine," that some of the local "sporting set" who knew Ben Ahakuelo had seen him at Waikiki Park Saturday night and later on Beretania Street early Sunday morning. Sam Kahanamoku, well known and respected in Honolulu, had apparently gotten the story from a young fellow known in the Honolulu sporting world as "Tuts" Matsumoto.

Detective Lucian Machado was sent out to get in touch with Sam Kahanamoku and pick up Matsumoto. They found Matsumoto and his friend, Bob Vierra, at the corner of Bethel and Hotel Streets, a well-known gathering place for the sporting blood of the city. Machado brought them in for questioning.

Matsumoto remembered seeing Ben Ahakuelo at Waikiki Park about the time the dancing stopped in the pavilion, but he did not see him leave the park. Vierra had been busy looking for a girl, Sybil Davis, who came to the park with them, and he also did not see when Ahakuelo left, but he recalled that another girl with them, Margaret Kanae, had mentioned seeing "Benny."

"She was riding with us," Matsumoto volunteered. "She is Frank Kanae's daughter. She said they left just before we did."

McIntosh jotted this down in his notes.

"Have you talked with Ben Ahakuelo since Saturday night?"

Matsumoto shook his head. He had seen the stories in the newspapers about the attack on "the *haole* girl," and he wanted to tell the police what he knew.

McIntosh sighed. "You think it was about half past twelve?"

"At Fort and Beretania Street, yes. About that time. The other time when Bobby [Vierra] jumped off my car, I was driving. I could not look back, but when this car came alongside Bobby jumped to the running board."

85

"I see," McIntosh said. "You saw Ben Ahakuelo later, though?"

"Yes, at Fort and Beretania Streets. We stop to see what is going on. The police was there and somebody had an accident or was fighting. That's when I saw Benny."

"What time was this?"

"I do not know exactly, but I know how long that was from Waikiki. It must have been about 12:40. We were going slowly and then stopped at Fort Street."

McIntosh knew it must have been earlier, because the boys were at King and Liliha Street at 12:37. He called in John Jardine again, and went over the situation.

"It had to be earlier," he said. His face was twisted in a scowl. "This throws the time off pretty much. It means Mrs. Massie must have left the inn earlier—let's say around 11:45 P.M. She could have been picked up around 11:55 instead of 12:05 as we figured. Taking five minutes for the pick-up and driving out to the quarantine station, and 20 minutes for the assault—as Mrs. Massie said—it would mean they could have gotten away from the quarantine station at 12:15 and still have been on Beretania Street by 12:30."

McIntosh scribbled a few more figures on his pad. Then he said to Jardine:

"Check the time again, John—from the quarantine station up to Beretania around Thomas Square."

Jardine sent Arthur Stagbar on this mission; and later he reported it required about ten minutes, with another five minutes needed to get to King and Liliha Streets. This would enable the boys in Ida's car, on a split-second schedule, to have left the quarantine station at 12:15. But at this point another complication ensued. Detectives had reported that young "Peter" Correa, the son of the Supervisor, and his sister, Wilhelmina Correa, had seen two of the accused boys—Ben Ahakuelo and Joseph Kahahawai—at the Correa home "around 12:30."

This could add another few minutes to the time. It began to appear that Thalia Massie must have left the Ala Wai Inn a good deal earlier than she said she had, probably around 11:35 P.M., which—as McIntosh knew from the statements of Massie and her other friends at the inn—was the last time anyone remembered seeing her.

The reports of George Goeas and his wife, and Alice Aramaki, who saw "a girl in a green dress" on John Ena Road about 12:10 A.M., had not come in at this time; and McIntosh felt certain that if the time of Thalia Massie's departure from the inn could be pushed up a bit, the whole thing would fall into place.

There was one point however, that disturbed him—not because it constituted a significant breach in the theory of the case, but it would probably prove to be a defect in the case for the prosecution. That was the identification of the car itself. On Sunday afternoon, after Thalia Massie had returned from the hospital, McIntosh had driven Horace Ida's Ford up to Kahawai Street to see if she could identify the automobile in which she presumably was abducted.

In her statement early that morning at the police station, he had asked her: "What make was the car which they had?"

"It was a touring car," she said. "I can't say what make it was, but I think it was a Ford."

Earlier that morning, when Detectives Furtado and Harbottle questioned her at her home, she had seemed less certain. Harbottle gave this version:

> He [Furtado] asked whether she could identify the car or give the numbers [license number] so we could get in the way of picking up this car, and she said the only way she could see was to give us a description of the car, which I stated a little while ago, the back of the car, the top was flapping, and it was an old car. She said it sounded like an old car, between a Dodge and a Ford.[5]

Earlier than that, according to George Clark, Sr., who was riding in the car of Eustace Bellinger that picked up Thalia Massie on the Ala Moana and drove her home, "when we asked her about the car these boys rode in, she said it was either a Ford or a Chevrolet. She did not remember any car numbers."

Furtado himself later recalled—although he did not make a note of it at the time—that when she described her abduction, she said that "while [she was] walking along John Ena Road about 200 or 300 feet from Kalakaua Avenue, a bunch of boys who appeared to be

Hawaiians, in an old-model Ford or Dodge touring car, stopped alongside of her, grabbed her and pushed her into the car."

The car that McIntosh drove up to the Massie home on Sunday was a 1929 Ford Model A touring car, in apparently good condition at the time, with nothing loose or "flapping" on the top or back. This was Horace Ida's car.

Ida's car had come into the possession of the police early Sunday morning, about three hours after the assault took place. The license number had been known to the police since approximately 12:45 A.M. Furtado in his later report, said:

> I asked her if she knew the number of the car in which she had been abducted, and she told me she did not.[6]

There is nothing in the police records, or any statement or testimony by police officers, or anyone else, to the effect that the license number of the car was passed on to Thalia Massie either at her home or at the Emergency Hospital, where she was examined. Nevertheless, in her statement to McIntosh at the police station early Sunday morning, when he asked her if she knew the number of the car, she had replied:

> I think it was 58–805. I would not swear to that being correct. I just caught a fleeting glimpse of it as they drove away.[7]

It will be recalled that Detective John Cluney came into McIntosh's office at the time and showed McIntosh a card on which the license number of Ida's car had been written. McIntosh had pointed to the number Thalia Massie had just given him.

As McIntosh later explained: "As far as I was concerned, that cinched it." She knew the license number and they had the right boys. The only problem was to build a case that would stand up in court.

It was this information, printed in the Honolulu *Advertiser* Monday morning, that contributed substantially to the belief in the public mind that the Honolulu police, acting with unusual expedition, had arrested "the right boys."

Politics in Paradise

The first news of the assault on Thalia Massie reached the people of Honolulu on Monday morning, although there were many in the city who knew about it earlier from the swift course of grapevine reports and rumors. The headline in the Honolulu *Advertiser* read: "Gang Assaults Young Wife . . . Kidnaped in Automobile, Maltreated by Fiends!"

The unusual part of the story, which aroused the horror, and to some extent the excitement, of the people of Honolulu was that it was a respectable white woman who was assaulted. There had been other cases of assault in Honolulu, usually "attempted rape"; for example, an attack had occurred a few years before on a girl on the steps of a school in the Kakaako neighborhood, one of the poorer sections of town. In that case a gang of a dozen boys participated in the assault, but the sense of public outrage was not so noticeable. In the case of Thalia Massie, however, the victim was described as "a woman of the highest character."

The story in the *Advertiser*, which did not identify the victim, was preceded by a bulletin in boldface type linking the Ala Moana attack to the Peeples incident at King and Liliha Streets on the other side of town. This bulletin noted that "a man said to be one of the suspects in the Ala Moana case jumped out of a car in which he was riding with three other men, dashed up to the Peeples car and struck Mrs. John Peeples a violent blow in the face. He then ran back to his car and the quartet hurriedly drove away."

Aside from the fact that this was not the way Mrs. Agnes Peeples reported the matter, the account gave the impression that a wild and unruly gang of hoodlums had ranged through Honolulu on Saturday night, attacking women wherever they appeared. The main story of the Ala Moana attack went on:

> After being kidnaped by a gang of young hoodlums as she was walking along one of the principal streets of the Waikiki district late Saturday evening, a young married woman of the highest character was dragged to a secluded spot on the Ala Moana and criminally assaulted six or seven times by her abductors, who fled in an open touring car and left her half-conscious on the road. She was picked up by occupants of a passing car as she staggered along the Ala Moana toward Waikiki in the early hours of Sunday morning and was taken home. She was later transferred to the Queen's Hospital.
>
> Seven suspects, one arrested early Sunday morning by Detectives John Cluney and Thurman Black, and the other six Sunday afternoon by Detective Lucian Machado, are being grilled by Chief of Detectives John McIntosh. One of those held is said to be the owner of the car which the gang used to abduct the women, and two of the others are said to have jail records, one having previously been arrested for rape and one for robbery.[1]

The story continued with a description of the woman "dining with her husband and a party of six at a Waikiki restaurant" and said she had "gone for a walk to get some fresh air." While walking along the street, she was seized by the occupants of a car which had driven up behind her, "forcing her to get into the car where she was held by two of her assailants who stifled her cries for help and struck her brutally in the face when she struggled to escape."

The story is noteworthy for a number of reasons. The description of the event assumed that it happened exactly as the victim described it, a pardonable form of journalistic license; yet it is probable that the writer was familiar with John Ena Road where the kidnaping occurred—"one of the principal streets of the Waikiki district." If so, he would have known that it was next to impossible for such an abduction to have taken place, unless by professional kidnapers, in an area that was continually crowded from early evening until past midnight.

It is also noteworthy that the unidentified victim is referred to as "a young married woman of the highest character" and the supposed attackers are described as "a gang of young hoodlums" and referred to in the headlines as "fiends." This again is pardonable journalistic license; how else would one speak of the perpetrators of an assault such as the one described? There appeared to be no question in the mind of the reporter who wrote the story that everything happened precisely as described.

The story continued:

> She declared that she pleaded with her captors to release her, and even offered them money if they would take her back to her husband. According to her story, they asked where her money was and she replied that it was in her purse, and finding that it did not contain any large amount of money, they drove her along the Ala Moana, turned into a clump of bushes, pulled her from her car and assaulted her. She declared she was assaulted six or seven times.

> Mayor Fred Wright, Sheriff Pat Gleason and City and County Attorney James Gilliland were in conference with McIntosh Sunday afternoon, with Detective Arthur Stagbar, assigned to the County Attorney's office, and Edward N. Sylva, Deputy County Attorney.

> "My office will cooperate in every respect in this case," Gilliland stated. "I am fully determined to get those who perpetrated the crime and see that they are brought to justice." [2]

This all represented a wholesome public attitude, since all civilized people would be opposed to rape; and yet its effect was virtually to assume the guilt of whoever the suspects might be—an assumption that would not readily be erased from the public mind. Although these suspects were not identified until Wednesday morning, they were referred to as "fiends", "gangsters" and "hoodlums" —even before a full-scale investigation was under way; and when they finally were identified as two Hawaiians, two part-Hawaiians and a Japanese, there seemed even less reason for the better class of white people in Honolulu to question their guilt.

This attitude was borne out by a comment in the *Advertiser*, which noted editorially that "public feeling is thoroughly aroused over the dastardly assault by a group of thugs upon a young woman in the Waikiki district early Sunday morning." The editorial added this ominous thought:

> The safety of women and children of Honolulu is a precarious thing as long as such degenerates are at liberty.[3]

It is quite important to note that at this point the only information the police possessed that indicated the five suspects under arrest were actually the perpetrators of the assault was Thalia Massie's own story. Her principal evidence had been positive identification of four of the five suspects, under circumstances which were far from normal police procedures, since only the suspects were exposed to her. Her recollection of the license number was under such a dubious cloud of conflicting recollections that even the police must have been suspicious of its authenticity; and the evidence of the tire tracks was also of such an uncertain character that it was ultimately repudiated by the prosecution itself. Chief Inspector McIntosh later admitted that the string of jade-colored beads, first reported to have been found in Ida's car, were picked up at the site of the old quarantine station, which merely indicated that Thalia Massie had been there.

In spite of the one-sided nature of the evidence thus far, the two English-language dailies, the *Advertiser* and the *Star-Bulletin*, proceeded with classic disregard of the fundamental basis of judicial procedure to set up a public hue and cry against the "gangsters" and "degenerates" who, by implication, were the five youths arrested in the case.

This leads us to the second of two reasons, referred to in the previous chapter, as the underlying explanation of why the police arrested the suspects first, and then undertook an investigation. In order to understand this phenomenon, which was in many ways peculiar to Hawaii, we must trace back through what at first may seem to be irrelevant historical background.

A Bit of Hawaiian History

Hawaii had been a Territory of the United States for more than thirty years when the attack on Thalia Massie occurred;

but it bore little resemblance at the time to political and economic institutions with which Mainland residents would be familiar. Theoretically, it was part of the great American democracy; but actually Hawaii had never been a democratic society in the accepted sense of the phrase.

Until the last decade of the nineteenth century, it had been a monarchy. It was ruled by elected kings and a form of parliamentary government. Some forty years before the Ala Moana case, the monarchy had been disposed of by a small group of white people —sometimes called the "haole elite" but more often referred to as "the Big Five"—which had grown in strength and influence for nearly a century.

This group was born of a strange alliance of shrewd Yankee traders, English and German merchants, Scottish bookkeepers and American missionaries who came to Hawaii in the early nineteenth century to spread enlightenment among the natives. They had successfully manipulated the Hawaiian Revolution, which overthrew the royal dynasty; and had continued to exercise a kind of feudal suzerainty over their Hawaiian fiefdom even after the annexation of the Islands to the United States. Affairs in the Islands were controlled not by elected officials, but by this little collection of commercial and religious entrepreneurs known as the Big Five.

Since this group exerted an influence over almost everything that happened in the Territory, it is necessary to go back a little over a hundred years to the origin of the Big Five in order to understand the conditions under which the Honolulu police force was called upon to investigate the assault on Thalia Massie.

In the early years of the nineteenth century Honolulu was a roistering sailors' port. Its narrow, shallow harbor was surrounded by a small cluster of frame buildings and warehouses built on the waterfront. Behind these waterfront buildings, thatched roofs of native houses were set out irregularly among the trees for perhaps a mile and a half toward the foothills of Nuuanu Valley and the Koolau mountains, towering nearly four thousand feet over the city.

Ships threaded through the shallow sandbars and moored off the small jetties at the back of the harbor. Much of the cargo was lightered to and from the ships in long sharp-prowed outrigger canoes;

and along the shore bales and casks were piled in lean-to ware-houses. Access to the harbor, which was little more than a lagoon, had only been discovered in the year 1794, when Captain William Brown, skipper of a British fur vessel, was credited with having found a passage through the reef into the otherwise landlocked habor.

On April 4, 1820, a boatload of missionaries from Boston an-chored in the brig *Thaddeus* off the village of Kailua on Hawaii, the largest island of the group. They found the Islands in the throes of an international struggle for commercial advantage among Rus-sians, English and Americans. All had perceived that this little group of tropical islands, with lush lowlands and a strategic loca-tion in the middle of the Pacific Ocean, might have consider-able future value as a "crossroads" of the Pacific.

In 1826 a Yankee ship's master, Captain Charles Brewer, not only perceived this strategic importance, but took steps to take some advantage of it. He formed C. Brewer & Co., Ltd., a small trading firm and shipping agency. This was the first of the Big Five.

While the missionaries were consolidating their crusade to evan-gelize the Hawaiian people, planting a small contingent in Hono-lulu, the traders were trading and building along the new harbor. In 1845 an astute young Welshman with great vision—Theophilus H. Davies—became a partner in a firm in Honolulu that was on the verge of bankruptcy, and within a short time he owned the busi-ness, changing its name to Theo. H. Davies & Co., Ltd.—the second of the Big Five.

Some four years later a German sea captain, Henry Hackfeld, ar-rived in Honolulu and joined with a trading firm known as B. F. Ehlers Company; and out of this merger of various commercial in-terests they formed H. Hackfeld & Co., Ltd., establishing a place of business near the waterfront. The successor to that company—Amer-ican Factors—still occupies the site today at the foot of Fort Street, having acquired the principal assets of H. Hackfeld & Co. after some peculiar dealings with the American Alien Property Custodian during the Great War of 1914–18. At that time the German-owned Hackfeld properties were seized and the assets sold to a select group of American businessmen in Honolulu—all accredited members of the Big Five—thus creating American Factors, Ltd., the third member of the Big Five.

Up to about 1850 the commercial establishments in Honolulu were strictly commercial. However, the missionaries who had arrived with the prayerful admonition of the American Board of Commissioners for Foreign Missions of the Congregational Christian Churches to "open your hearts wide and set your mark high" had observed certain signs of secular as well as spiritual improvement. In the year 1851, a former Connecticut bookkeeper, Amos Starr Cooke, who had joined the Hawaiian missionary group as a teacher, decided to participate in the secular improvement. He resigned his post with the missionaries and rejoined the world of business, forming a partnership, known as Castle & Cooke, Ltd., with another missionary, Samuel N. Castle. In his first entry in the journal of the new company the Reverend Mr. Cooke wrote an illuminating explanation of his deviation from the orthodox pattern of missionary work:

> The foreigners are creeping in among the natives, getting their largest and best lands, water privileges, building lots, etcetera. The Lord seems to be allowing such things to take place. This is trying, but we cannot help it. It is what we have been contending against for years, but the Lord is showing us His thoughts are not our thoughts, neither are His ways our ways . . . Honolulu has never looked so green and pleasant. Our large plain of sand is covered with vegetation and is laid out in lots. I am proposing ere long to purchase some of them . . .[4]

Having consoled himself with this poignant expression of his new interpretation of the Lord's will, Cooke and his partner, Castle, engaged in providential and profitable dealings with some of the new plantations that were beginning to emerge in the broad, fertile valleys of Oahu, the island on which Honolulu is located. Several of these new ventures found themselves on the verge of bankruptcy; and Castle and Cooke helped them out generously, also acquiring control of the plantations.

Thus did the fourth member of the Big Five come into being— actually the first to be organized by brothers of the cloth.

The American Board of Commissioners for Foreign Missions apparently was not insensitive to temptations the Lord was likely to fling in the path of His chosen vessels in Hawaii. Early in the 1850s the board issued a mild warning to the missionaries that "if any of your members shall be betrayed into a spirit of worldliness and acquire property, that would become a most painful source of scandal." [5]

Painful as it may have been, the firm of Castle & Cooke went right on acquiring property, until it became one of the largest and most powerful agencies in the Islands, holding contracts with plantations and all manner of business enterprises.

Meanwhile, in the year 1875, two young sons of missionaries, who were also engineers of a sort, observed that the configuration of land on the island of Maui was such that a large trench could carry water from the rain-soaked highlands to the flat, arid saddleback of the island, thus providing irrigation for sugar growing. The two young men, S. T. Alexander and H. P. Baldwin, formed a company known as Alexander & Baldwin to handle their potential sugar business, and completed the digging of the huge Hamakua Ditch, which poured forty million gallons of water a day upon otherwise arid areas. So began the great Maui sugar empire of the Baldwin family, which today controls the island as if it were a feudal estate. This was the fifth member of the Big Five.

Thus there was created the core of a curious power structure—a small group of white men who began to form a nucleus of economic control over what had been a rambling assortment of tribal chieftains, kings and advisers of one sort and another who had ruled this tropical paradise for seven hundred years.

Later others joined the clique. In 1865 an American sailor, Benjamin F. Dillingham, was stranded in Honolulu when he had the good fortune to fall off a horse and break his leg, and could not join his ship's crew when it sailed. As a result, he met Emma Louise Smith, daughter of a missionary, who read to him in the hospital. He married her, and from this fortuitous beginning grew the great Dillingham interests, spreading landholdings all over Oahu, building piers, and finally constructing a railroad on Oahu. At the time of the Ala Moana case Walter F. Dillingham, the son of Ben Dillingham, was one of the most powerful members of the *haole* elite in Hawaii—although, in a strict sense, he was not one of the Big Five.

In 1850 an Irish cabinetmaker, Christopher Lewers, of Dublin, arrived in Hawaii and decided to set up a lumber yard in Honolulu. He joined with Charles Montague Cooke, a member of the missionary Cooke family and Lewers & Cooke became the largest supplier of building materials in the Islands. In 1882 Captain William Matson sailed the *Emma Claudine* into Hilo harbor, and liked what he saw so much that he set up a shipping firm to carry sugar from Hawaii to the mainland. Today the Matson Navigation Company carries sugar, pineapples, coconut candy, macadamia nuts and almost everything that is shipped to and from Hawaii, including tourists. These families and their enterprises all became aligned with the Big Five.

During this period of economic progress, undeniably useful to the growth of Hawaii, a new kind of political power began to rear its head. When King Kamehameha II was succeeded in 1815 by Prince Kauikaeouli, as Kamehameha III, the young king was only nine years of age. It was necessary that advisers be called in, and the missionaries were available for this service. One of these was the Rev. William Richardson, who became an unofficial "prime minister" to the young king. Later Dr. Gerrit Judd, a medical missionary, joined him as an adviser and also became prime minister in the latter years of the reign of Kamehameha III.

By a process of political osmosis, the power in Hawaii was gradually passing from the Hawaiians themselves into the hands of this small group of *haole elite*, largely Americans. By the middle of the century they dominated the royal rulers. The "Great *Mahele*," a sweeping declaration by Kamehameha III in 1848, made possible private ownership of land through grants or purchase; and this made possible the acquisition of land by *haoles*. It became increasingly evident that the Lord, as Amos Starr Cooke had suggested, was "allowing such things to take place." In the course of those things, the road was being paved to riches and power for the descendants of those intrepid savers of the human soul who set forth from Boston on October 23, 1819, on the long voyage around Cape Horn to the Sandwich Islands.

The Race Problem

Most histories dealing with Hawaii and its multiracial problems dwell principally on the rising tide of Oriental blocs—the Japanese, Chinese and Filipinos. The emphasis on Hawaii as "the melting pot of the Pacific" is largely in this context. Few concern themselves with the decimation and disenfranchising of the Hawaiian people. However, it was this internal racial problem which began to boil up when the *haole* elite took over the Islands at the end of the nineteenth century, and it was this racial conflict that most seriously affected the Ala Moana case.

In 1898, five years after the last monarch of Hawaii, Queen Liliuokalani, was overthrown by a political revolt led by the *haole* elite, predominantly American, the same group succeeded in having Hawaii annexed to the United States as a Territory. This transfer of power was virtually bloodless, but was not without racial repercussions. Two years after the Queen was forced to abdicate, there was an incipient revolt among the Queen's loyal followers, put down with the loss of only one life; but as a reminder that the new *haole* rulers of Hawaii meant business, the Queen was arrested and threatened with a fine of five thousand dollars and a sentence of "ten years at hard labor"—the sole purpose of which, the Queen afterward said, was "to terrorize the native people and humiliate me." By the time of the annexation in 1898 the dominance of the *haole* elite was firmly established.

Meanwhile the Hawaiians had dwindled not only in political influence in their own land, but in numbers. From a native population of approximately 300,000 in the Islands when the white man first arrived in 1779, the number of pureblooded Hawaiians had dropped to a fourth of that figure by the 1850s; and by the turn of the century there were fewer than 50,000 Hawaiians left. This decimation of the Hawaiian race was assisted by certain noneconomic factors, such as tuberculosis, smallpox and syphilis.

Earlier disagreements had cropped up between Yankee traders and missionaries as to acceptable reasons for acquiring property, but these differences had been merged pleasantly into a benevolent patriarchy, which assumed not only moral and economic responsibilities, but also political guardianship for the fast-fading Hawaiian people. This political influence took the form of the Republican Party.

In 1915, when Woodrow Wilson, a Democrat, was President of the United States, the influence of the Big Five was sufficient to have Lucius E. Pinkham, a Republican, appointed Governor of Hawaii. The political leader of the Hawaiian people at the time was Prince Jonah Kuhio Kalaniaole, the legitimate heir to the Hawaiian throne. There was a political slogan in vogue among Hawaiians at the time: *Nana i ka ili*, meaning "look at the skin." It was intended to draw the Hawaiian vote to Hawaiians, since it was the rather naïve belief of many Hawaiians that by capturing the Republican Party, Hawaiian voters would automatically recapture political control of the Islands. Instead, the Republican Party captured Kuhio. He joined the party, hoping to improve the lot of his people; and he became political handyman for the *haole* elite.

On one occasion, Prince Kuhio challenged the Big Five with a public statement that "the domination of Hawaii by the sugar plantations, in turn controlled by the agencies in Honolulu, has extended through the Governor's administration, and this fact has been winked at by Governor Frear." Walter F. Frear, the Governor, was a brother-in-law of Walter F. Dillingham.

Kuhio died in 1922; and after that, political resistance to the encroachments of the Big Five began to evaporate. The power of major economic interests was so closely linked with the Republican Party that the Hawaiians and part-Hawaiians turned to the Democratic Party.

Throughout the decade that preceded the Ala Moana and Massie-Fortescue trials, the differences in political as well as economic orientation of the Hawaiian-Democratic bloc and the Big Five-Republican clique had deepened and widened. The differences were not entirely racial, but they had racial overtones. At the turn of the century, shortly after annexation, the Hawaiian *Gazette,* a weekly newspaper devoted to the *haole* point of view, had warned the Hawaiian people not to "obstruct the progress of the white man in Hawaii" by forming a party of their own. "If any color is to rule any American territory," the *Gazette* announced, "the color will be white." This became the rule in the two decades that followed.

Several events during the decade of the 1920s had served to increase the resentment of Hawaiians. For a time they were led by Lincoln L. McCandless, a white man who had built a prosperous well-digging business but had never joined the Big Five. He was never entirely satisfactory to the Hawaiian voters, however, although later he was elected Delegate-to-Congress in the Roosevelt landslide of 1932. Meanwhile the Hawaiians were turning to their own, to men like John H. Wilson, a part-Hawaiian whose father had been a minister in the court of King Kalakaua, and who was elected Mayor of Honolulu in the latter 1920s. Mayor Wilson had told young Bill Richardson, part-Hawaiian descendant of the Reverend William Richardson, who had been an adviser to Kamehameha III: "Bill, you've got to do things for the Hawaiian people! You've got to work for them, and politics is the only way to do it!"

In the years immediately preceding the Ala Moana case, the City Hall of Honolulu was in the throes of political revolt under the label of a Republican-Reformist movement. By general agreement and historical precedent, the Territorial Government of Hawaii had been in the hands of the *haole* Republican group, and Honolulu had been run by the Hawaiian-Democratic element. However, a Reformist contingent of Republicans and disgruntled Democrats had turned Mayor Wilson out of the City Hall and reconditioned the Honolulu Police Department, electing Fred Wright mayor.

Much of the pressure for this reform came from the military installations in Hawaii—the Army and the Navy. They were the least permanent but most vocal of the *malihini haole* elements, the "new whites"; and because they exercised a powerful economic leverage on the business affairs of Honolulu, they were drawn inevitably into the orbit of the *haole* Republican clique, and the upper echelons of military command became quite friendly with the Big Five —and with Walter Dillingham.

Among these temporary residents of Hawaii was Admiral Yates Stirling, Jr., commandant of the Pearl Harbor Navy Yard, whose views became those of the Navy Department in Washington. Admiral Stirling gleaned his knowledge of Hawaiian affairs principally from discussions with members of the *haole* elite, who entertained him suitably in their mansions atop Pacific Heights and on the slopes of Diamond Head.

Before the sun had set on the Sunday after the assault of Thalia Massie, word had come down from the Navy to John McIntosh, through appropriate channels, that nothing less than immediate convictions of the hoodlums who had assaulted the white wife of a U.S. Navy officer would be tolerated. As Admiral Stirling put it, in a rather bizarre analysis of the situation: "American men will not stand for violation of their women under any circumstances."

On Tuesday, after the report of the attack on Thalia Massie— whose name and connection with the Navy was not disclosed by either of the English-language newspapers—Admiral Stirling and Captain Ward Wortman, commander at the Submarine Base, met with "twenty leading businessmen of the city," as it was later phrased by Walter Dillingham in a "private memorandum" on the Massie case. The meeting was given no publicity, although editors of the local newspapers were asked to sit in. The County Attorney, Jimmy Gilliland, was there, as were Sheriff Pat Gleason and Chief of Detectives McIntosh.

Dillingham's private memorandum, which will be referred to later in some detail, reported as follows:

> At this meeting the position of the Army and Navy in support of the complaining witness was emphatically stated. The local officials said positively that sufficient evidence had been secured to make the case a strong one. The prosecutor requested assistance, explaining that he was inexperienced in criminal cases and would welcome the help of three of our older and more experienced criminal lawyers, naming those he would like to have assist him in the handling of the prosecution. The meeting was unanimous in its emphatic support of the local officials in bringing the criminals to justice. A reward of $5,000 was offered for the apprehension of the guilty parties.[6]

It was thus that the County Attorney of Honolulu virtually abdicated his responsibility to the voters, turning over the work of his office to the "older and more experienced criminal lawyers" who were to be provided by a committee of "twenty leading businessmen." The Big Five had effectively taken charge of the Ala Moana case, and the Navy for the time being was placated.

The Alibi Witnesses

The problem of prosecuting the perpetrators of the Ala Moana outrage fell upon the unwilling shoulders of James F. Gilliland, the District Attorney for the City and County of Honolulu. The office of County Attorney was elective, and Jimmy Gilliland, a rotund, genial man, had won his way to this high office through the exercise of handshaking talents that were much greater than his knowledge of the law. He was a politician in every sense of the word; and up to this time he had managed to keep an even distance between the Hawaiian-Democratic voters and the *haole* elite. He did this by the simple process of not antagonizing anyone.

In this case, he was in a fair way to run into some political cross-currents, no matter which way he swam; so he did what any astute politician would have done: he assigned two deputies to handle the case. These were Griffith Wight, a former Army captain, who was on good terms with the folks on Merchant Street, the business community of Honolulu; and Eddie Sylva, a personable young Portuguese lawyer who had been graduated from Stanford and was acceptable to the Hawaiian-Democratic voters.

Both deputies were present when the five suspects were interviewed on Sunday evening, and presumably had full knowledge of what was said. It will be recalled that Horace Ida, when questioned about the route the five boys took into town, said:

"I do not know. We followed a car. Ben knew the boys in the car."

During the interrogation of Henry Chang Sunday night, he was even more explicit:

Q. What time did you leave the dance?
A. When the dance was over . . . about twelve o'clock.
Q. You all got in Shorty's car?
A. Me, Shorty, Ben, Mac and Joe.
Q. Who drove?
A. Shorty. I was in back, Ben sat in front, and *we followed a Ford, Matsumoto's car.*[1]

The fact that this did not pass entirely unnoticed by McIntosh was attested to by a question he put to Chang a moment later:

Q. You said you were following Matsumoto's car?
A. Yes, I know a fellow on the car and I know his name is Bob. He used to go to school with me.[2]

This statement, made Sunday night, September 13, was the first mention to be found, in any of the police records, of knowledge on the part of the police that a car driven by "Tuts" Matsumoto had preceded Horace Ida's car out of the park gate. While neither McIntosh nor Wight might have been expected to understand the significance of this information at that time, it would be reasonable to expect that the possibility of someone's having seen the Ala Moana boys—and thus providing an alibi—at a place where they could hardly have been present and still have been at the old quarantine station when Thalia Massie said she was assaulted there, would have stimulated some doubt as to whether they had the right parties.

There was no immediate reaction, however. This important possibility was passed over as if it had no particular significance; and it was not until the following day that it was considered important to pin down the time when the Ala Moana boys might have been seen on Beretania Street, miles from the scene of the assault. At that time Tuts Matsumoto and Bob Vierra were brought in for questioning, after a critical delay of twenty-four hours.

Planning the Prosecution

It was not until Monday afternoon that McIntosh first heard that Sam Kahanamoku had some interesting information that might prove useful in the case. When he realized that it concerned the fellow "Matsumoto," who had been mentioned by Henry Chang the night before, he immediately sent Detective Lucian Machado to find Matsumoto and bring him in.

Even when Tuts Matsumoto and Bob Vierra came down to the Detective Bureau, and gave their stories, the questioning was perfunctory and inconclusive. There was not even an effort to pin down the actual time—which would appear to have been of the greatest significance.

However, the first stirrings of uncertainty seemed to have been creeping into the Chief Inspector's mind when Griffith Wight arrived at the Detective Bureau on Tuesday for a conference. Wight was a bristling, energetic man, and he walked into McIntosh's office with a bouncing step and a smile that seemed to radiate confidence. As he came into the room, McIntosh was sitting at his desk staring glumly at a sheaf of notes and tapping his pencil on the desk. He was radiating anything but confidence.

"Well," Wight began, cheerfully. "It's about time we tracked all these things down and got ready for the grand jury."

He glanced around the room. There were three men there, besides McIntosh. One was Deputy Inspector Jardine, who sat beside his chief. On the other side, facing toward the desk, was a smooth-faced man whose cherubic countenance radiated practically nothing. This was Sanford B. D. Wood, better known as "Sandy" Wood. He was the United States Attorney for Hawaii, and his connections with the *haole* elite in Honolulu were outstanding. He was named for the late Sanford B. Dole, the first President of the short-lived "Republic of Hawaii" who was, in a way, the George Washington of the Hawaiian Revolution. Young Wood had belonged to one of the most distinguished law firms in Honolulu until he was elevated to the post of Federal Attorney for the Territory. He had come down, as he said, "to sit in and see how things are going."

"The Navy is involved in this, you know," he told McIntosh.

The other person in the room when Wight entered was a tall, heavily built man with a handlebar mustache and the expression of a St. Bernard dog. He was Arthur McDuffie, McIntosh's predecessor as Chief of Detectives, who had been removed after some unpleasant disclosures in a graft scandal in the Honolulu Police Department a few years before. McDuffie was now head of a private detective agency in Honolulu, and had been called in to assist McIntosh in the crisis, at the suggestion of Walter Dillingham.

McIntosh looked rather sharply at Wight; but the Deputy County Attorney went on: "We expect to be ready for trial in two weeks—as soon as we can get a grand jury indictment and have a trial date set."

The Chief Inspector's frown deepened.

"Two weeks? I don't think we'll be ready by that time, Griff."

"Why not?" Wight snapped. "You've got the right boys. The evidence is all there, and Mrs. Massie has identified four of the boys. The fifth was with them, so that's no problem. This town won't stand for any delay in this matter, John. I've talked with Admiral Stirling. He feels the sentiment at the Harbor and at Washington won't brook any delay."

McIntosh shrugged.

"Why not let the Navy try the case, then? We're still looking for facts, and there are quite a few things to check out. We're doing it as fast as we can."

Wight's tone became sharper.

"What in hell is there to check on?" His face assumed an expression of professional authority. "Look here, you've done an outstanding job, John. An outstanding job! Rounding up these boys in less than twenty-four hours—it's commendable! I doubt if many Mainland departments could beat that. Now it's our job—Jimmy's and mine—to get a conviction."

McIntosh smiled slightly at the reference to "Jimmy." It was rumored around town that Wight had his eyes on Jimmy Gilliland's job, and might run against him in the next election. The Chief Inspector had a suspicion that was the reason Gilliland had assigned Wight to the case. There were still a lot of Hawaiian voters in Honolulu.

He tapped his pencil a moment, and then said in a low voice:

"We've checked into that story about Tuts Matsumoto, Griff. You were here when one of the boys mentioned following Matsumoto's car out of the park, weren't you?"

The Deputy County Attorney looked slightly puzzled; but he nodded.

"Yes, of course—but that was just Henry Chang's statement. We certainly don't intend to rely on the stories these fellows tell us, do we?" Wight laughed, although he seemed distinctly annoyed. "They've already lied enough so we know they are covering up."

McIntosh nodded, but he said:

"We have to check them out, all the same. We've already checked out part of that story, Griff. There are some details we need to pin down, but we've got to have time to do that. We don't want to take this case before the grand jury half-cocked, do we?"

Wight arose from his chair and walked around the room. McIntosh waited patiently for him to sit down again.

"There's nothing half-cocked about this," Wight finally said. "It's open and shut!"

"There are a few complications," McIntosh finally said. "Let me tell you what they are."

"There are always complications, John," Sandy Wood put in mildly. "You have to expect them, but they usually iron themselves out."

McIntosh recited briefly the matter of Tuts Matsumoto and his friend, Bob Vierra. He spread his notes on the desk and read the joint statement of the two. Wight came over and stared at the notes.

"When did you talk with these boys?" he asked.

"Last night. Lucian Machado talked with them first. I don't know what he said."

"Did Matsumoto or Vierra talk with any of the boys you're holding?"

McIntosh shook his head.

"Not unless it was early Sunday. All five have been in custody since Sunday afternoon. I don't think there was any chance to talk."

Wight looked worriedly at McIntosh; then he snapped his fingers.

"Don't check anything further," he said. "We won't need this testimony, John. We've got enough to convict—and that's what we're interested in."

McIntosh looked shrewdly at the Deputy County Attorney. He put the tip of his pencil against his teeth and twirled it. Then he shook his head.

"We're checking out Tuts Matsumoto's story, anyway," he said. "Even if we don't use it." He turned and glared for a minute at Sandy Wood. "That satisfy you, Sandy? Or don't you think people will be interested in how we get a conviction, as long as we get it?"

Wood was aware that the patience of the Chief Inspector was being stretched. He shook his head quickly, and said: "We want everything checked out, John, of course."

McIntosh turned again to Wight, and asked: "Did you know Bill Heen was representing the five boys?"

Wight shook his head, and said a bit testily: "You know damned well we want everything checked out, John. But these boys are guilty as hell, and we don't want some fool with a cock-and-bull story to upset things. What these boys did put the Territory in a bad light, John. The fleet's coming down this fall, you know. Nothing must stand in the way of getting a conviction, and showing fellows like Britten and Crisp in Congress that we can handle things down here."

McIntosh was well aware of the significance of this reference. For many years the specter of "Commission Government" for Hawaii had been held up by the *haole* elite as a good reason for Hawaiians not to rock the boat in Washington over issues of home rule. Recently, Representative Fred A. Britten, of Illinois, Republican Chairman of the House Insular Affairs Committee, had suggested that Hawaii, as a place of strategic importance to the United States, be placed under military rule. This horrifying notion—as odious to the *haole* elite as it was to the Hawaiians—had received unexpected support from Representative Charles R. Crisp, a Democrat of Georgia, who opposed a resolution recently introduced on behalf of the Hawaiian Delegate to Congress, Victor S. K. Houston, asking for a vote for Hawaii in the House. McIntosh tapped his pencil on the desk. "You can forget the political speeches,

Griff," he said. "We've still got to build a case, and that's my job."
He paused and looked narrowly at Wight. "Maybe you didn't hear
me when I said Bill Heen may represent some of the boys?"

Wight snorted. But his eyes showed he was worried. Judge Heen
was one of the most widely known Hawaiian lawyers in the Territory, and was popular with his people.

"We can't let politics enter into this," Wight finally said.

McIntosh smiled, without much humor.

McIntosh had already received some additional information,
about the public reaction in Honolulu, which he did not want to
divulge to Griffith Wight at the time.

Signs of Trouble

Earlier in the day McIntosh had taken a sudden step,
on an impulse, which might have been regarded as reckless, and
even dangerous. He had called in a man who—although a *haole*—
would be more closely aligned with "the other side"—that is, the
Hawaiian-Democratic group, than with the *haole* elite. This was
Jack Snell, a former newspaperman, and one-time bureau manager of
the Associated Press in Honolulu.

Snell was not in politics, although he was now working for the
City and County, in the Engineer's office; but he knew about everything political that went on at the City Hall. He had married Kaui
Wilcox, a part-Hawaiian girl of the missionary Wilcox family; one
of her forebears was Robert Wilcox, who had led the "royalist
uprising" in 1895 in an effort to restore Queen Liliuokalani to the
throne.

Snell was a dark-haired, soft-spoken Irishman with quick black
eyes, a sharp sense of humor and an even sharper sense of the
"smell" of news. He had the reporter's instinct for knowing what
was going on behind the scenes. McIntosh knew that Snell was
familiar with all the back alleys of Hawaiian politics. He was closer
to the real sentiments of Hawaiians in Honolulu than any other
white man McIntosh knew. If there were storms ahead in this case,
Snell—who was a personal friend of the Chief Inspector—would
know about it.

McIntosh said, over the telephone: "I've got a problem, Jack—and I was wondering if you would drop over a few minutes to talk about it."

"Is this an official call? Do I have to come—or are you going to send for me?"

"This hasn't anything to do with you personally, Jack—although you ought to stop being Mama-san's best customer. One of these days the 'prohi' squad is going to raid that place, and you'll be in the middle."

Snell laughed. "Mama-san" was a well-known Japanese lady bootlegger whose place was patronized by the local newspaper fraternity.

"Quit kidding. Mama-san knows when they're coming before they do."

"Okay—but will you come over? I've got problems."

"I've got problems, too," Snell said. "But I think I know what yours are. I won't be able to give you much help—but I'll be over."

Snell arrived at the police station a half hour later. He was well aware of McIntosh's "problem." There were already evidences of rising differences of opinion in Honolulu. The Monday newspapers had carried the story of Honolulu's "shame" in lurid word-pictures. The *haole* elite were loudly demanding quick action, and immediate conviction of the hoodlums who had marred Hawaii's reputation by assaulting the white wife of a U. S. Navy officer. Among other elements in town, however, there was a rumbling resentment. The Hawaiians had the old feeling that this was another case where the *kanakas* were going to get the "dirty end of the stick." Even the language of the *Advertiser* and *Star-Bulletin* editorials were reminiscent of the "kangaroo justice" dealt out by the Committee for Public Safety during the days of the Republic of Hawaii.

When Snell had seated himself, sprawled out in a chair across from the Chief Inspector, McIntosh remarked: "I've got a tiger by the tail, John."

Snell looked from under his eyebrows.

"In what way?" he asked mildly. "I thought from what I read in the papers that you did some real fancy work—running these boys down in just a few hours. I understand Sandy Wood is coming in to help Genial Jimmy."

McIntosh grunted.

"Sandy Wood is a horse's ass," he said. "You can tell him I said so."

"In spades," Snell said. "But he represents Walter Dillingham and Al Castle and the boys—and don't you forget it!"

"I'm not likely to," McIntosh said morosely. The power of Walter Dillingham in Hawaii—as well as in Washington—was well known. A synthetic member of the local aristocracy, who could trace his ancestry all the way back to his father, the sailor with the broken leg who had married into a missionary family, Dillingham was regarded as the real power of the *haole* elite, even though he was not an accredited member of the Big Five. He was known as an "independent industrialist," but he could make Governor Lawrence Judd jump through a hoop at the crook of his finger. He had long tentacles of power reaching all the way back to Washington; and the Hawaiian Construction Company, founded by his father, Ben Dillingham, had substantial contracts with the Navy at Pearl Harbor. He had already arranged the meeting at the Chamber of Commerce, attended by "leading citizens" as well as Admiral Stirling and General Wells, and it was evident Dillingham meant to "see the case through."

Snell, watching the Chief Inspector with some amusement, his mouth twisted in a slight smile, asked: "Have you got the right boys, John?"

McIntosh nodded.

"I'm damned sure of that! Everything fits—at least most everything. The Japanese boy lied—twice. People that aren't guilty don't lie. These are the boys, all right—I'm sure of it!"

"You'd better be," Snell said shortly. "Some of the boys at the City Hall aren't so sure. They think these fellows you picked up are just handy suspects. I hear some of your own boys aren't too sure, either."

McIntosh looked steadily at Snell for several seconds.

"I can't very well discuss the evidence," he said, quietly. "That's got to be my job. But I've had a dozen telephone calls already on this. I won't tell you who they were, but they all said the same thing. They want action, and they want it right away." The Chief Inspector arose from his chair, and walked around his desk. "They don't want to wait for us to build a case. They say we've already got a case. What's your idea of the situation, Jack . . . around City Hall, I mean? Do you think we'll get a lot of pressure from the other side? We've still got a lot of Hawaiian boys in the Police Department."

Snell nodded, his mouth still twisted in a slight smile.

"So I hear. Nobody is going to back these boys if they were really the attackers. Hawaiians don't need to attack women, John . . . They get paid for it. Did you know the beach boys had a meeting last night?"

McIntosh nodded.

"I saw it in the *Advertiser* this morning. They want to be sure they aren't linked to this thing."

Snell laughed shortly, and shook his head.

"No, John . . . They just want to be damned sure nobody gets the idea Hawaiians need to attack young ladies. They've got professional pride, too. Do you know what the *kanakas* are saying at City Hall? They're saying this is going to show up the *haoles*—not the Hawaiians. This is the first time in the twenty years I've been down here that the *hanaka* vs. *haole* business is right out in the open, John."

McIntosh nodded. "I wish I knew what the hell to do—to keep that sort of thing from getting mixed up in this case."

"It's your problem, John . . . and I think it will be a tough one. I talked with Bill Heen this morning. I think he and possibly Bill Pittman are going to represent the boys. You're going to have to have a damned good case to get a conviction."

McIntosh nodded again.

"We know that," he said. "We'll have a good case . . . These boys are guilty, but I don't want to get too much pressure from the other side—the Hawaiians, you know. It makes things bad all around."

"You know what I think, John?"

111

"That's why I asked you to come over. I'd like to know what you think."

"I think you're going to have a real tough time—whatever you do. You're going to get it from both sides, John . . . and you'll be the guy in the middle. Your only chance is to have a case so strong nobody can question it—and from what I've heard, you haven't got that kind of case."

The Time Factor Changes

After Snell left his office, McIntosh sat for some time looking over the notes he had written. If Tuts Matsumoto's statement was correct, the time schedule needed considerable revision. He had asked Stagbar to make another run over the route from the old quarantine station to King and Liliha Streets, going by way of Beretania. It required eleven minutes, which would place the time of departure from the quarantine station at about 12:25 A.M. But there was one more factor that had to be taken into account. Wilhelmina Correa and her brother, Peter, presumably had spoken to the boys when they stopped off at the Correa place about half past twelve. This report could be readily checked out, and if it turned out to be true, it took off another four or five minutes from the time of departure from the quarantine station, putting it back to 12:20 A.M.

This would make it necessary to re-examine Thalia Massie's own story. If she was wrong about the time, could she have been wrong about the identification?

McIntosh realized that the time Thalia Massie left the Ala Wai Inn was becoming critical. Up to this point most of the evidence indicated she had left "around 12 o'clock," and McIntosh had accepted this since it confirmed his own theory of what happened—that she had been picked up shortly after midnight, driven to the site of the old quarantine station, where she was attacked; and the boys who attacked her had left in time to reach King and Liliha Streets at 12:37 A.M.

It wasn't too plausible a theory, and it required close connections; but it fitted the facts he had gathered thus far. However, the information supplied Monday afternoon by Tatsumi Matsumoto and

Bob Vierra altered this schedule. If it should be definitely supported by Peter and Wilhelmina Correa, it would require that Thalia Massie have left the Ala Wai Inn earlier than she said she did.

Peter Correa had come into the station Tuesday morning; but he was unable to fix the time he talked to Ahakuelo and Kahahawai when they returned to the *luau,* except that it was "after midnight."

"They asked for some more beer, and I said there was no more beer," he said. "I don't know how long they were around there. I was out behind. I just told them we had no more beer."

Later McIntosh and Wight went up to the Kauluwela School, near the Correa home and talked with Wilhelmina Correa. She was more specific.

> Q. [By Wight] Now on Saturday, September 12th, your father and mother gave a luau?
> A. Yes, for my sister's wedding.
> Q. And Joe Kalani was there the early part of the evening?
> A. Yes.
> Q. And he left, didn't he? Then later he came back again?
> A. Joe and Ben Hakuole [probably Ahakuelo] and—
> Q. Shorty?
> A. The short fellow, that's just come back. [Ida had been in Los Angeles for several months prior to this.]
> Q. And that time, as near as you can figure, was about 1:30?
> A. Yes.[3]

Wilhelmina's recollection as to time obviously was in error, since Horace Ida was found asleep at his home at about 1:30 A.M. when Detective Cluney called to pick him up for questioning. McIntosh realized, however, that he might have returned to the Correa house *after* the Peeples incident.

On the other hand, if the five boys had driven directly to the Correa place after meeting Tuts Matsumoto and Bob Vierra on Beretania Street—as appeared likely from the reports from these two obviously independent sources—it would add at least ten minutes, and perhaps more, to the elapsed time between their departure from the quarantine station and arrival at King and Liliha Streets at 12:37 A.M.

McIntosh sat with Jardine and Stagbar at the Detective Bureau that afternoon, rearranging the time schedule. They first worked out the reverse schedule for the five boys, beginning with the time of the Peeples incident:

Time of accused at King and Liliha Streets	12:37 A.M.
Elapsed time from Correa home	3 min.
Time spent at Correa home	6 min.
Time of arrival at Correa home	12:28 A.M.
Elapsed time from Fort and Beretania Streets	3 min.
Elapsed time from Waikiki Park to Fort and Beretania	7 min.
Time of departure from Waikiki Park	12:18 A.M.

The latter time would conform generally to the time Tuts Matsumoto had driven out of the gate into John Ena Road—within a minute or so—and if the car driven by Ida had actually followed the Matsumoto car all the way into town, this would indicate the assault on Mrs. Massie had occurred much earlier—probably between 11:45 A.M., the time she probably was picked up on John Ena Road, and 12:15 A.M. This, on a split-second schedule, would have allowed time for the five boys to have driven to the quarantine station site, assaulted Thalia Massie "six or seven times" and driven back to Waikiki Park in time to follow Matsumoto's car out of the gate. However, it required considerable shifting of the time of her departure from Ala Wai Inn.

At this point, Inspector McIntosh had in his possession a document that has been reproduced in facsimile in these pages. It was the original statement of Thalia Massie, which McIntosh took down in his own handwriting at 3:30 A.M. Sunday, September 13. It differed from the report later released in one important respect. The later statement, purported to be a true copy of the statement given by Mrs. Massie, said:

"Around 12 midnight I decided to go for a walk and some air."

The photostatic copy of her statement, as it was written down by Inspector McIntosh early Sunday morning, after the assault, read:

"Around 12:30 or 1 A.M. I decided to go for a walk and some air."

This difference in the time factor had troubled McIntosh from the beginning. It was quite evident that the error in time—a half hour, if his original estimate was to be used; a full hour if the infor-

*Statement of Mrs. Thalia
H. Massie made to
John H. McIntosh at
the Detective's Bureau
at 3.30 a.m. Sept 13
1931.*

*Q Your full name?
A Thalia Rabbard
Massie.
Q Where do you live?
A 2850 Kahawai St.
Q Will you relate
to me what happened
to you tonight.*

*... together, around 12.30
or 1 a.m. I decided
to go for a walk and
some air. I walked
along Kalakaua to
Crossed the bridge
over the canal and
then down John
Ena Road and
walked a block
or so down a car
about 8 up behind
me and stopped
two men jumped
out from the car*

Thalia Massie's original statement to Inspector McIntosh. The notebook
containing the statement was taken secretly from the Honolulu police station, photographed and returned. Shown here are the first page, and the
page on which Mrs. Massie gave her time of departure from the Ala Wai Inn
as "around 12:30 or 1 A.M." At the trial she testified that she left "around
11:35 P.M."

115

mation supplied by Matsumoto and Vierra were taken into account
—required a complete reappraisal of the case.

The reappraisal would have been comparatively simple if the
investigation of the Ala Moana case had been a normal affair, and
the only objective of the Honolulu Police Department was to bring
the guilty parties to the bar of justice. It would merely have required an analysis of all the evidence produced thus far to determine whether the Ala Moana boys actually were the guilty parties;
or whether the partial alibi presented by the information obtained
thus far was airtight.

However, by Tuesday afternoon there was no possible way of
backing up on the case. The Police Department of Honolulu—and
John McIntosh in particular—were *already committed to the theory
that the five Ala Moana boys were guilty*. The only course of action
open to McIntosh under the circumstances was to "build a case"
that would stand up in court.

It is interesting to note at this point the enormous rift that was
beginning to develop in Honolulu between those representing the
so-called *haole* element—both the "new whites" and the "old whites"
—and the Hawaiians, part-Hawaiians, Portuguese and other citizens
of the lower economic and social strata. Walter Dillingham's famous
"private memorandum" expressed at least one viewpoint, in these
terms:

> On Monday, following the Saturday night on which Mrs. Massie was
> assaulted, the morning papers carried headline items to the effect
> that the wife of a Naval officer had been assaulted; that five boys
> of mixed races had been apprehended; and, that it was believed the
> guilty parties were locked up. The name of the young woman was
> not given.
>
> Within twenty-four hours, and possibly because of the withhold-
> ing of the name of the complaining witness, rumors became rife as
> to whom [sic] she was, what she was, and whether there was some-
> thing being withheld about the affair. These rumors spread rapidly
> through the community. Within a few days there was common gossip
> to the effect that: "she was drunk," "out looking for trouble," "was a
> depraved character," "was a sex pervert," "a dope fiend," "a brother
> Naval officer had been beaten up by the outraged husband," "the
> Admiral was not behind the prosecution of the criminals," "someone

connected with the Navy had been found guilty by court-martial and shipped out of the Territory." Many other vile rumors, heavily embroidered, were freely discussed in social groups as in other groups of the community. It is interesting to note that during the trial of the gangsters the defense admitted that Mrs. Massie had been assaulted, but no scintilla of evidence was produced to show the truth of any of the vile rumors which had been circulated detrimental to her character, habits or standing.

An effort was made by the leaders of the Chamber of Commerce to ascertain the position of Army and Navy officials, and the statement to the effect that the Navy was disinterested was emphatically denied, as were all other stories derogatory to the character of the woman.[4]

Aside from the *non sequiturs*—such as the reference to the failure of the defense to produce evidence that the complaining witness was a drunk, a depraved character or a sex pervert, which would have been questionable tactics in any case—Dillingham's commentary provides an important sidelight. He assumes two specific points: first, that the defendants were "gangsters," and second, that they were guilty.

These two assumptions had become fixed in the minds of the *haoles* of Honolulu; and it was the effect of these two assumptions that, in a sense, pretried the case. It was also the continuing effect of this fixed opinion after the trial that not only made possible but virtually motivated the tragic events that followed.

There was one other aspect of this public pretrial of the case that is worth noting. That was the complete indifference of the two English-language newspapers as to who, or what, the five accused youths were. The *Advertiser*, on Tuesday, September 15, referred to them as "gangsters," two with "police records."

The normal practice of newspapers making reference to such matters as police records is to dig out the facts and print them. Anyone called in to explain anything to the police may be said to have "police records." The most that was reported was that Joseph Kahahawai, "alias Joe Kalani"—which happened to be the name he used as a professional boxer—had been "convicted on a robbery charge"; and Ben Ahakuelo was described as a "convicted rapist."

The background of these two prior cases is interesting. Kahahawai was accused by a Japanese, Toyoko Fukunaga, of having robbed him on September 20, 1930—about a year before the Ala Moana assault case. He had received a sentence of thirty days in jail, which was suspended when the complainant admitted there was some dispute as to whether it was robbery or merely a disagreement. Ahakuelo was neither charged with nor convicted of rape; he was originally tried for attempted rape of a Chinese girl and sentenced in 1929 to a year in Oahu Prison. Ahakuelo was at that time eighteen years old; and after he had spent four months in Oahu Prison, the parole board released him on the recommendation of character witnesses, including his physical instructor at school, a playground supervisor and several other citizens of some standing. It is also noteworthy that the charge was finally changed from "attempted rape" to "fornication involving a minor."

Whatever the details of these cases may actually have been is lost in the limbo of court records; but it was upon the basis of these reports that the two suspects were referred to as "ex-convicts with prison records." Neither of the English-language newspapers found the background of the five "gangsters" sufficiently interesting or germaine to the situation to bother about tracing their history beyond the bare reference to their "prison records."

The Mystery Witnesses

The grapevine of rumor, gossip and plain scandal-mongering is usually a livelier means of communication than newspapers; and Honolulu was no exception. Within three days after the attack on Thalia Massie, the two big daily newspapers still had not printed the name of the victim of the assault, but her identity was known all over town, together with her connection with the Navy. As Walter Dillingham had noted, "rumors became rife."

Part of this was due to one newspaper which did publish Thalia Massie's name and the fact that her husband was a U. S. Navy officer. This was a Japanese newspaper with an English section, the *Hawaii Hochi*. On Tuesday, September 14, this newspaper disclosed not only the names of those involved, but gave the first indication that the five suspects might have a "water-tight alibi." It reported that "a youth is declared to have followed their [the suspects'] automobile from the time it left Waikiki Park until it was picked up two hours later by the radio squad." While the report was inaccurate as to detail, it furnished the first public intimation that the arrested suspects might not be guilty.

The following day the same newspaper printed a report that two other people—the son and daughter of Supervisor Sylvester P. Correa—had talked with the suspected rapists sometime after midnight, several miles from the scene of the assault; and it also carried a report quoting Chief Inspector John McIntosh as having said the string of jade beads, supposedly found in the car of one of the suspects, had actually been picked up at the scene of the assault.

These matters are noted not for the purpose of assessing their value as evidence, or even their veracity, but to indicate a phenomenon that would play an important part in the divided public feelings about the case. One segment of the population of Honolulu was getting information as it developed and was gathered by reporters; while the other—by far the larger—segment was getting only what the *haole* newspapers saw fit to print, based entirely on the theory that the five arrested "gangsters" were the guilty parties.

Perhaps the most astounding example of this selective reporting of the investigation in the *Advertiser* and *Star-Bulletin* was the complete disregard of certain so-called "mystery witnesses." These included Alice Aramaki, the Japanese girl who lived on John Ena Road behind the barber shop where she worked; George Goeas and his wife; Eugenio Batungbacal, Roger Lieu, Charles Chang and James Low, all of whom saw a woman who answered Thalia Massie's description on John Ena Road about 12:15 A.M. Sunday.

On the Monday following the assault, Sam Kahanamoku had been told by a member of the Honolulu Police Force, Traffic Officer George Sato, that a Japanese girl named Alice Aramaki had read the story of the assault in the morning paper and had some information that might be useful. On Wednesday, September 16, Alice Aramaki was brought to the Detective Bureau and questioned at length by McIntosh and Wight in the presence of Detective Stagbar, Lieutenant Massie and Harry Hewitt, the Attorney General of Hawaii.

She said she was standing in the store next to the barber shop where she worked, watching people pass by. She saw a white woman, answering generally the description of Thalia Massie, walk past the front of the store about 12:15 A.M., with a white man following her. She said she spoke of this to Sam Kahanamoku, when he came to her place on Monday; and that on the following day two other

120

men had talked to her—apparently the United States Marshal, Oscar Cox, accompanied by Traffic Officer Sato.

On the following day George Goeas, the Dillingham Insurance Company executive who had been at Waikiki Park with his wife that night, came to Police Headquarters voluntarily, believing he might have information that would be helpful in solving the case. As previously noted, Mr. and Mrs. Goeas saw a woman generally answering to the description of Thalia Massie, walking "with her head bent down" along John Ena Road, with a white man following a yard or two behind her; and this also was about 12:15 A.M.

Another of these "mystery witnesses" who saw approximately the same thing at about the same time was James Low, a former Supervisor on the Island of Hawaii. Low, it will be recalled, was riding in the car of Eugenio Batungbacal and two other men—Roger Lieu and Charles Chang—on the night of the assault. They did not appear in the Police Headquarters until November 9, a week before the trial; and as had been noted, their stories differed in certain essential respects.

The fact that Alice Aramaki and Mr. and Mrs. Goeas had seen a woman of Thalia Massie's general description, followed by a white man, walking down John Ena Road shortly after twelve o'clock would have had little significance immediately after the arrest of the five suspects; it merely would have confirmed certain details of the police theory of the case.

But this information was not obtained by McIntosh until Wednesday, September 16; and the story of George Goeas and his wife was not obtained until the following day. Thus, while it fitted the police theory of the case on Monday prior to the interrogation of Matsumoto and Vierra, *it did not fit the case after that*. If Thalia Massie was on John Ena Road as late as 12:15 A.M. Sunday, and the events of the kidnaping occurred as she said they did, it would have been impossible for the five suspects to have been her assailants.

The existence of the first three "mystery witnesses" was known not only to the police but was mentioned in the *Hawaii Hochi* on Friday, September 18. Yet no report of this possible contradictory evidence was published in either the *Advertiser* or *Star-Bulletin*.

Again, the selective reporting of news left a large number of people in Honolulu completely unaware that there was evidence in the possession of the police which might conceivably exonerate the five suspects.

Alice Aramaki was questioned for nearly an hour, particularly as to her description of the man walking behind the woman in the green dress. She offered little that was specific; she could not recall the exact color of the dress the woman wore, and she thought the white man following her did not wear a coat. He had a white shirt and dark trousers.

The significance of her story was the time element, and the fact that on the following day George Goeas and his wife appeared at McIntosh's office and told an almost identical story, both as to the description of the woman and the man following her, and as to the time it happened. In both cases, there was no indication of any violence on the part of the man following her, or by anyone else.

None of these witnesses was subpoenaed to testify for the prosecution of the Ala Moana defendants. Some six weeks later, Eugenio Batungbacal, Roger Lieu, Charles Chang and James Low came into the office of Deputy County Attorney Wight and gave their stories. All their accounts were almost identical as to the time the woman in the green dress was seen walking down John Ena Road —about 12:15 A.M.—and her general appearance. There was considerable difference, however, in their accounts of what happened. In the case of Batungbacal, who was questioned by Wight:

Q. Did you drive down John Ena Road [on the night of September 12]?
A. We'd been down to the Orange place, and we drove towards the Ala Moana.
Q. As you were driving down John Ena Road, did you notice anything?
A. It looked like four or five men were forcing a woman into a car.
Q. How many men first grabbed hold of her?
A. I think two with both hands, and there was one behind.
Q. Did she yell?
A. Well, it looked the way she acted, it looked like she was trying to get away.[1]

Roger Lieu's statement was quite similar:

122

Q. When you drove down John Ena Road, what did you see?
A. We saw two men talking with a lady, and they grabbed her by the arm and pulled her into a car.
Q. What did she do when they grabbed her?
A. She was fighting, moving her arms and tried to pull away.
Q. And what did they do when she tried to struggle?
A. She can't get away from the boys and they made her get in. They pushed her in.[2]

The story told by Charles Chang was substantially the same. He was asked what he saw, and he said he saw "several boys—they were dragging a woman—an Occidental woman." Asked how they were dragging her, he said: "They was pulling her by the arms."

Q. How many men actually had hold of her?
A. At least two.
Q. What did she do when they were dragging her?
A. She was standing in the middle of that crowd.
Q. How was this car [he had previously said the boys had gotten out of a car] when you saw this woman?
A. They was on the sidewalk, in front, on the right side of a parked car alongside the sidewalk.[3]

James Low's account, as was previously noted, made no mention of a struggle, although he said that there was a car alongside the curb where he saw "a lady who looked like she was drunk—intoxicated—and immediately behind her was a man following her."

James Low, Alice Aramaki and Mr. and Mrs. George Goeas were not called by the prosecution to testify at the trial. But Eugenio Batungbacal, Roger Lieu and Charles Chang—whose stories differed only in that they described a woman struggling against several men, being dragged into a car, all in the midst of a crowd of merrymakers leaving Waikiki Park shortly after midnight—were all called to present their evidence for the prosecution.

The fact that the time element in the case of the three who were called to testify was identical with those who were not called seemed to have been overlooked in the vividness of their description of the event, which corresponded almost exactly to the story told by Thalia Massie. The explanation of the failure to call the other four, as rendered later by Griffith Wight, was that Thalia Massie must have left the Ala Wai Inn some time before midnight—which, of course, would have also made the testimony of Messrs. Batungbacal, Chang and Lieu equally irrelevant.

This distinction was not observed by the defense, however. All four of the "mystery witnesses" were called as defense witnesses in the Ala Moana trial.

Detective's Dilemma

Even before hearing the stories of Alice Aramaki and George Goeas and his wife, McIntosh had begun to have significant doubts about the time element which he had established early in the investigation. He was confronted with two different and utterly contradictory possibilities: If Thalia Massie left the Ala Wai Inn at midnight or later, as she originally told him, it would now appear to be virtually impossible for the five suspects to have been her assailants—in the light of Tuts Matsumoto's story. It would have to be shown that both Matsumoto and Vierra had lied.

On the other hand, if she left earlier it would also mean that the five suspects would have had to leave earlier—around 11:45 P.M.; and this of course was contradicted by the testimony of several people who saw Ben Ahakuelo and David Takai on the dance floor at the time of the last dance.

McIntosh decided it would be necessary to talk with Thalia Massie again and pin down as closely as possible her time of departure. If he could be shown that she left as early as 11:35 A.M., they would then have to disregard any testimony that placed the five boys in the park between 11:45 P.M. and 12:15 A.M.—the time they would have had to leave the site of the assault on the Ala Moana in order to be at Fort and Beretania Streets by 12:25 A.M. McIntosh had a conference with Jardine and McDuffie, outlining his problem.

McDuffie was an old war horse in the detective business. He came from a school of criminology in which there were few refinements; if a man was suspected of a crime, it was assumed he was guilty; and if he refused to confess his crime, the truth, or an approximation of it, was usually shaken out of him. McDuffie's own experience with crime in Honolulu had been largely confined to running down small burglaries or picking up Aala Park hoodlums who had gotten

124

into fights. Few of these affairs impinged upon the conscience of the community as a whole, and they were not regarded as more than interesting tidbits in the news by the *haoles* who lived on the lofty slopes of Pacific Heights, in Manoa Valley or the expensive homesites beyond Diamond Head.

"You're going to have to fix this one good," McDuffie bluntly told McIntosh. "Just like Griff Wight said—nobody is going to stand for any delay."

That afternoon McIntosh met with Wight and Wood again at the Queen's Hospital, where Thalia Massie was now recovering from surgery on her jaw. Wood undertook most of the questioning this time; and her jaw hurt so badly she was permitted to write out answers.

Q. [By Wood] Now my understanding is that you went upstairs to where Mrs. Fish's party was, at the Ala Wai Inn. You were there with Mrs. Fish and Mrs. Stogsdall up there [in the booth] and then they went home.

A. Yes [nodding].

Q. How long was it after Mrs. Fish and Mrs. Stogsdall left—did both leave at the same time?

A. [Shaking head] No.

Q. Will you write which one of the two left first?

A. [Writing] Mrs. Fish.

Q. Will you indicate how many minutes it was after Mrs. Fish left that Mrs. Stogsdall left?

A. [Writing] I can't remember . . . Mrs. Fish left before Mrs. Stogsdall, I believe.

Q. When you say, "Mrs. Stogsdall was still there when I left," do you mean you left the premises and started out?

A. Yes.

Q. Do you recall approximately how long after Mrs. Fish left that you left?

A. Five minutes.

After brief questioning by Griffith Wight, Wood resumed:

Q. Do you recall when Mr. McIntosh, or some other officer, asked you the number of the car the boys were driving—at that time had you heard from any other source whatever any number that would make you give that certain number, which you saw on the car, to the police?

A. No.

125

Q. You didn't hear it over the radio—or from people talking—that night?

A. No.[4]

McIntosh, sitting in a chair beside the bed, listened and chewed on his pencil as he took notes. He was becoming more and more aware—as Griff Wight perhaps was not—that a new time element had to be "proved." He had already had a short talk with one of the guests at the Ala Moana—Mrs. Stogsdall, the wife of the Lieutenant Stogsdall who had been slapped in the face by Thalia Massie. Her story indicated that she had departed from the Ala Wai Inn about twelve o'clock, because she was home at twelve-thirty and she figured it required thirty minutes to get home. She said Thalia Massie was there when she left. This story had fitted in with McIntosh's original time schedule very neatly.

However, it no longer fitted in; and no one was more acutely cognizant of this than the Chief Inspector of Detectives. It had become absolutely essential to place the time of Thalia Massie's departure from the Ala Wai Inn at about 11:35 P.M. To this end, he arranged to question several of the guests at the Ala Wai Inn the night of the assault.

On September 21 he questioned Lieutenant Massie himself at the County Attorney's office:

Q. When did you first miss her?

A. Between 11:30 and 12 o'clock. That's as near as I can judge—depending on hearsay.[5]

The following day he questioned Lieutenant and Mrs. Fish and got only the vague answer from Susan Fish that "it must have been near eleven-thirty" that she left the inn. Thalia Massie and her husband were still in the booth vacated by Commander Miller, his wife and his party. Under the circumstances it was possible for the prosecution to establish that Thalia Massie was not actually seen at the Ala Wai Inn—except by Mrs. Stogsdall—after about 11:35 P.M. Mrs. Stogsdall agreed to change her statement, apparently to conform with the others. However, it was not possible to establish this at the trial for a very simple reason: Not one of these people was subpoenaed by the Territory to testify at the trial, including Tommy Massie!

In the final analysis, the prosecution had to rely on the testimony of Thalia Massie herself. On September 21 McIntosh and Wight went to the Massie home, with Detective Stagbar, to obtain a final summary of her statement. Up to this time she had identified four of the five accused (David Takai was not identified, but the prosecution contended that since he admittedly was with the other four all evening, this was equivalent to identification).

She sat with her husband, her face still bound with white bandages. The hurt look that had been in her eyes earlier had now given way to an angry and resentful stare. As McIntosh later said: "She looked as if she was beginning to get sore about the whole thing."

Wight asked:

Q. Were there any pedestrians on the road that night?
A. I didn't pay any attention.
Q. Did you notice any cars parked on the side of the road?
A. No.
Q. How many drinks had you had that night?
A. About a half a drink.
Q. Mrs. Massie, there was a dance at Waikiki Park that night—that is, across the street from the side where you turned down, by the pink store—you turned down by that pink store, didn't you?
A. Yes.
Q. After you got down about half way—there was a big dance and a lot of cars there. When you went by, was the music playing?
A. I don't remember any music.
Q. Were there lots of cars coming out of the park?
A. I didn't look over there.
Q. Did you hear a lot of cars?
A. I didn't hear especially—no.
Q. The street is quite light?
A. It is lots lighter than Kalakaua Avenue.[6]

At that point Wight asked Thalia Massie about her identification of the five suspects at the time they presumably stopped their car and dragged her into it. She said she was walking down "the right hand side of the street," which would have been opposite the entrance to Waikiki Park on John Ena Road:

Q. How far away from the corner were you when you were picked up?

A. About from here to the door [18 feet].

Q. Do you know what men of that crowd grabbed you and pulled you into the car?

A. Yes, Henry Chang and Joe Kalani.

Q. You don't know whether there were four or five in the car?

A. Well, there were four. I thought there were five.

Q. The front seat was quite light, wasn't it? You could see those two. Did they turn their heads and talk at all?

A. That one, Benny, did.

Q. You could see he has a funny mouth?

A. He has a gold tooth. In the back it was dark. As soon as I got in the car I went down so I couldn't see anything.

Q. When you were down in the car, did they bend forward so you could see their faces?

A. Yes. They were holding me down.

Q. Now, this Mac—is he a short man?

A. A short, slim, lean—

Q. Shorter than Henry Chang?

A. I thought there was another short one there—a lean, slight man.

Q. At any time in the evening—before talking to Inspector Mc-Intosh—did anyone mention the number of an automobile to you?

A. No.

Q. Did you by any means whatever—from your husband, or from any person, over the radio—hear the number 58-895 mentioned?

A. No.

Q. And that number was the number of the car—you got as they fled?

A. I said 58-805.[7]

It will be recalled that when Detective Bill Furtado had first questioned Thalia Massie, with George Harbottle standing by his side, he asked: "Would you be able to identify the boys who attacked you?" and she said, "Only by their voices." When he asked her if she heard any names, she replied, "No . . . except one called 'Bull.'" When he asked her if she remembered the license number of the car, she said, "I'm sorry. It was dark. I didn't see much. I don't remember the number of the license."

When she gave her first statement to Inspector McIntosh at the

Detective Bureau early Sunday morning, not more than three hours after the attack, she still did not recall the names or description of any of her assailants, except the name "Bull." In the ensuing days, when she had been given an opportunity to see them and talk with them, her recollection improved and she was able to remember Ahakuelo's gold tooth and Horace Ida's leather coat.

Perhaps her most remarkable delayed recollection was the license number—which she missed by only one figure. She had told Dr. David Liu, when he was examining her at the Emergency Hospital shortly before three o'clock Sunday morning, about two and a half hours after the assault, that "she could not recognize the men because it was too dark." But she later told McIntosh that as the car drove away, she saw the license number and remembered it, except for one figure; and she was able to repeat the number with the exception of that one figure—a cipher instead of a nine.

On September 24, Dr. Liu made the following statement to Deputy County Attorney Wight:

Q. Was any car number mentioned in your office?
A. No, not in the office, but they were talking about some number on the porch outside. I heard talking but I did not pay attention to that part. Several people and officers were there, but I just stayed inside so that nobody could talk to me.[8]

It was at this time, as Officer William Seymour later reported, while Thalia Massie was in the emergency room, that Deputy Inspector Jardine stood on the verandah outside talking with Massie. "During their discussion a radio car stopped in front of the Emergency Hospital . . . Shortly thereafter a dispatch was broadcast from headquarters in regard to automobile 58-895 having been picked up."

Griffith Wight did not know how much of this information was known to the defense attorneys, Judge Heen and Bill Pittman; but he suspected quite a lot was known. There was a "faction," as it was later described, in the Police Department that appeared to be devoted to having the facts known, even if they favored the defendants. How deep this rift was would be demonstrated at the trial itself.

129

Pretrial Problems

There was one serious defect in the prosecution's plans that McIntosh recognized but the legal talent at the County Attorney's office apparently overlooked. That was the requirement under Hawaiian law that corroborative evidence be introduced in a case involving criminal assault. Three lawyers—Pittman, Harold E. Stafford and Gerald R. Corbett—had already filed with Judge A. E. Steadman, in the Territorial court, a motion to quash the indictment on the grounds that the grand jury indictment did not present a bill of particulars which offered any substantial complaint except the testimony of Mrs. Massie herself. There was a good reason for this: there actually was no evidence other than Thalia Massie's statement.

The motion was dismissed, however, and Judge Steadman set the trial date for Monday, November 16, 1931. This was more than eight weeks after the assault. Meanwhile, the public, as represented by the *Advertiser* and *Star-Bulletin*, had been clamoring for action. Why were not these "fiends" brought to trial? What sinister undercurrents of political and perhaps racial animosities were preventing the suspects from being brought to the bar of justice and formally condemned? There were broad hints of a feud in the Police Department. Some members of the force, presumably Hawaiians and Portuguese, were reported to have "leaked" information to the defense, and also to the Japanese-English newspaper, the *Hawaii Hochi*.

Griffith Wight was beginning to recognize what John McIntosh had recognized from the start. As the Chief Inspector later said, "We really had a hell of a weak case at that time." The case for the prosecution, devoid of the emotional background provided in news accounts in the *Advertiser* and *Star-Bulletin*, consisted of these essentials:

1. Thalia Massie's story, in which she told how she had been abducted, driven to a lonely place on the Ala Moana, and raped six or seven times.
2. The supporting story of Eugenio Batungbacal, given some weeks after the event, indicating he had seen a woman

dragged into a car at about 12:15 A.M. on John Ena Road.

3. Thalia Massie's identification of four of the five suspects.

4. Thalia Massie's recollection of the license number of the car in which the five suspects were known to have been riding.

5. The tire tracks found at the scene of the attack, showing the marks of a Goodyear All-Weather tire and Goodrich Silvertown cords, which were known to be the tires on Horace Ida's car.

6. The string of jade-colored beads, the purse and other items found at the old quarantine station site.

7. The "police record" of two of the accused, Ben Ahakuelo and Joseph Kahahawai.

McIntosh was aware that every one of these points was vulnerable to attack. Thalia Massie's story alone was not sufficient to convict; there must be corroborating evidence. The discrepancies in the time factor would tend to reduce the effect of her story; it would be difficult to establish whether she left the Ala Wai Inn "around midnight" or about 11:35 P.M.; and in either case there were confusing elements that would shake the confidence of the jury in her story.

As to the identification of the five accused as attackers, and the license number of Horace Ida's car, there were points of vulnerability that even Griff Wight had begun to recognize. As McIntosh said years later:

"We weren't ready for trial. There simply were too damn many chinks in the Government case that hadn't been filled. The fact that Mrs. Massie's identification came after she had seen the boys, not before, was natural enough under the circumstances. How in hell would she be able to identify them until she had seen them? There was the fact that she had told some of our detectives earlier that she couldn't identify them—when she was half hysterical, in shock, or under sedation. We knew this was going to be a factor in the effectiveness of her story. But we had to go ahead. There was too much pressure, and we had no choice."

As to the "pressure," it may be well to quote Walter Dillingham's famous "private memorandum":

Unfortunately, Mrs. Massie's physical and mental condition prevented her appearing in court for several weeks, but as soon as she was able to appear the case was set.

The proceedings were hardly under way before it became evident that the prosecution was pitifully handicapped through the attitude of the Police Department and its failure to produce evidence. A worse bungling of facts cannot be imagined.

As is true, I think, of many cities, the Honolulu Police Department had become riddled with petty graft. It was under the complete control of politicians and the Sheriff [Patrick Gleason] was a pitiful figure in a so-called organization, which not only lacked a head, but was divided into groups. These groups were competing with each other to destroy efficiency in the effort for political advancement.

Two able lawyers represented the gangsters. The brother of one of these attorneys was a member of the Grand Jury which found the indictment, so it is reasonable to suppose that all the evidence produced at the first hearing became available to an attorney for the defense. During the court proceedings it developed that the star witnesses for the defense were members of the police force.[9]

These comments, in spite of the rambling and illogical arrangement of the ideas set forth, are again interesting for the same two reasons noted previously. The commentary assumes that the defendants were "gangsters," and that they were the guilty parties. In addition, however, it furnishes an excellent insight into the mentality, and also the civic morality of some of the "leading citizens" of Honolulu. The "efficiency" of the Police Department was equated with the assumption that the accused were guilty, and the "bungling of facts" was cited as proof of police inefficiency. What was this "bungling of facts"? The only supporting evidence that could have positively corroborated Mrs. Massie's own story was the finding of tire tracks, supposedly made by Horace Ida's car at the scene of the assault. This alone would have been sufficient to prove the Government's case. Even the identification of the five accused as attackers, and the license number and description of the car, were merely part of Thalia Massie's own statement, and not the responsibility of the police.

The beads, the purse, the mirror and other bits of evidence that may or may not have been found at the scene were irrelevant, since they did not in any way implicate the five boys. There was no one except Mrs. Massie who could identify them as having been at the scene of the attack. The tire tracks, therefore, were the sole link that could have justified conviction—and we shall see, in the account of the trial itself, how this evidence was "bungled," and who bungled it.

Walking on Eggshells

There was one other element in the prosecution's case which was perhaps the most delicate and difficult to define of all the evidence available to the Territory. That was the most fundamental question of all: Was Thalia Massie actually raped?

That she was badly beaten was beyond question. The bruises on her face and the cut in her upper lip bore testimony to that. According to her own story one of her assailants had struck her on the jaw while he was raping her. She said she had been assaulted "six or seven times" in a space of twenty minutes. Under the circumstances it is hardly conceivable that her clothing, as well as her person, would not have borne some marks of this brutal assault.

Under most circumstances involving a criminal attack upon a woman, the "corroborating evidence" required to support her complaint includes an indication, from a medical examination within a short time after the event, that the rape actually has taken place; and in addition, evidence of the condition of the victim's clothing to support this claim.

In the case of Thalia Massie, the report of the first examining physician, Dr. David Liu, at the Emergency Hospital, made at the County Attorney's office on September 24, indicates that he did not make a complete examination of her body, and the result of his examination of the pelvic area was largely negative. However, Dr. Liu did not exclude the possibility she had been raped. As previously noted, he said he had discussed the matter with Dr. Robert Faus, the City and County Physician, and he had said it was "possible."

Due to an unfortunate mixup in information, the two physicians who examined Thalia Massie shortly afterward—the Navy doctor, Lieutenant Commander John E. Porter, and Dr. Paul Withington of Honolulu—were under the impression that Dr. Liu had made a complete physical examination, and therefore neither of them made more than a superficial examination, since they were more concerned with her mental and nervous condition.

Thalia Massie was admitted to the Queen's Hospital at 3:23 P.M. on Sunday, September 13—about fifteen hours after the attack—and the record of the hospital states:

> Patient came into hospital with fractured jaw and contusions and abrasions. General condition fair, except patient quite upset following accident.[10]

A month later, Thalia Massie was taken to the Kapiolani Maternity Home at the suggestion of Dr. Withington to determine whether she was pregnant. An examination was performed and Dr. Withington's diagnosis was negative.

As a result, there was no positive evidence available to the prosecution at the time of the trial, as far as medical testimony was concerned, that indicated one way or another whether she had been criminally assaulted. There was ample evidence, however, that she had been severely beaten.

The second phase of this investigation involving the condition of her clothes was undertaken almost immediately after the report of the attack on her. At three o'clock Sunday morning—while Thalia Massie was in the office of Chief Inspector McIntosh—Deputy Inspector Jardine and a detective—George Nakea—returned to the Massie home with Lieutenant Massie. Nakea's report of this follows:

> About 3 A.M. Lieutenant Jardine and Mr. Massie came back to the house and I walked into the house with them. Lieutenant Jardine picked up Mrs. Massie's dress, the one she had worn to the Ala Wai Inn. This dress was in Mrs. Massie's bedroom, hanging over the back of a chair. Lieutenant Massie picked up the dress and handed it to Lieutenant Jardine who took charge of it. Lieutenant Jardine asked Mr. Massie if that was the dress and Lieutenant Massie told him yes. I did not see Lieutenant Massie hand Lieutenant Jardine any other clothes. The color of this dress was green but I did not notice if there was any fur on it . . .

I saw Mrs. Massie's dress, the one Mr. Massie handed to Lieutenant Jardine, first before Massie handed it to him and it was not rumpled and appeared to be in good condition.[11]

The dress was subjected to a complete physical and chemical examination. It consisted of a green silk jacket, with short sleeves trimmed with brown fur; and a dress of the same material as the jacket, except that the upper part was white silk. A sworn statement by Captain R. O. Griffin, chief identification officer of the Honolulu Police Department, states that except for a bloodstain on the right sleeve, and a small bloodstain on the sash of the jacket, there were no other marks or tears in the outer garment. The dress itself showed what appeared to be a bloodstain on the front and another stain on the right side, "an indefinite stained area, giving the cloth at that point a stiff texture." There were also a couple of "small, dark stains, probably blood" near the bottom of the dress.

There were also a few stains on an underslip and a girdle, which were carefully examined. Blood spots were found on the slip and stains were also found on the girdle which the report said "might be seminal material." There were also small bits of foliage on her silk stockings which might have been from ironwood trees. An examination of the area at the site of the quarantine station disclosed a scattering of foliage and leaves similar to "pine needles" of ironwood trees.

As McIntosh later said: "It was completely inconclusive—neither corroborating nor denying her story. We had to assume her story was correct. In any case involving a complaint by a woman that she has been criminally attacked, it is like walking on eggshells. You can't prove anything and by the same token you can't disprove anything, either. Thalia Massie wasn't on trial—these boys were."

This, of course, had to be the position of the defense, also. The lawyers for the accused boys had no reason to attack the Government's contention that Thalia Massie had been criminally assaulted, since they were not trying to disprove this point. They were merely trying to prove their clients were not the guilty parties.

Unfortunately, this was not the viewpoint of the people in the streets of Honolulu. Those who had supported Thalia Massie's story, hearing that she had been taken to the Kapiolani Maternity Hospital, immediately assumed she was pregnant, and the public furor against the perpetrators of the outrage grew more intense and sinister. Those who did not believe her story found their beliefs amply supported by rumors of negative results at the hospital.

On October 15—a month after the attack on the Ala Moana—the *Advertiser* contributed to this public bitterness with a rather odd news story, under a heading: "Alarming Apathy . . . Community Aroused for Protection of Women from Attack."

The story went on to describe the "alarming apathy" of Honolulans in the matter of sex offenses. Although it was carried as a news story, printed on the front page, the article editorially charged that a "public frame of mind" had been created that "has emboldened sex offenders to a point where women are not safe outside their own dooryard."

"There is no disposition to try the Ala Moana case" the story said; and it added that "foully false stories have been circulating over tea tables." The newspaper, having accused the public of apathy and the police and county attorney of negligence, found that there was "a changed attitude toward public gossip that puts the injured person on trial." [12]

The text of the story, which was more of an editorial than a news item, was somewhat reminiscent of the "private memorandum" which Walter Dillingham printed and circulated among an exclusive circle of friends some time later. It failed to explain that the reason for the delay in the prosecution of the Ala Moana case was primarily because there actually was very little evidence on which to prosecute. And the charge that sex offenders had been "emboldened" by this laxity was hardly supported by facts. There were seven cases of sex offenses on record in the City and County of Honolulu in the year 1931. Of these, only one was a charge of rape (not counting the Ala Moana case); four were cases of attempted rape and two were charges of improper conduct with a female under sixteen. And only two of these incidents occurred after the Ala Moana assault and prior to the date the charge of laxity appeared in the *Advertiser*. The character of these cases is worth recording:

The first occurred on September 27, a Sunday night, two weeks after the attack on Mrs. Massie. A young girl met a youth at a Saturday night dance and went riding out to Koko Head with the boy and two of his friends. She later accused them of attacking her. The case drew little attention in the newspapers, since the girl was not a *haole;* and the upshot of it was that Police Judge Brooks threw the case out of court.

The second incident involved a twenty-year-old Japanese housekeeper, who said she was picked up by four boys who drove her up to the Nuuanu Pali and tried to assault her. She managed to escape; but the information she could give police was so scanty they could not find her assailants. This case, also, was given short shrift in the newspapers.

Nevertheless, it was apparently on a basis of these two cases—the only ones on the police records since Thalia Massie was attacked—that the *Advertiser* launched its crusade against "public apathy" and expressed a "revulsion of public feeling" against such a state of affairs. The editorializing reporter must have had two different "publics" in mind—one of which condoned rape and similar offenses, while the other did not.

The *Advertiser* unfortunately did not include a distinction between those who believed in guilt by accusation and those who did not; and it was in the midst of this general turmoil that the five accused boys in the Ala Moana case went to trial on November 16, 1931.

The Ala Moana Trial

On Monday, the sixteenth of November, the five boys charged with criminally assaulting Thalia Massie sat in the dark-walled courtroom in the old Territorial Courthouse, ready for trial. This queer old structure, a combination of ornate baroque and late nineteenth-century neoclassic design, with columns and a Victorian clock tower, had the appearance of a controversy between several schools of architecture. In front of the building stood the statue of Kamehameha the Great, the conqueror of all Hawaii. Underneath the black figure with its golden cape, on a pedestal supporting it, was carved the motto of Hawaii: *Ua Mau Ke Ea O Ka Aina Ika Pono;* which, loosely translated, means. "The life of the land is preserved in righteousness."

There was a great deal of righteousness represented inside the courtroom, but it is questionable whether it was the kind that would preserve "the life of the land." Judge Steadman, a mild-mannered man with a sound knowledge of the law and a reputation for firmness, was on the bench. In the audience were the usual groups of onlookers, mostly women. They were largely of the virtuous variety that dote on rape trials. Many of these women had carried on a constant cabal against the Honolulu Police Department and the County Attorney ever since the assault was first reported, presumably for not having had the suspects lynched forthwith. Now they sat watching everything with eager, beady eyes, awaiting the moment when Thalia Massie would take the stand and tell her own story of the experience of being raped. Most of the women stared from time to time at the five defendants, some covertly, others openly, as if the suspects were animals in a cage. The psychological amalgam of virtuous indignation and prurient curiosity is probably a phenomenon natural to rape trials, particularly in a hot area like Hawaii.

The heat of public emotion had grown rather than abated during the weeks preceding the trial. There was hardly anyone in Honolulu who regarded the matter with calm and objective judgment: either the boys were "gangsters" and "fiends," as the *Advertiser* had labeled them at the beginning; or they were members of an exploited race, ground into the soil of their own land by the intransigent arrogance of the intruding white man, and therefore the whole case must be a frame-up.

The truth obviously was somewhere between these extremes; but under the circumstances, few residents of the Islands could regard the affair with rational moderation. For this reason, selection of a jury that would be able to try the case fairly was an almost impossible task. The defense counsel, Judge Heen and Bill Pittman, relentlessly attacked the prejudice of "white supremacy," seeking to cull out of the veniremen those who held to a fixed point of view that the suspects must be guilty or they wouldn't be on trial; and Griffith Wight and Eddie Sylva sought with equal persistence to weed out those who were sympathetic to the Hawaiians or held an "anti-*haole*" point of view, and might vote to acquit the defendants on the theory that they had a bad shake anyway, just being Hawaiians.

Heen and Pittman themselves presented a curious contrast. The Hawaiian lawyer had striking eyes, dark and sharp; it was the face of a born fighter. Pittman, in contrast, seemed almost sleepy at times; he sat back in his chair, slightly paunchy, and calmly interrogated the witnesses in a slow, drawling voice, with a low-key courtroom manner. This was deceiving. Bill Pittman seldom raised his voice above a conversational pitch, but those who had witnessed his courtroom performances were well aware of the whiplash in his words. He spoke at times with a low, persuasive tone; and at times his words rang out with anger and scorn and biting sarcasm.

Two other attorneys appeared for the defense—Robert Murakami, a Japanese lawyer, who represented David Takai; and Ernest Kai, a young Hawaiian from Hilo, who assisted him. Ahakuelo and Chang were represented by Heen, and Kahahawai and Ida by Pittman.

It required the better part of two days to select the jury. In the cross-fire of questions and challenges, it became apparent that the racial issue was being clearly drawn by the defense, if not by the prosecution. Were the five accused boys, four of Hawaiian blood, to be given a fair trial, or were they to be convicted in order to placate the United States Navy? The issue was never quite stated; and it was ignored by the *haole* newspapers. But it was evident in the questions asked by Judge Heen and Bill Pittman, both able and conscientious lawyers and neither of them particularly awed by the *haole* elite of Honolulu. Walter Dillingham noted in his "private memorandum" that "the jury, from the time of its selection, was considered by the community a favorable jury for the defendants."

In point of fact, the jury consisted of seven white men, including one Portuguese who might have been regarded as aligned with the Hawaiian-Democratic bloc; two Japanese; two Chinese; and only one Hawaiian. The jury was actually a typical cross section of Honolulu. The single Hawaiian was employed in the City Engineer's office; the others were scattered through various mercantile or city government offices in Honolulu.

Since the makeup of the jury acquired some importance, particularly in later accounts in mainland newspapers and in the attitudes of certain members of Congress, it may be well to list the members of the jury for the record:

Charles H. Baker, white, a retired police captain.
Hee Wai, Chinese, employed by the City of Honolulu.
John Watson, white, employed by the Mutual Telephone Company.

John G. Botello, Portuguese, employed by the Honolulu Iron Works.
William Brede, white, also an Iron Works employee.
Robert French, of the Schumann Carriage Company, also white.
Jan Yip Lee, Chinese, working for the Hawaii Shoe Company.
Matsuo Matsugama, Japanese, employed by Theo. T. Davies Ltd.
William E. Paikuli, Hawaiian, employed by the City Engineer.
Takeo Kuamoto, Japanese, working for American Factors.
Ernest H. Fountain, white, of Aloha Motors.
William Blaisdell, white, an executive of the Von Hamm Young Company, and a brother of the present Mayor of Honolulu.[1]

Thalia Massie's Story

During the first day of jury selection Thalia Massie was not in the courtroom, and the more avid curiosity seekers were thus disappointed. A few were even disgruntled, apparently holding to the view that the complaining witness in a rape case, like a stage trouper, ought not to disappoint her audience. One middle-aged lady, on leaving the court, was heard remarking: "She should have been there to face the brutes."

Thalia Massie remained in court during the latter part of the second day, sitting with her husband and a few friends; and the third day—November 18—she took the stand as the Territory's first witness. She wore a light tan suit, and her hair was fairly short, combed back from her forehead. Her eyes were set wide apart in what had been a rather plump face, but was now almost gaunt. They seemed heavy-lidded and expressionless. Her face was drawn and white, with almost no makeup. The carved lines of her cheeks reflected the weeks of harrowing tension she had gone through, at the hospital and at her home. As the *Advertiser* expressed it:

> Her face scarred, her body bent and wracked with anguish, her voice trembling at times with emotion and fatigue, she bravely faced the ordeal.[2]

When Thalia Massie walked to the stand, every seat in the courtroom was filled. The majority were women, and most of these were white. A scattering of Hawaiian and Portuguese were there, but they sat at the rear of the courtroom, watching quietly and unobtrusively. Some of the white ladies had even bribed the bailiff to hold seats for them—a matter that later came to the attention of Judge Steadman when complaints were made by those who came on time but could not find seats.

Griffith Wight, with a courtliness seldom observed in a prosecutor in a criminal trial, met Thalia Massie as she walked up the aisle and escorted her to the witness chair. After a few perfunctory questions, in which she identified herself, he gently asked her to recount the events of Saturday night, September 12.

Thalia Massie sat rigidly in the witness chair, her mouth pursed in a hard line. Her eyes were bright, and at times she stared at the lawyers who questioned her in a way that seemed to reflect an inner anger, or resentment. She spoke in a low voice, almost throaty at times; and she appeared to be fighting to maintain her composure. Her hands rested in her lap, and now and then she twisted her fingers before she answered.

"Mrs. Massie, where were you shortly after 11:30 P.M. the evening of September 12?"

"I was at the dance at the Ala Wai Inn and I left shortly after 11:30."

"Why did you leave?"

"Because I was bored and tired of the party."

"Did you leave alone, or was someone with you?"

"Alone."

She said she walked down Kalakaua Avenue toward Waikiki until she came to the corner of John Ena Road. Because it was better lighted, she turned down this road toward the beach. She did not remember whether or not there was a dance at Waikiki Park; she passed a few stores but did not notice whether they were open. She said she had no idea that the entrance to Waikiki Park was across from the sidewalk on John Ena Road, along which she was walking.

Wight asked her how far she walked.

"I walked to a spot within twenty feet from where the road turns to go into Fort De Russy. I had intended to walk a little way down the road and then turn back and return to the Ala Moana."

At that point, she said, a car drove up beside her and two men jumped out. One of the men struck her on the side of her jaw, she said. The other man pulled her into a car.

"Would you be able to identify those two men?" Wight asked.

She looked at the five boys sitting in chairs behind the lawyers' table. She pointed to two of them. Judge Heen turned and asked the two to stand up. They were Joseph Kahahawai and Henry Chang.

Wight continued:

Q. After they dragged you into the car as you have described, what happened next?
A. I tried to talk to them but every time I did Kahahawai hit me. I offered them money if they would let me go.
Q. Was the car still or in motion at that time?
A. In motion. As soon as they dragged me into the car they started immediately. They were holding me in the back and I begged them to let me go. Whenever I spoke he would hit me.
Q. Who?
A. Kahahawai. Chang hit me too. I offered them money; I told them my husband would give them money if they would let me go. I said I had some money with me they could have. When I said that he turned around and said, "Take the pocketbook," and one of them took it from me.[3]

It was at this point that she identified the third of the group—Ben Ahakuelo. She said he was the one who had turned and said, "Take the pocketbook."

"How did you recognize him?" Wight asked.

"He turned around several times and grinned and I saw his face; I also saw he had a gold tooth."

"Where?"

"A gold filling—about here." She pointed to her teeth.

"You saw this gold filling?"

"Yes. When he turned around the first time—I think it was when he said that about taking my pocketbook."

She described what happened in the car as they drove down the Ala Moana toward town, and finally turned into the open space surrounded by trees. Her voice remained calm as she spoke, but it was evident that she was under great tension—which was to be expected. At times she paused and seemed to bite her lip before she answered; but as the *Advertiser* noted in its account of her testimony, Judge Steadman showed her "every consideration, ordering recesses when she showed evidence of breaking under the strain."

In her original statement to Chief Inspector McIntosh, it will be recalled that Thalia Massie told how her abductors drove the car into the undergrowth on the right-hand side of the Ala Moana and dragged her out of the car and into the bushes, assaulting her "six or seven times."

At that time McIntosh had asked her what nationality her attackers were, and she said, "Hawaiians I would say." He asked her the make of the car and she said: "It was a touring car, I can't say what make it was, but I think it was a Ford." She made no effort to identify any of her assailants at that time, although she had been asked by several detectives if she would be able to recognize them, and had replied, "Only by their voices."

However, on direct examination at the trial she was able to supply many of the missing details. When Wight asked her who dragged her out of the car, she replied: "The two holding me in the car. [Chang] and Kahahawai."

After they dragged her several yards into the bushes, she said, "Chang assaulted me."

Q. How did you know it was Chang?
A. Because he was holding me in the car and he dragged me over there; he helped the others drag me over; he never let go of me.
Q. Did you consent to this act?
A. Certainly not. I tried to get away but I couldn't. I couldn't imagine what was happening. He just hit me; the others were holding me—holding my arms.
Q. And when Chang completed this act what happened next?
A. Then one of the others did it—I don't know which one.
Q. Now, what happened after that?
A. After that, Kahahawai assaulted me.
Q. How did you know it was Kahahawai?
A. Because he had been sitting beside me in the car and I recognized his face; he had a short-sleeved shirt on; he knocked me in the jaw; I started to pray and that made him angry and he hit me very hard; I cried out, "You've knocked my teeth out," and he told me to shut up. I asked him please not to hit me any more.

144

Q. He hit you when you started to pray?

A. Yes.

Q. During the time you were in the woods with these men do you know how many times you were assaulted?

A. From four to six times. I think Chang assaulted me twice because he was standing near me and he said he wanted to go again. The others said all right, and a little later he assaulted me.

Q. Mrs. Massie, do you know any other individual besides these two men who assaulted you?

A. Ida.

Q. How do you know that?

A. I felt his coat against my arm.

Q. What was your physical condition when this was going on as to strength?

A. They hit me so much that I was sort of dazed.

Q. Did you or did you not hear any remarks—any language from these defendants?

A. Yes, the others talked to each other in some foreign language. They spoke in English—they said a lot of filthy things to me. . . . They called each other by name.

Q. What names were they?

A. I heard the name "Bull" used, and I heard the name "Joe." I heard another name—it might have been "Billy" or "Benny," and I heard the name "Shorty." Then I heard one of them say, "Hurry up, we have to go back out Kalihi way."

Q. Now, when these acts were completed, what happened then?

A. One helped me to sit up; he pointed to something and said, "The road's over there," then they all ran off and got away, and I turned around and saw the car—the back of the car towards me—and I saw Ida get in the front seat of the car.

Q. How did you recognize him?

A. Someone had turned on the headlights and I saw his leather coat.[4]

Judge Heen conducted most of the cross-examination. He spoke in a low, conversational tone, touching only briefly on those parts of her testimony which involved the assault. He seemed to be more interested in the time element.

Thalia Massie had said under direct examination that after her attackers left, she "wandered around in the bushes and finally came to the Ala Moana. I saw a car and ran toward the car, waving my arms. The car stopped; I ran to the car and asked the people in it if they were white."

"How long were you wandering around through the bushes and trees?" Heen asked.

"I don't know."

"A matter of a few minutes?"

"I don't know. I was just beginning to realize what had happened to me and I wasn't thinking of the time."

Heen paused and looked at her.

"What do you mean by saying that you just happened to realize what had happened to you? . . . Didn't you know what was happening to you all the time?"

"I couldn't believe people actually did things like that."

In the course of her direct testimony, Thalia Massie had identified each of the defendants, except David Takai. She testified that she had particularly recognized Ben Ahakuelo because "he turned around several times and grinned and I saw his face. I also saw that he had a gold tooth."

Whether the defense counsel had access to the prosecution's pretrial statements is not certain; but it is probable that some of the results of the interrogations at the police station and at the County Attorney's office were known to Heen and Pittman.

At any rate, Heen began to probe more directly into her identification of the suspects.

"Do you recall asking David Takai his name, when you were identifying the boys?"

She shook her head.

"I don't remember having done so."

Q. Do you recall asking him if he was Hawaiian?
A. I don't recall what I said to him.
Q. How did you know their names?
A. Evidently someone told me. I may have read them. They are familiar to me now.
Q. When you identified Ahakuelo—by his gold tooth—did you mention it to anyone?
A. I saw him twice; I think it was the second time.
Q. The first time you didn't mention it?

A. The first time, as I told you, I had been given drugs and don't remember much about it.

Q. Was it the second time that you mentioned it?

A. I don't remember.[5]

Pittman, who was representing Ida, arose and walked over to the witness. He stood for some time, looking at Thalia Massie, until Judge Steadman prompted him by tapping his gavel on the bench.

"Please proceed, Mr. Pittman."

"Oh, yes . . . When was it that you saw the automobile that Ida was supposed to have driven on the night of September 12?"

"You mean, when did I see it?"

"After the assault?"

"I saw it Sunday afternoon . . . about two or three o'clock, I think."

"Where did you see it?"

"At my home."

Pittman seemed to be reflecting again. He stared at the witness for several seconds before he put the next question. Then he asked:

"Did you recognize the car, Mrs. Massie—at that time?"

She nodded. "It was just like the car I had seen the night before —just like it."

"What color was the car?"

"It was sort of brown."

It will be recalled that on Sunday afternoon, Inspector McIntosh drove Horace Ida's car—a 1929 black Ford Phaeton—up to the Massie house. In her statement earlier that morning, at the Police Station, she had told him, in reply to his question as to the make of the car: "It was a touring car . . . I can't say what make it was, but I think it was a Ford."

It is interesting, at this point, to compare her testimony with that given later by the Chief Inspector when he was on the stand under direct examination by Wight:

Q. [By Wight] Mrs. Massie told you that if she saw the back of this car and the back seat of this car she might recognize it?

A. She did.

Q. Did you show her the back seat of this car?
A. I did.
Q. Were there any distinguishing marks in the back seat of the car?
A. Not in that particular car.
Q. Did you show her the Ida car—No. 58-895?
A. I did.
Q. Was she unable to point out anything in this car?
A. *She wasn't able to identify the car.*[6]

Judge Heen jumped up at this point, requesting that the car be brought over to the courthouse for the inspection by the jury. It was driven under a huge banyan tree, and the jury filed past it, each juror examining it carefully. The car was almost new, a 1929 Model A Ford touring car. There was nothing loose or flapping in back; and the color was definitely black—not brown.

Time Rears Its Ugly Head

It was near the end of Thalia Massie's second day on the stand. She appeared weary and almost on the edge of breaking. Judge Steadman frequently ordered recesses, to give her an opportunity to recover her composure.

Heen and Pittman had questioned her with extreme tact; yet it was evident they were boring relentlessly into her story. The women in the courtroom were getting restive, murmuring audible whispers of complaint whenever it seemed that the attack on the girl's story was becoming sharp and severe.

Just before the end of Thalia Massie's cross-examination, Judge Heen picked up a paper, looked at it briefly, laid it down, and then walked over to the witness chair.

"You testified, Mrs. Massie, that Inspector McIntosh took your testimony in shorthand—at the police station?"

"I think he was taking it in shorthand. He was writing, anyway."

Heen walked back to the counsel's table and picked up the piece of paper he had been looking at. Then he turned, and this time his voice became even more gentle and persuasive.

"You have testified, Mrs. Massie, that you left the Ala Wai Inn around 11:30 or shortly afterward. Is that correct?"

"Yes."

"What do you mean by 'shortly after'?"
"Five minutes."

Q. About what time was it then that you left the Ala Wai Inn?
A. It was about 11:35.
Q. How do you recall that time?
A. Because some friends of mine left the dance hall at 11:30 and I left the party a few minutes after they did.
Q. Did you look at any clock or look at a timepiece so as to know your friends left at 11:30?
A. No.
Q. How did you happen to know it was 11:30?
A. My friend told me later she had looked at her watch and it had been 11:30.
Q. Several days later?
A. I don't remember.
Q. What is your best recollection as to that?
A. I don't remember.
Q. You don't remember whether it was the next day or a week after?
A. No, I don't remember when it was.
Q. Did you tell your husband that you were going out from the inn at the time you left the inn?
A. No.
Q. Did you tell any other member of your party you were going?
A. No.[7]

There had been no witnesses subpoenaed from among the Navy couples who were at the party at the Ala Wai that Saturday night, with one exception: Lieutenant Thomas M. Brown and his wife, Mary Anne Brown, were called in to testify that they had not seen Thalia Massie after 11:30 P.M. Mary Anne Brown later took the stand to lend a somewhat negative corroboration of Thalia Massie's estimate of the time she left. She said she had "gone upstairs at about 11:35 to see if Thalia was still in the booth, and she wasn't there."

While Judge Heen stood in front of Thalia Massie, waving the paper and asking her questions, it was apparently assumed by the County Attorney's staff that this estimate would be accepted. However, it could not have been so assumed by John McIntosh, for reasons that will appear.

Griffith Wight was either unaware of the contents of the paper

Judge Heen held in his hand, or was singularly obtuse as to the trend the testimony was taking. He sat at the table, making no effort to divert the witness's attention by objections or interruptions. The significance of Thalia Massie's words became evident later in the trial, when Inspector McIntosh was under cross-examination.

At that time, Judge Heen's voice was neither gentle nor persuasive. It had a cutting edge. McIntosh had testified on direct examination that he had taken down Mrs. Massie's statement at the Police Station in longhand. "I do not write shorthand," he said.

Heen asked: "Did Mrs. Massie tell you it was about midnight when she left the Ala Wai Inn?"

McIntosh stared at the Hawaiian lawyer. Then he replied:

"Around midnight, I think she said."

Heen went back to the table and picked up a sheet of paper—the same sheet he held in his hand when cross-examining Thalia Massie. The Chief Inspector straightened up a bit more rigidly in the chair. Heen walked toward him, holding up the paper, and said:

"This is a copy of her statement to you, Inspector—as you say you took it down. Your copy of her statement, which you wrote down, said along about 12:30 or 1 A.M. she left there. Is that correct?"

Griffith Wight made no move. He merely looked at the paper which Judge Heen waved in his hand.

"That would be her statement, then," McIntosh said evenly. "I wrote it down as she made it."

The importance of this bit of testimony was never made apparent in the newspaper reports of the trial. Neither Heen nor Pittman seemed disposed to follow it up. Yet it laid bare a basic flaw in the prosecution's entire case. If Thalia Massie left the Ala Wai Inn "around 12:30 or 1 A.M.," as she said in her original statement, it would have been impossible for the five accused youths to have been her assailants. The records of the police themselves would have provided an alibi.

The paper from which Judge Heen read what was purported to be Thalia Massie's first statement to McIntosh was not offered in evidence; nor was it asked for by the prosecution. The original of the statement, in Inspector McIntosh's handwriting, likewise was never introduced. The notebook upon which it was written apparently was destroyed, since the phrasing is misquoted in later official reports of the investigation by the Pinkerton Detective Agency, to read: "Around midnight I decided to go for a walk and some air." The handwritten statement said: "Around 12:30 or 1 A.M."

Nevertheless, the handwritten record was not completely lost. The notebook was taken from the police station by one of the investigators and photographed. The notebook was returned and it is doubtful if the fact that it had been photographed was ever known to the police or to the City Attorney's office. The photostatic copy, as previously noted, is reproduced in this book, together with a copy of the excerpt from the Pinkerton report.

Had Thalia Massie's original statement gone into the record, it would have contradicted every theory the prosecution had to offer. It would have made it extremely difficult to explain exactly what happened between "around 12:30 or 1 A.M." and the time the car driven by Eustace Bellinger picked her up, wandering along the Ala Moana Road, at about one o'clock in the morning.

Above all, it would have provided an unimpeachable alibi for the five boys accused of the rape, since they were known to have been at King and Liliha Streets at about 12:35 A.M.

The Tire Tracks

It became evident as the case progressed that the defense would rely on three basic points: the uncertainties and vagueness of Thalia Massie's identification of her assailants and the car they used; the confused time factor; and the "alibi witnesses," Tuts Matsumoto and Bob Vierra, supported by Peter and Wilhelmina Correa. Only one bit of evidence stood in the way of such a defense: the tire tracks at the old quarantine station.

Shortly after Thalia Massie completed her testimony, and medical evidence was introduced to show the nature of her injuries, Police Officer Claude Benton was called to the witness chair. It will be remembered that early Sunday morning, while Inspector McIntosh was still taking Thalia Massie's statement at the Police Station, Benton and Radio Patrolman Percy Bond drove down to the site of the old quarantine station to look for tire tracks.

Benton took Ida's car, in order to examine its tires and compare the tread with any tracks found at the place where the assault was believed to have taken place. Later he reported to McIntosh that he had found tracks of two kinds of tires—Goodrich Silvertown cords and Goodyear All-Weather tires. These corresponded to the tires on Horace Ida's car.

When Benton took the stand, it was late Friday; and his testimony had to be carried over into Monday. This, of course, permitted the defense time for inquiries of their own, based on Benton's direct testimony.

When Judge Heen took over the cross-examination of the witness on Monday, it was evident to those in the courtroom that this was a crucial moment in the trial. At one point Judge Steadman had to admonish the audience to "remain quiet or the courtroom will be cleared."

There was little doubt from the determined way in which both Heen and Pittman attacked Benton's testimony that they knew their case hung on this evidence. If Benton were able to establish beyond question that tire tracks corresponding to those on Ida's car had been found freshly made at the site of the old quarantine station it would contradict every bit of testimony the defense could produce, including the "alibi witnesses." It would also provide the supporting evidence necessary for a conviction on a charge of criminal assault.

Heen paced up and down before the witness before he spoke to Benton. He went over to the defense counsel's table and conferred briefly with Pittman. The latter turned to where the five boys were sitting, staring stolidly at the proceedings, and motioned to Horace Ida, who owned the car. The Japanese boy jumped up and went over to the defense lawyer's table. They whispered for a few seconds, and then Heen turned to Benton:

"When you went back to look over the so-called tire tracks—this was Monday morning, wasn't it."

Benton nodded, and said, "Yes." He had testified under direct examination that after his first visit to the old quarantine station grounds early Sunday morning, he had returned later with Sammy Lau and Horace Ida, in Ida's car, for the purpose of taking pictures of the tracks. Meanwhile Assistant Chief of Police Bill Hoopai

152

and Police Officer George Cypher had also driven down to the site; and even McIntosh, as he later admitted, had also driven down sometime Sunday in Horace Ida's Ford. Hoopai reported having seen some tire tracks, which could have been made by Ida's car when Benton drove it down earlier in the morning. The welter of confused testimony on this matter made it difficult to establish when the tracks were made; and Heen and Pittman were not slow to seize on this confusion.

Heen asked Benton:

"Did you run Ida's car alongside the tracks and ask Lau to photograph them?" Samuel K. Lau was the Police Identification Officer and official police photographer.

"Yes," Benton said, "but he did not do it."

"Did you tell him not to photograph the tracks because they were not the same tracks you had seen earlier?"

"I did not."

"Did he come to your home and talk to you about the matter?"

"He came the other night and we discussed it."

Later, when the defense presented its case, Sammy Lau was called to the stand as a defense witness—a matter that provoked an assortment of rumors that certain police officers had "defected to the defense" and was cited widely by the *haole* contingent in Honolulu to prove that the "Hawaiian faction" in the Police Department had "betrayed" the prosecution.

Lau, as a matter of fact, was Chinese, not Hawaiian; but he had grown up in Honolulu, attended McKinley High School there, and could be regarded as a "local boy." He had been on the police force for several years.

Lau testified, under direct examination by Judge Heen, as follows:

Q. When you went to the Ala Moana with Ida and Benton, did he tell you all the tire marks he had seen on Sunday morning had been obliterated?

A. No. He said "erased."

Q. Did he point out one?

A. I saw that mark. It was about a foot from the end of the road, in the grass.

Q. That mark was the only one that corresponded to the tires on Ida's car?
A. The only one.
Q. Did you tell Benton you knew Ida?
A. No. I did not know Ida then.[8]

There was no doubt in Griffith Wight's mind that his case literally hung on Claude Benton's testimony. Thalia Massie's story had no other support that actually placed the suspects at the scene of the attack. The supreme effort to discredit Sammy Lau's testimony could readily be understood; but what was not understandable was the effort to discredit Lau himself.

Wight, in his cross-examination, tried to show bias in favor of the defendants, and in fact a deliberate betrayal of the Police Department.

"Isn't it a fact," he asked, "that you were sore at the County Attorney's office because your testimony in previous cases was discredited?"

Heen jumped to his feet.

"The effort to discredit this witness," he told the Court, "is not only irrelevant, but malicious. The testimony stands on what Mr. Lau observed and what he did—not on what he thought."

Whatever the justification may have been for Wight's bitter attack on Sammy Lau, the result of his testimony, together with the cross-examination of Benton, struck an almost mortal blow at the prosecution's case. The demonstration of "bungling," as Walter Dillingham had described it, was almost incredible. Why had Benton driven Ida's car down to the site of the attack in the first place? Why had McIntosh gone back on Sunday and driven over the area, perhaps obliterating all tracks that had been made by the attackers? What did Bill Hoopai do when he and Officer George Cypher drove down Sunday morning?

And perhaps most important of all—why did the police proceed solely on the theory that it had to be Horace Ida's car that was to be identified by the tire tracks?

It probably would have been obvious to an objective investigator that the purpose of a police investigation is to find out who committed the crime—not to arrest suspects and then find the evi-

dence upon which to convict them. But as previously noted, the
Honolulu Police proceeded in the reverse of this order, for reasons
that have been dealt with in some detail, and not all of which can
be ascribed to police inefficiency. The "bungling" of the tire-track
evidence began from the moment it became necessary to find suit-
able suspects and arrest them—and that moment occurred almost
at the time Thalia Massie first told her story to the police.

The "Woman in Green"

The closing effort of the prosecution was devoted to
presenting the testimony of three witnesses, rather carefully culled
from a group of seven who were available, to provide evidence that
"a woman in a green dress" had been dragged into a car on John
Ena road "around midnight" of September 12. These witnesses
were Eugenio Batungbacal and two of his three Chinese friends,
Roger Lieu and Charlie Chang.

In describing the incident, Batungbacal said:

"I see about four or five men with one girl. Two mens holding
the woman with hands and one is following. They look like they
force the woman to bring it [her] into the car."

Wight asked, "What kind of a car?" and Batungbacal shrugged.
"I don't know what kind of a car, but I am sure it is touring."

Heen, on cross-examination, asked:

Q. What kind of dress did the woman wear? A green dress?
A. I don't know what the green dress, or what color, but I see the
   woman, that's all. I don't know the color of her dress.
Q. What kind of color did you think it was?
A. I don't know. Night time is hard to tell.
Q. Wasn't there light enough?
A. There is light there but you never can tell. I am not interested to
   see what kind of color her dress. I just know I see her, and I
   don't know what kind of dress.
Q. What kind of hair she have?
A. I don't know.
Q. Black?
A. I don't know.
Q. You saw this woman walking?
A. Yes, walking with the men—[9]

Griffith Wight broke into the questioning, apparently in some consternation.

"Walking with the men—what?" he asked.

"I saw the girl walking with the men the first time. I thought they go together; just go with the party. The girl is just a little drunk, you know. I don't think the mens were—we don't pay any attention."

Judge Steadman suddenly interrupted:

"Judge Heen, you are examining the witness."

Heen shrugged and grinned.

"He has answered my question. I didn't ask him for all these things."

Wight sat down. He had opened a small Pandora's box of questioning, and Heen was not slow to take advantage of it.

"You said the woman walked as if she was drunk?" he asked.

"She looked like she was drunk because two mens held this arm and she tried to get away from these men. That is what make me believe she is drunk."

"And you said it looked as if they were all walking together at first?"

"You asked me first if I said the woman was walking," Batungbacal said. "Yes, she is walking with the men. Mens holding her in both arms and some following and some stay behind. I don't know. That's all I saw."

Heen walked up and stood directly in front of the witness. He asked:

"When you saw these men walking that way, you were surprised, were you not?"

"What do you mean?"

"You were surprised. You know what 'surprised' means—"

"I don't pay no attention. The first time I think the woman go with those boys. I thought she was drunk and those boys just help her in the car. That is what I thought the first time."

Heen nodded. "That's all," he said.

Roger Lieu's story was about the same, but less ambiguous. He described the woman as "struggling" with the men; and Charlie Chang said much the same thing. However, when Chang was under cross-examination, Heen asked:

"When you saw that these men were trying to get this woman into the car . . . did you become excited?"

"Well, no, I did not."

"You didn't think it was strange?"

"I thought they were just a bunch of friends."

"You didn't get excited when you thought they were dragging her into the car? You didn't say to anybody in the car, 'Look at those boys dragging that woman'?"

"No."

James Low, the fourth member in the Batungbacal party, was not called by the prosecution, but he was a witness for the defense. He said he had seen the woman about 100 feet from the *saimin* stand on John Ena Road. They had just left the dance hall at Waikiki Park, after he and Charlie Chang had gone into the pavilion a few minutes before the last dance. He estimated it was about 12:15 A.M. when he saw the woman walking slowly down the sidewalk.

Q. [By Heen] And at that time did you see anybody else?
A. There was a man following immediately behind her.
Q. . . . About how far behind was this man from that woman, as near as you can judge?
A. About two or three feet.
Q. And how was this woman walking at that time?
A. She, well, she was drunk, I presume it was; she was walking like a drunken person.
Q. How was her head?
A. Head down.[10]

There was never any evidence presented that would indicate definitely, one way or the other, whether the woman was Thalia Massie, except for a description of her clothes. Alice Aramaki, in her testimony for the defense, described her as wearing a lighter-colored green dress than the one she wore that night; James Low said he thought the dress was "blue"; but Mrs. Goeas, perhaps more qualified than any of the others to describe the dress, said in her testimony: "It was a dress with sleeves to the elbow, tight around the waist, full around the skirt and ankle length."

"Were you questioned by police officers about this matter?" Heen asked.

157

"Yes . . . at our home a few days after the accident."

"At that time did they show you a dress similar to this?" He held up before her the dress Thalia Massie had worn the night of the attack.

"After they had asked questions, they showed us the dress," she said.

Q. Your husband was there at the time?
A. Yes.
Q. Did you examine the dress at the time?
A. We looked at it when a man placed it in front of us.
Q. Including the top, like this?
A. Yes.
Q. Did you recognize that dress as being the dress this woman had on that night?
A. Yes.[11]

It is scarcely to be expected that the prosecuting attorney, in any case of the importance of the Ala Moana trial, would disclose in advance any evidence contrary to the Government's theory of the case. Nevertheless, it is a matter of record that the Chief Inspector had the report of Deputy Inspector Jardine on September 17—four days after the assault—giving complete statements made by George Goeas and his wife. If he had taken this into account in planning the case against the five Ala Moana defendants, it might have changed the entire course of events.

If Mrs. Goeas' story was to be accepted at its face value—and there was no reason whatever to doubt it—this strongly indicated that Thalia Massie was the woman who was walking down John Ena Road at about 12:15 A.M. Sunday. This time had fitted the earlier theory of the prosecution; but it made the case against the five Ala Moana suspects utterly improbable in the light of later developments.

This information was allowed to lie dormant until the defense brought it out at the trial; and it may be regarded as another of the links in the chain of events directly responsible for the tragic happenings that followed.

Conflicting Stories

Since the entire structure of the prosecution's case was founded on the testimony of Thalia Massie—if the apocryphal evidence concerning the tire tracks may be disregarded for the moment—it is worth while to inquire at this point into exactly what she said in her pretrial statements, and what was said in sworn testimony at the trial.

There were two elements that Chief Inspector McIntosh noted at the beginning of the investigation as the basis for the Territory's case:

1. The time factor.
2. Identification of the suspects and their car.

Early Sunday morning, when McIntosh questioned Thalia Massie in his office, she was reported to have said she left the Ala Wai Inn "around midnight." The actual statement, as attested by the photostatic copy of the statement McIntosh wrote down in his own handwriting, was "around 12:30 or 1 A.M."

In her direct testimony at the trial, she had been asked:

Q. Where were you shortly after 11:30 P.M. the evening of September 12th?
A. I was at the dance at Ala Wai Inn and I left shortly after 11:30 P.M.[12]

In cross-examining her, Judge Heen sought to pin this down by asking the witness on what basis she had estimated that she left the Ala Wai Inn at 11:30 P.M.:

Q. How did you happen to know it was 11:30?
A. My friend told me later that she had looked at her watch and it had been about 11:30.[13]

This presumably referred to Susan Fish or Mary Anne Brown; yet Susan Fish did not testify at the trial, and Mary Anne Brown had only a vague recollection that she went upstairs "about 11:30" to look for Thalia Massie, and Thalia was not in the booth where she had last been seen.

Therefore the entire structure of the time element, as presented by the prosecution, depended on the statement of the complaining witness. No one had come forward, either before or during the trial, to give any positive evidence as to where Thalia Massie was, or what happened to her, from a few minutes after 11:30 A.M. when she was last seen at the Ala Wai Inn, until she was found an hour and a half later, her face bruised and her body showing signs of a physical beating, wandering along the Ala Moana. The nearest to any tangible evidence were the reports of the seven people who saw "a woman in a green dress" walking slowly along John Ena Road about a quarter of an hour after midnight.

As to the identification of the suspects, the most significant aspect seems to be the chronological order in which Thalia Massie was able to increase her recollection of additional details. The police officers who questioned her at her home were Detectives William Furtado, Frank Bettencourt, George Harbottle and George Nakea, and Traffic Officer William Simerson. When Furtado asked her if she could recognize the boys who had attacked her, she replied: "Only by their voices." Later she said, "I am sure they were Hawaiians. There were four or five—I'm not sure how many."

In the office of Inspector McIntosh later that Sunday morning, she was asked if she could identify her attackers, and she replied: "I don't know." McIntosh asked if she heard any names mentioned, and she said, "I heard the name 'Bull' used several times and some common name like Joe."

At the trial, she was asked by Griffith Wight:

Q. What names were they?
A. I heard the name "Bull" used and I heard the name "Joe." I heard another name, it might have been "Billy" or "Benny" and I heard a name "Shorty" . . .[14]

When Judge Heen questioned her at the trial as to her earlier efforts to identify her attackers—or rather her inability to identify them—she suddenly seemed to have very little recollection of what had happened. Heen asked:

Q. Before Mr. McIntosh appeared on the scene were you asked by some of the other officers what happened that night?
A. I don't remember much. They took me to the hospital.
Q. Do you recall being asked by either Mr. Furtado or Mr. Harbottle what happened that night?

A. No. My husband explained it all.

Q. Do you remember telling the police officers who first arrived at your home that night that these boys had grabbed you and pulled you into the car and that one boy held your mouth and beat you while in the car? Do you remember telling the officers that?

A. No. I remember telling Mr. McIntosh that.

Q. And you don't remember telling any police officers the same thing, prior to telling Mr. McIntosh?

A. They came in, a whole lot of them. My husband explained to them . . .

Q. Do you remember saying on that same occasion something to this effect—that you didn't hear any names except "Bull"?

A. No. That wasn't so.[15]

With reference to the identification of the car that Horace Ida had driven that night, she displayed a similar vagueness of memory as to what had happened earlier in the evening of the attack, before she gave the license number to Inspector McIntosh. Heen, again cross-examining her, asked:

Q. Do you remember stating upon questioning that you couldn't identify the car—that you weren't sure what kind of car it was?

A. I didn't think much about the car. Mr. McIntosh asked about it.

Q. Have you seen this car since that night?

A. Yes . . . It was the next day. They brought the car up.

Q. Now I ask you whether or not you remember making a statement to this effect on that night when the police officers arrived, that you thought it was a Ford or a Dodge touring car? An old car?

A. I don't remember saying anything as to the age of the car.

Q. Do you remember saying anything to these officers before you saw Mr. McIntosh that the top in back of this car was loose?

A. No.[16]

Detective George Nakea, later called as a witness for the defense, said in direct testimony:

I asked Mrs. Massie—I went to her, right at her head [she was then lying on a couch] and she was looking at me. She was holding a handkerchief over her mouth, and I told Mrs. Massie, I said, "What is the matter?" and she said, "I have been assaulted." I said, "Who was you assaulted by?" and she says, "Some Hawaiian boys." I asked her, "Do you remember the place where you was assaulted at?" and she said, "Yes, the other side of the Ala Wai Inn."

Q. Did she tell you or say anything about who assaulted her?
A. No, she just told me it was Hawaiian boys.
Q. What else, if anything, did she say as to the identity of the boys, of the Hawaiians, rather?
A. She did not make no identification about the boys to me, but all she said was Hawaiian boys.
Q. Did she say anything at the time as to whether or not she could identify these Hawaiians?
A. She said she could not . . . All she knew was Hawaiian boys.[17]

Detective Nakea's account confirms with the reports made to Inspector McIntosh by Furtado, Harbottle and Bettencourt following their first interview with Thalia Massie, namely, that she remembered only that they were "Hawaiian boys" and she could not identify the car.

Less than an hour after they talked with her, when she was at the Emergency Hospital, the nurse who attended her, Agnes Fawcett, asked her what happened and she said "six men" had assaulted her. Miss Fawcett was also called as a defense witness at the trial, and she testified that "Mrs. Massie said six men—Hawaiians —had assaulted her." She did not identify any of them by name.

Miss Fawcett added: "She said it was so dark that she would not be able to recognize any of them."[18]

The one man who might have presented for the prosecution a story that would support Thalia Massie's testimony at the trial was John McIntosh. He had talked with her within three hours of the assault; he had the experience of a trained investigator; and he should have been able to present the case for the Territory in its strongest light.

Only two of Thalia Massie's friends who were with her at the party at the Ala Wai Inn were in court to testify. These two Navy witnesses were Lieutenant Brown and his wife, Mary Anne Brown, who had "gone upstairs at about 11:35 P.M. to see if Thalia was still in the booth, and she wasn't there." That was all she remembered. Tommy Massie did not testify; nor did Lieutenant Jerry Branson, who, according to the Navy, was away at sea during the trial, or his wife appear as witnesses.

There was only the one witness left who could lend credence to her story, and that was the Chief Inspector. He had talked with her when her recollection presumably was clear; and he had conducted the investigation. It is interesting to note what he said under oath at the trial.

The Prosecution Closes

McIntosh was aware that the two points of greatest vulnerability, which the prosecution must prove, were the time factor and the identification of the suspects and the car. After he had described the investigation in a rather concise way on direct examination, he turned to face Judge Heen on cross-examination.

"Did Mrs. Massie tell you the back of the car [Horace Ida's car] was loose and flapping?" Heen asked.

"No."

"Didn't she tell you one of the men she grabbed wore a leather coat?"

"She did not."

"Did you get reports from the officers who questioned her at her home?"

"Yes," McIntosh replied. "The County Attorney has the statements."

Heen stared at the Chief Inspector in surprise.

"Who made the written reports?"

"No written reports were made," McIntosh said calmly. "They made statements and I took them down and turned them over to the County Attorney."

"Do you mean all this evidence—these statements—were made verbally to you and you turned them over to the County Attorney?"

"That is right," the Chief Inspector said.

Heen shifted quickly to another point—the matter of the beads which were identified by Thalia Massie and supposedly had been found in Horace Ida's car.

"Did you tell Ida you found the beads in his car?"

"Yes," McIntosh replied.

"Didn't he say that if they were in his car, they were planted there?"

163

"He did not. He said they might have belonged to his sister."

In the written report of the questioning of Horace Ida on Sunday night, September 13, at the police station, with Wight and Sylva present, McIntosh had asked:

"These beads"—showing Ida a string of jade-colored beads—"are the ones that were picked up in your car."

Ida had replied: "I don't know."

The fact that this incident was known to the newspapers became a sensitive point for the prosecution, and led to a bitter denunciation of "certain members of the Police Department," whom Wight accused of "leaking information to a Japanese newspaper." The *Hawaii Hochi* on November 23 published a story to the effect that Inspector McIntosh had told Horace Ida the beads had been found in his car. As he explained it, "I wanted to see if Ida would crack." Since it was not an unusual police practice, and had little importance anyway, it is quite probable that McIntosh himself told the *Hochi* reporter.

The final questioning of the Chief Inspector on cross-examination involved the controversial exchange between Detective John Cluney and Horace Ida. It will be recalled that it was Cluney's report on this matter that—as McIntosh later said—"cinched the case" in his mind. According to Cluney's story, the Japanese boy had admitted he knew about the assault on Mrs. Peeples at King and Liliha Streets—after first denying any knowledge of the matter; but he said he knew nothing about an attack on "the white woman." It was after this that McIntosh called Ida into his office, pointed to Thalia Massie, and said:

"Now look at your beautiful work!"

At the trial, Heen asked McIntosh:

"Did Cluney at any time tell you that Ida admitted the Peeples incident, but denied assaulting the white woman?"

McIntosh shook his head firmly.

"He did not."

The Chief Inspector's reply may be compared with Cluney's own testimony earlier at the trial. He was asked on direct examination by Wight:

164

Q. What did you do when you took Ida to the police station [the night of the assault]?

A. I took Ida over to the Detective Bureau and waited to turn him over to McIntosh or Jardine.

Q. What did you say to Ida?

A. I told him it looked pretty tough. He told me he was ready to admit one of the boys in his car struck the Hawaiian woman, but they had nothing to do with the white woman.

Q. Had you told him about the white woman?

A. I had not. I had instructions to keep that under cover.

Q. Did you put that in your report?

A. No. *I told McIntosh.* Wight said it was "good stuff." [19]

This "good stuff," like Claude Benton's testimony on the tire tracks, might have had sufficient corroborative weight to convict the five youths. Had it been definitely shown that Horace Ida had denied knowing anything about an attack on "the white woman" before he could have had any knowledge that such an attack had occurred, it would have lent substance to McIntosh's own conviction that he had the guilty parties and this might also have persuaded a jury.

Yet, McIntosh, under cross-examination, declined to confirm that such an incident occurred. And Cluney, himself, under cross-examination by Pittman, admitted that he was "not sure" whether or not Detective Thurman Black, who had been sitting beside the Japanese boy in the police assembly room, might have told Ida of the other assault case involving a white woman before Cluney talked to him.

In his final cross-examination of McIntosh, Heen asked the Chief Inspector questions relating to the identification:

Q. Did she [Mrs. Massie] tell you she could identify one of the boys by a gold tooth?

A. She did not.

Q. You are certain Ben [Ahakuelo] was not asked to open his mouth so she could see his gold tooth?

A. Not while I was in the room.[20]

The matter of Ben Ahakuelo's gold tooth had not been mentioned in any of the numerous statements Thalia Massie gave to the police;

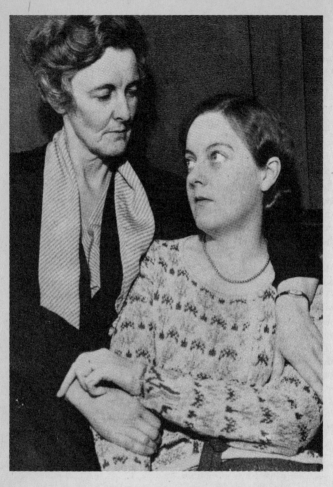

Mrs. Grace Fortescue with her daughter, Thalia Massie.

but at the trial she said that "the one called Benny" had turned around at one point and laughed and she saw his gold tooth. On cross-examination, Heen again elicited this testimony:

Q. You stated, I believe, that at one point Ahakuelo turned around and laughed?
A. Yes.
Q. Did you see his facial characteristics at that time?
A. Yes.
Q. And you also saw a gold tooth, or a gold filling at that time?
A. Yes.[21]

In spite of this, Inspector McIntosh denied that the matter of Ben Ahakuelo's gold tooth ever came up in his presence. It was becoming apparent that the Chief Inspector had no intention of directly supporting anything Thalia Massie said that could not be verified as a fact from other sources. He was, in fact, "backing away" from the prosecution's theory of the case.

Why? The answer seems to lie in the very structure of the prosecution case, which by now depended entirely on Thalia Massie's story. There had been many rumors and suspicions of fabricated evidence circulated through Honolulu; and while John McIntosh, as a police officer, may have tried to "build a case," it was quite evident he did not intend to participate in an effort to sustain the prosecution's theory, while under oath, beyond stating the facts as he knew them.

The Chief Inspector was well respected in Honolulu. He had been literally forced into presenting a case before it was properly prepared; and he had become painfully aware that it was cracking at the seams. His testimony, as to both the time element and Thalia Massie's identification of the suspects, added virtually nothing to an already weakened case. And it was on this note that the prosecution rested.

The Bitter Fruit

On Thursday night, November 26, Judge Heen and Bill Pittman held a conference with the five Ala Moana boys at Heen's office. Ben Ahakuelo's mother was there, a quiet, gray-haired woman; and so was the father of Joseph Kahahawai, an old Hawaiian from the "windward side" of Oahu, with a seamed, leathery face and the stolid expression of an Indian. Heen turned to Horace Ida.

"Shorty, you'll be on the stand tomorrow. The Territory ought to close its case around noon. Now I want one thing understood, and I want it understood damned well. It isn't just you boys that are on trial. It's the Hawaiian people—my people as well as Joe's and Benny's and Mac's and all of you. If there is anything you boys haven't told me, no matter what it is—I want to know it now!"

Horace Ida shook his head.

"There ain't nothing, Judge. These boys were with me all night—except when Ben an' Mac was in the dance hall. I drove all of them home. You remember, Judge, I told you about them two *haole* fellows at the College of Hawaii." (The University had been a college up to a dozen years earlier, and was often referred to as "College of Hawaii.") "Them boys saw us at the park. I picked them up that night, before we left Ben an' Mac. They saw us an' they will tell it in court if you want them to, but they don't want to get mixed up in this, that's all."

Many years later, Judge Heen recalled the grilling he put the five defendants through that night. "Griffith Wight couldn't have been rougher on them than I was," he said, with a chuckle. "I told Ida he had lied once, he'd damned well better not lie again. He admitted it. He said he didn't want to get mixed up with Joe's fight with that *kanaka* woman, and that's why he told Johnny Cluney he wasn't out that night. It was the second time I put them through a cross-examination, and I can tell you I didn't spare the horses. But their story held together and I was more sure than ever that these were not the boys."

There were several minor points on which their story was not clear, however. There was the misunderstanding about the route they took back from Waikiki Park into town. Ida pointed out that he had been on the Coast when the Kalakaua "Extension" was built, and he had been confused when he tried to recall the route they had taken, and thought they must have turned down King Street to Keaumoku.

The matter of Horace Ida's jacket was also confusing. He had first denied he wore the jacket; later he said he had thrown it into the car, and put it on when Detective John Cluney came to his house shortly before two o'clock in the morning. But there was one report that he wore it during the evening.

In the statement Joseph Kahahawai made to Inspector McIntosh at the police station Sunday night, September 13, McIntosh had asked:

Q. How were you dressed?
A. Same pants [indicating his pants], blue denim pants, blue silk shirt, and had short sleeves.
Q. After 12 o'clock when you left the dance hall how was Shorty dressed?
A. He had a leather coat on. He wore a white silk shirt and a kind of white pants, till he dropped off at Correa's.
Q. Correa's?
A. Yes, Sylvester Correa's place at the wedding party.[1]

169

Judge Heen questioned Kahahawai on this point, but he denied he had said anything to McIntosh about Horace Ida's leather jacket. "When I see that statement, I scratch it out," he said. "They put that down and I scratched it out."

This was also Kahahawai's testimony at the trial.

The following day the prosecution closed its case, and Heen summarized the position of the defense. He said witnesses would account for every minute of time the defendants had spent, from early in the evening until after one o'clock the morning of September 13. He said Horace Ida had driven his car to the Correa *luau* early in the evening; he had met Joseph Kahahawai and Henry Chang and another part-Chinese boy, "Buster" Chang, at the *luau*. Later he had agreed to drive "the other Chang" home and had also agreed to drive Ben Ahakuelo and David Takai, who were also at the *luau*, out to Waikiki Park where they wanted to go to the "Eagles' dance."

He had driven them out and then drove over to a place in Waikiki to pick up "two *haole* fellows" from the University of Hawaii; he had returned to the Park with them and then had driven back to the *luau* with Kahahawai and Chang. About 11:30 P.M. he had returned to Waikiki Park to pick up Ben Ahakuelo and David Takai. Both Kahahawai and Chang were with him.

Heen recited the events of the last few minutes before midnight. He said he would produce witnesses who saw Ben Ahakuelo and David Takai in the dance hall about the time of the last dance. He would also produce witnesses who saw Horace Ida, Joseph Kahahawai and Henry Chang outside the dance hall, standing near Ida's car, about midnight. He said certain of these witnesses drove back to town over the route covered by Horace Ida's car, between approximately 12:10 A.M. and 12:25 A.M. on Sunday morning— the time the Territory had sought to establish as the time the assault on Mrs. Massie occurred, and they saw the accused boys en route to town.

"We are not trying Thalia Massie in this case," Judge Heen said, his voice ringing sharply as he paced back and forth in front of the jury box. "We are not trying the Navy. We are not trying the *haoles*. We are trying five boys—five local boys—who have been accused of a foul and vicious crime, and we will prove they were not the ones who committed that crime."

The defense testimony was brief. It consisted mainly of the stories of the "alibi witnesses"—Tuts Matsumoto and Bob Vierra, together with the other youth, George Silva, and two girls, Sybil Davis and Margaret Kanae, who rode in the car with them. In addition, the defense called William V. Asing, a clerk at the Territorial Board of Health, who had been at Waikiki Park Saturday night. Judge Heen questioned him.

> Q. While you were out there at Waikiki Park I will ask you whether you saw Benny Ahakuelo or not?
> A. I saw Benny out there.
> Q. About how long after you got there was it when you saw him?
> A. About 15 minutes after I got there, I saw Benny. [Asing had testified that he had arrived at the park at 11:30 P.M.]
> Q. . . . Did you see him later than that?
> A. I saw him later than that.
> Q. When?
> A. After the dance.
> Q. After the dance was *pau?* [*Pau* is the Hawaiian word for ended, or finished.]
> A. Yes.
> Q. . . . Where?
> A. . . . Outside of the dance hall.[2]

Wight, on cross-examination, asked Asing how well he knew Ben Ahakuelo. The witness replied that he knew him only slightly, but two girls who were with him at the dance- Alice Kam and Agnes Kam—had known Ahakuelo well and also recognized him. "I will have them come into court if you wish," Asing said.

Wight shook his head. "It won't be necessary."

Two other witnesses—Tomomi Murada and Charles Kalami—both testified they knew Ahakuelo and saw him at the park "about the time of the last dance." Murada said he spoke with Ahakuelo "just before the dance was over." George Lum, who knew David Takai, said he first saw the Japanese-Hawaiian boy about 10:30 P.M. at the dance and later talked with him "near the last dance."

The one witness who might have established definitely the time Ahakuelo and the other four boys drove out of the Park was the

Hawaiian girl, Margaret Kanae, who was in Tuts Matsumoto's car. Her testimony developed into a bitter exchange between Heen and Wight, each of whom accused the other of "coaching" and "misleading" the witness. Margaret Kanae first recalled seeing the Ford car, with Ahakuelo riding in it, as it was driven out of the park entrance. Under cross-examination by Wight, however, she became utterly confused and changed her story several times.

Heen had asked her, on direct examination:

Q. When you went to the car where Sybil Davis was [Tuts Matsumoto's car] did you notice anybody there?
A. Yes.
Q. Who?
A. Ben.
Q. Benny Ahakuelo?
A. Uh huh.

Earlier, in his direct examination of Tuts Matsumoto, Heen had asked:

Q. Now after you came out of the dance, did you see Ben Ahakuelo?
A. No. I was sitting in the car talking to the girl there, one of these girls sitting on the side of me [evidently Sybil Davis] but when this other girl came in the car, I heard her mention Benny's name—she looked, and said, "Benny I think is over there."
Q. You didn't look?
A. No, I did not look.[3]

Matsumoto had testified that it was "about ten minutes after the dance ended" that he drove out of the gate into John Ena Road and headed toward Kalakaua Avenue. He said, "We were about the last. There was very few cars left there." Thus, as previously noted, the only witness who said she actually saw Ben Ahakuelo, riding in Horace Ida's car as they left the park, was Margaret Kanae.

She testified that she saw Ben Ahakuelo again on Beretania Street, as they were driving toward town, and it was then that she called out to Tuts Matsumoto: "Benny and them is following us!" She also described the incident in which Bob Vierra had jumped over to the other car to talk with Ahakuelo; but when Wight began his cross-examination her replies became vague and indefinite.

"Did you see Benny inside the dance hall?" he asked.

"Yes . . . he was drunk."

"Now, didn't I ask you, down at the office, when you next saw Benny, and you said it was down on Beretania Street?"

"Yes."

When Heen got her back on redirect examination, he asked:

"This morning, when you told us you got on Tatsumi's [Matsumoto's] car, you turned around and saw Benny nearby, standing near his car?"

"Yes."

Wight jumped up and accused Judge Heen of trying to impeach his own witness.

"It's not impeaching at all," Judge Steadman said. "She answered 'Yes.'"

Heen went on:

"Now, if you told Mr. Wight that the only time you saw Benny was out on Beretania Street, is that a mistake—if you saw Benny standing near his car outside the pavilion after the dance?"

Wight jumped up again, as if he had been stung.

"This is outrageous," he said. "I shall object to anything further along this line of questioning."

"It was a mistake?" Heen asked the girl, calmly.

"Yes."

Heen turned to the Deputy County Attorney:

"Mr. Wight, may I have a copy of that statement—the one this witness made in your office?"

"No!" Wight snapped.

The Mystery White Man

After this potpourri of frustration and obfuscation, everyone including the jury seemed glad to drop the matter. Margaret Kanae, a dark-haired girl in her teens, with an open, friendly face, appeared to be the only person in the courtroom unperturbed by the ramifications of her testimony. She smiled and nodded at every question, no matter how contradictory. Had her story been clear and unconfused, it might have settled beyond question the issue of the Ala Moana case; because Harold Godfrey, the manager of Waikiki Park, whose testimony could not have been challenged, had stated unequivocally that when he left the park shortly after closing, at midnight, he saw Tuts Matsumoto's car and two others just leaving the park.

There was one point in the story of the "alibi witnesses" that might have been enlightening to any member of the prosecution staff gifted with psychological insight, had there been any such capability in the prosecution staff. That was the critical testimony of Tuts Matsumoto and Robert Vierra on the car-jumping incident. If any single event of the night would have impinged itself on the recollections of witnesses, it would be this.

On direct examination by Judge Heen, Tuts Matsumoto testified as follows:

Q. Now do you remember at any time, as you were going along Beretania, Robert Vierra leaving your car?

A. Yes. I was not really sure, I could not look back . . . He was sitting in the back, but when this car came alongside of our car Bobby jumped over to this car . . . You see when he left my car I don't know how he left it. He was sitting in back. Whether he got on the other car from my fender, I do not know. We were going slow and . . . I remember hearing the girls say that [this car was following us] . . . But when Bobby jumped back on my car I was driving and there is that windshield, and well, he got on my car, on the running board, holding the windshield.[4]

Later in the examination, after a wrangle between Wight and Heen as to what the witness could and could not testify that he heard, Heen asked:

Q. At about what point was it when you noticed Robert Vierra getting back to your car from the other car? On Beretania Street?

A. I am pretty sure it was around, well, on Thomas Square, around there some place, say about Thomas Square . . .

Q. At the time you talked to Robert Vierra, who talked to you when he got back on your car, did you happen to look around to see who was on the other car?

A. No, you see I tried to, but I am going this way, and Bobby standing on the running board here, when this car came right alongside of my car he jumped on my car. There wasn't much traffic at the time. We could have gone this way for quite a ways when Bobby jumped on my car and we kept on going. Once—I am not sure whether it was this car or not, he passed us, and

then we passed this car again; I am not sure whether it was
their car or not. I was not—I didn't think anything like this would
happen. I was not paying attention to every car that we passed
or that passed us.[5]

The significance of Matsumoto's testimony could not have been
overlooked by the prosecution. Its value to the defense lay not so
much in exactly what was said, but *how* it was said. If Matsumoto's
testimony had been rehearsed, it is doubtful if he could have delivered it with such an obviously sincere effort to describe exactly
what happened. Breaking down his testimony was absolutely essential to the prosecution, yet no effort whatever was made to impeach his story. It was simply disregarded.

The only other testimony of importance offered by the defense was
the report of the "woman in a green dress" who was observed walking down John Ena Road at about 12.15 A.M. Sunday.
George Goeas, obviously ill-at-ease and not anxious to be involved
in the case one way or another, nevertheless gave a straightforward
report.

Under direct examination by Heen, he said:

I noticed the way she [the woman in the green dress] was walking
at the time. It seemed kind of funny to see a white woman in that
kind of condition and I thought she might be under the influence of
liquor and noticed the way she held her head down, and it made me
think they had a quarrel or something.[6]

The word "they" referred to the white man seen by Mr. and Mrs.
Goeas and Alice Aramaki, and also by James Low, the Supervisor
from Hawaii. He had been walking a few feet behind her. In his
final summation to the jury, Bill Pittman called attention to the
"mystery white man" in what seemed to be the only significant
reference to this important item of testimony:

There can be no question but what the white man who was following
the white woman that night on John Ena Road knows what happened. He is the man that can explain the crime. Why wasn't he
found?[7]

This question—Why wasn't he found?—illustrates the underlying
question, and perhaps explains the tragic blunder, of the entire
Ala Moana case. Why did the Honolulu Police, as represented by

John McIntosh; the County Attorney, as represented by Griffith Wight and Eddie Sylva; the legal power of the Territory, as represented by Attorney General Harry Hewitt; the "public," as represented by the *Advertiser* and the *Star-Bulletin;* the "business community," as represented by Walter Dillingham; the United States Navy, as represented by Admiral Yates Stirling, Jr.—why did they all close their eyes to every possibility except the theory that the five boys hastily arrested that Sunday in September must be the "guilty parties"? Why didn't they investigate a half dozen clues that pointed in other directions?

There may be no real answer to a question such as this—at least no single answer. There were many factors: the prejudice and obduracy of the "dominant minority" of *haole* elite in Hawaii, to borrow a phrase from Arnold Toynbee; the stupidity not only of the Honolulu police, but of those who controlled the policies of the police; the "superiority complex" of a small group of white people who, in effect, ruled this island community; the ignorance and arrogance—a combination that seems to go hand in hand—of the *malihini haoles*, the "new whites." Or it may have been a combination of all these things. Bill Pittman, in his final words to the jury, described the *haoles* of Hawaii as "servile sycophants, the servants of an outmoded caste of people who rule Hawaii, even though they are unfit to rule."

Whatever the answer to Bill Pittman's question may have been, it was evident as the trial wound toward its conclusion, that the investigation and prosecution of the Ala Moana case was, as Pittman described it, "the most damnable piece of bungling in the history of the Territory."

There was one final spasm on the part of the prosecution. Just before the attorneys were about to present their summation to the jury, Griffith Wight received a note as he sat at the lawyer's table. He read it and jumped up, motioning to Judge Heen, Bill Pittman and Robert Murakami, to follow him to the bench.

"May we approach the bench?" he asked Judge Steadman. The judge nodded.

After a whispered consultation, Judge Heen shrugged and said, "Why not?"

Judge Steadman then announced that trial would be adjourned until Saturday morning in view of certain "new evidence" that had just come to light and which the County Attorney's office wished to present.

The *Advertiser* announced in screaming headlines on Saturday morning that "new evidence" had been found. Two "mystery witnesses" would present it at the unusual Saturday morning session of the court. The story hinted broadly that the new testimony was likely to strike at the very foundations of the defense.

Judge Heen's remark, "Why not?" might have been "So what?" The "mystery witnesses" were a Mr. and Mrs. George M. McClelland. George McClelland was manager of Honolulu Stadium. Mrs. Mc-Clelland had to be brought into court in a wheel chair; she had suffered an accident and was unable to walk. She testified, however, that she had walked down John Ena Road on the night of September 12, shortly after the dance ended at Waikiki Park; and she "remembered she was wearing a green dress."

The new evidence which was supposed to have rocked the defense was refuted in almost a single sentence. George Goeas was recalled to the stand by Heen and asked whether the "woman in the green dress" might have been Mrs. McClelland.

"I know Mrs. McClelland," he said. "She was not the woman I saw."

Harold Godfrey, the manager of the park, was also recalled as a witness. He said he knew Mrs. McClelland, too, and he saw her at the park that night. She was wearing a white silk dress, not a green dress.

This revelation furnished the basis for one of the most remarkable suggestions in the entire case, offered by Griffith Wight in his closing address. The Prosecutor observed, in connection with the Mc-Clelland testimony: "Why shouldn't there be a number of women with green dresses? There may have been scores of them on John Ena Road that night." In his effort to minimize the importance of the testimony of the Goeases, Alice Aramaki, James Low—and even his own witnesses, Eugenio Batungbacal and his two Chinese friends—Wight painted a picture of a veritable St. Patrick's Day Parade of ladies in green dresses, all wandering down John Ena

Road that Saturday night in September, shortly after midnight.

The *Advertiser* referred to the Deputy County Attorney's summation to the jury as a "strikingly effective closing argument." In many ways, it was. If there had been any doubt in the mind of an objective juror as to the fumbling ineptitude of the Territory's presentation, Griffith Wight's final address would have erased it. With reference to the time element, for example, he suggested that the time the five defendants left Waikiki Park was "not actually relevant."

"Perhaps they left earlier," he suggested. "The attack may very well have occurred long before midnight, and these five boys could have completed their dastardly work, left this poor woman beaten and helpless on the road, and returned to the park *before* the last dance!" Since Thalia Massie was definitely known to have been at the Ala Wai Inn until about 11:35 P.M., this would have required that she be kidnaped, rushed down to the old quarantine station site, raped six or seven times, and the attackers would then have driven back to the park—all within a space of twenty minutes!

For the most part, Wight's summary was a labored defense of the prosecution's case. He spoke of the "horror" of rape, and referred to those who committed it as "beyond the pale of human pity." This was not disputed by anyone. Pittman, in his closing remarks, called is "the lowest and vilest in the category of crime—a work fit only for human reptiles." But he said the contention of the defense was that "nothing in the case presented by the Territory can possibly connect these boys with this vicious attack."

Pittman bitterly upbraided Claude Benton for what he said was "deliberately and maliciously manufactured testimony." Wight had previously referred to several of the members of the Detective Bureau—Lucian Machado and George Nakea—who testified for the defense; and Sammy Lau, the identification officer, as having "betrayed their oath of office."

"What is this oath?" Pittman roared. "To send men to prison— whether or not they are guilty? Is that the code of the Honolulu Police?" He turned and pointed at Benton, who sat at the table beside Wight. "That man sought deliberately to frame these defendants, to create evidence that did not exist! If honest officers had not come forward, that testimony—if it had not been contradicted—would have sent these boys to the penitentiary."

Pittman spoke of "the conspiracy of the white people—the small group of hypocritical *haoles*, more anxious to satisfy the Navy than to seek justice." The *Advertiser* referred editorially to this, with a queer sense of virtue, as being "the first note of racial prejudice introduced into this trial."

Judge Heen, in the final summation to the jury, threw down the racial gauntlet, which the *Advertiser* had chosen to believe did not exist, even more heavily. He stood before the jury, his feet apart and his voice again ringing out in the courtroom. "If we are to accept the theory of the prosecution," he said, "we must believe that every witness in this case, except the complaining witness, must have been lying! Are we to accept only the testimony of *haoles* in this court? Are we to disregard witnesses for the defense simply because they are Hawaiian, Chinese, Japanese or Portuguese?"

Judge Steadman gave the case to the jury at 3:40 P.M. on Wednesday, December 2; and it was not until the following Saturday afternoon that the jury, through its foreman, William Bede, indicated that it was at an impasse. There had been sounds of loud voices raised in argument in the jury room, and indications of scuffling were reported by the bailiff. Foreman Bede asked if Judge Steadman would come into the jury room.

The judge, a tall, mild-mannered man, spoke to the jurors for some time. Later, when he emerged, Judge Heen immediately entered a motion to declare a mistrial on the grounds that if there had been physical fighting in the jury room, regardless of the verdict, this was *prima facie* evidence of "coercion and intimidation." Judge Steadman ruled against the motion. He explained that he had told the jurors that "the strongest indication that you are seeking sincerely and honestly to reach a verdict lies in the fact that for seventy-two hours you have not appealed to me for dismissal of the jury."

Meanwhile, the eruption of violent reactions in the streets of Honolulu was already in evidence. Police dispersed crowds of sailors and soldiers who had gathered in Aala Park; and the area around the Territorial courthouse was patrolled day and night.

In Walter Dillingham's famous "memorandum" he made this rather weird comment:

In the minds of many people there was considerable doubt as to whether those charged with the crime were guilty. The law of probability would convict, but the weak and unconvincing character of much of the testimony gave opportunity for reasonable doubt, in spite of the fact that Mrs. Massie's testimony was of the most definite character.[8]

This critique on judicial procedures did not explain exactly how the "law of probability" would be invoked in a criminal trial; but the comment is remarkable for the curious bit of logic that admits there was a reasonable doubt but assumes that since Mrs. Massie's story was "of the most definite character," the defendants were "probably" guilty and therefore were not entitled to the "reasonable doubt."

On Sunday night at ten o'clock, more than four days after the jury had been given the case, Foreman Bede sent a note to Judge Steadman:

"It is impossible for this jury to reach a verdict."

The judge declared a mistrial. This was on December 6. In less than a week after that, the Ala Moana case began to bear its first bitter fruit.

The Kidnaping of Horace Ida

On the evening of Saturday, December 12, Horace Ida was standing in front of a small "beer place" on Kukui Street, near his home on Cunha Lane. He was talking with a friend, Bobby Wong, when several cars drove by, slowing up as they passed the place where Ida was standing.

A man leaned out of one of the cars, pointed at Ida, and said: "That's the guy!"

The cars turned at the end of the block and came back. Several men jumped out of the cars and gathered around Ida. He tried to break away, but they held his arms and shoved him toward one of the cars. Bobby Wong looked around for help, and then ran into the "beer shop." By the time he came out with a couple of men from the beer place, the cars had driven off.

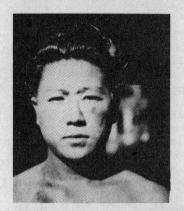

Horace Ida after his beating.

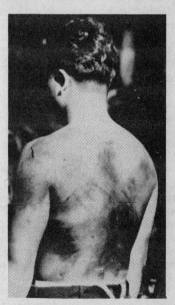

This was about eight o'clock. Less than two hours later, Horace Ida dragged himself into the small police substation at Kaneohe, on the windward side of the island, looking more dead than alive. His face was a mass of cuts and bruises, his shirt torn to ribbons and his back covered with bruises and raw welts, apparently from whips or belts.

Ida told the police he had been forced into one of the cars with a pistol jabbed in his side, and had been driven up the Nuuanu Pali Road and across the Pali—the famous cliff that divides the eastern and western sides of the Island of Oahu, with a sheer drop of nearly twelve hundred feet on the windward slope. Ida said he had been driven down to the base of this cliff, along a small side road, and ordered to get out of the car.

The men pulled off their belts and began to lash the Japanese boy across his face and shoulders and on his back. Bloody welts on his body testified to the severity of the beating. He finally fell down and pretended to be unconscious.

"They think I pass out," he told the police. "Finally when they ask a lot of questions, like 'Who am I to attack the white woman?' and 'Why did I do it?' but I don't say nothing, and they go away. I think they think I am dead."

Ida said he remained still for some time, fearful that some of them might come back; then he made his way down the slope of the mountain toward the village of Kaneohe, several miles beyond the place where he was beaten. When he reached the Pali Road, the main highway across the island, a passing car stopped and the driver took him into the village.

The Kaneohe police drove Ida back to Honolulu, arriving at about 10:15 P.M. Meanwhile reports of the kidnaping spread through the city, and riot calls began to pour into the police station. Two of the other Ala Moana defendants—all of whom were out on bail pending retrial of the case—were at Waikiki Park, and police were sent there to guard them. Both boys, Ben Ahakuelo and David Takai, were taken home under police guard. Henry Chang was found at his home, and a police guard was stationed there. Joseph Kahahawai was picked up by a patrol car and taken to his home in Palama.

The Honolulu *Advertiser* noted piously the following morning, along with large headlines describing the kidnaping and beating of Horace Ida, that "unofficial vengeance, no matter what the provocation, is a grave offense."

Walter Dillingham, in his "private memorandum," went a little beyond this admonition. He said the Governor had been "strenuously urged" by Rear Admiral Yates Stirling, Jr., the Navy commandant, to have the five defendants "locked up and not permitted the freedom of the city." The memorandum, which was probably the best evidence of the attitude of the *haole* elite in this crisis, went on:

> The Admiral felt it was extremely hazardous, considering the temper of the rank and file of the Navy, for these men to be where they might be molested. The Admiral told me that the Governor said it was impossible for him to take any action as the Attorney General had advised him that it was wholly within the jurisdiction of the court. . . .
>
> Not long after this Ida, one of the five indicted, was kidnapped and it was reported that a confession had been secured. This, however, was never corroborated. Ida was never able to identify any of the personnel of the Navy who were lined up for his inspection as being guilty of his kidnapping, nor was he able to identify the automobile used by the kidnappers.
>
> Again it was urged that these boys be locked up for their safety and for the welfare of the community. No action was taken.[9]

It was evident to Walter Dillingham, at least, that the solution of the entire matter was to lock up the boys. It seems to have escaped Dillingham's notice that the United States Navy presumably is a well-disciplined organization and its personnel are not usually permitted to roam the streets, kidnaping suspected people and beating them with belts to extract a "confession." The implied suggestion that Admiral Stirling was incapable of running his organization with the controls usually regarded as necessary for military discipline also appears to have passed unnoticed by the Admiral.

In any event, on the following Monday—December 14—Admiral Stirling cabled Admiral William V. Pratt, Chief of Naval Operations in Washington, that it would be "inadvisable" to send the Pacific Fleet into Hawaiian waters for its winter maneuvers due to the outbreak of violence in Honolulu.

The visit of the Fleet was not merely a gala occasion for Honoluluans. It was a source of considerable revenue for Hawaii's business establishments. The "bitter fruit" of the Ala Moana case thus was not merely having a poisonous effect upon the morale of the people and the honor of Hawaii; it was likely to create serious indigestion in an area where the *haole* elite and the business community were most sensitive; that is to say, in the pocketbook.

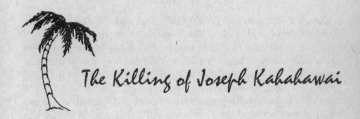

The Killing of Joseph Kahahawai

The good people of Honolulu may have comforted themselves, following the kidnaping and beating of Horace Ida, with the notion that this was merely a flare-up, a release of tension. A convicted murderer, Daniel Lyman, had escaped from Oahu Prison around Christmas Day of 1931, and the National Guard was called out, thus diverting everyone's attention from the Ala Moana affair. However, the "bitter fruit" was still ripening.

On Thursday morning, January 8, 1932, Joseph Kahahawai left his home, a small frame house on Queen Street in lower Palama, at about 7:30, to go downtown to the Territorial courthouse where he had to report twice a week to William A. Dixon, the Probation Officer. This was required of all five defendants in the Ala Moana Case, who were out on bail.

A cousin of Kahahawai, Eddie Ulii, had come over to his house, where he lived with his mother, Mrs. Esther Anito, to meet him and walk down to the Territorial courthouse, a distance of perhaps three miles. It was about 8:30 when they reached the courthouse, across King Street from Iolani Palace, the former home of Hawaii's kings and now the Territorial capitol. Eddie Ulii later said: "We saw a woman standing on the sidewalk, looking at Joe and me, but I didn't think anything about it at the time."

Kahahawai went into the courthouse and into Dixon's office, while Eddie Ulii sat on a bench outside. A man stepped out of a black Buick sedan across the circular paving in front of the building, and walked over and stood beside the woman. She was wearing a trim, blue serge dress and had gray hair.

"After Joe came out, as we walked out of the courthouse, the woman was still standing there," Eddie Ulii said. "We walked about fifty feet, and I looked back. The woman was pointing at us."

It was about this time that he first called his cousin's attention to the pair watching them, but Kahahawai did not seem particularly concerned. They crossed the sidewalk, and started toward King Street, intending to walk back to Palama.

As they started walking along King Street, the main thoroughfare which passes between the courthouse and Iolani Palace, Eddie Ulii noticed the Buick car following them.

"It turned into King Street without even making a boulevard stop," he said. "The driver of the car was a man wearing goggles. He leaned out and opened the door. The man I first saw with the woman came up behind Joe, and said, 'Get in the car. Major Ross wants to see you!'"

Major Gordon Ross was at that time High Sheriff of Honolulu and commander of the Hawaii National Guard, which had been called into active service after the rioting that occurred when Horace Ida had been kidnaped three weeks before, and was then engaged in the manhunt for the escaped killer, Daniel Lyman.

The man handed Kahahawai a white paper with a gold seal in the lower right-hand corner. He said, "Get in the car—on the left-hand side, back seat."

Eddie Ulii said that Kahahawai called to him, as he was partly shoved into the car: "Eddie, get on the car!" He tried to step on the running board, but the man inside said, "We'll be back soon," and the car drove off, leaving Eddie Ulii standing on the sidewalk. It was the last time any of Joseph Kahahawai's friends saw him alive.

The so-called summons later proved to be a queer document. It was printed in rough, awkward letters, evidently by hand. At the top were the words "Territorial Police"—misspelled; and underneath, the words: "Major Ross—Commanding." Under that was printed, "Kahahawai—Joe."

Beside the semblance of the seal in the corner were pasted these words, evidently clipped from a newspaper or magazine:

Life is a Mysterious and Exciting Affair and Anything Can Be a Thrill if You Know How to Look for It and What to Do With Opportunity When It Comes.

TERITORIAL POLICE

MAJOR ROSS COMMANDING

SUMMONS TO APPEAR

Kahahawai Joe

Life Is a Mysterious and
Exciting Affair, and Any-
thing Can Be a Thrill if
You Know How to
Look for It and
What to Do With
Opportunity
When It Comes

The fake summons that was handed to Joseph Kahahawai.

Eddie Ulii was worried about his cousin's departure, and finally he went back into the courthouse and talked to Frank Bettencourt, the bailiff. He said he thought Kahahawai may have been pushed into the car. Bettencourt apparently thought little of the incident, and did not report it to the police; so Eddie Ulii went back to Dixon's office and told him what had happened. Dixon immediately called the Honolulu Police.

All this required perhaps fifteen or twenty minutes; and it was another twenty minutes before the police got into action. The first alarm was broadcast about 9:30 A.M., asking patrol cars to be on the lookout for a black Buick sedan with Joseph Kahahawai as a captive inside the car. The situation was complicated to some extent by the fact that the police were also looking for another man—the escaped prisoner, Daniel Lyman.

Whether Kahahawai actually read the fake summons or got into the car in the belief that it was authentic could never be determined. The gray-haired woman was Mrs. Grace Fortescue, the mother of Thalia Massie; Tommy Massie was the driver; and in the back seat, with a gun in his hand, was the one who invited or shoved Kahahawai into the car, Albert O. Jones, a Navy enlisted man from the Pearl Harbor Submarine Base.

Whether Jones held the gun at Kahahawai or not was never quite ascertained; but it was hardly likely that the tall, powerful Hawaiian, who had been a football player at St. Louis College and a professional boxer, would have sat quietly at young Massie's bidding. In any event, they arrived at a cottage on Kalawalo Avenue, in Manoa Valley, which Mrs. Fortescue had rented shortly after her arrival in Honolulu the previous October. It was only a few blocks from the Massie home.

The events of the next few minutes will undoubtedly remain officially uncertain forever, since those involved were understandably vague in their story of the affair, told later at the trial. However, it seems evident that Joseph Kahahawai was taken into the house, tied to a wicker chair, and for several minutes questioned by Tommy Massie.

One of the men in the room held a .32-caliber Colt pistol, pointed at Kahahawai.

The identity of the person who held the gun was never clearly determined. Later Tommy Massie, by implication, seemed to have assumed that role for himself, but there were other more or less apocryphal reports that indicated that one of the other two men in the room—Jones and another enlisted man from the Navy, Edmund J. Lord—held the gun.

At one point, according to these unconfirmed stories, Massie called Kahahawai a "black son of bitch"—a name that would anger most Hawaiians; and the muscular Hawaiian lunged toward him, dragging the chair. In the scuffle and confusion, the gun went off and Kahahawai collapsed with a bullet in his chest.

The events of the next few minutes are likewise wrapped in mystery. About 10:15 A.M.—more than an hour after the "kidnaping" of Kahahawai at the courthouse, but only about forty-five minutes after the alarm was spread—Detective George Harbottle was on patrol duty on Waialae Road, the main highway leading out of the city toward the southern end of Oahu. He saw a black Buick sedan heading out toward Koko Head, a volcanic promontory near the southern end of the island. The car was traveling at a fairly high rate of speed.

With Harbottle was Patrolman Thomas Kekua, on a motorcycle. As the two cars raced along Waialae Road, Harbottle flagged another police radio patrol car, coming from the opposite direction; it whirled around and joined the chase. The radio cars finally overtook the Buick going up a long, curving slope over the saddleback of Koko Head. Harbottle pulled out his pistol and fired two shots in the air. The motorcycle passed the Buick going up the slope and blocked it at the top of the hill, overlooking Hanauma Bay—a blue stretch of water about a mile wide between two claws of land jutting into the Pacific. Harbottle pulled up behind; he and Kekua, who had stopped at the top of the hill, waved their guns at the three people in the Buick.

Harbottle opened the rear door of the Buick and saw a white bundle on the floor, a roll of canvas. There were dark splotches on the canvas, and sticking out of one end of the bundle was a human foot.

The woman and two men were ordered to get out of the car. The former—Mrs. Grace Fortescue—walked quickly to the side of the road and stood there rigidly, gazing out at the blue waters of the Pacific Ocean. Harbottle walked over to talk with her, but she smiled frigidly, and went over to a rock alongside the road and sat down. She was wearing the same blue serge suit she had worn in front of the courthouse that morning, and seemed completely calm and un-ruffled by the events which were taking place.

The two men were searched for weapons. Meanwhile the radio car advised Police Headquarters they had found Joseph Kahahawai —dead in a car driven by a woman and two men, who gave their names as Massie and Lord. Mrs. Fortescue had refused to identify herself.

The geographical location of the bluff overlooking Hanauma Bay is about twelve miles south of the Honolulu city line; and about three miles farther south, toward the tip of Oahu, is a well-known tourist attraction known as "the Blow Hole." This is a crevice in the volcanic rock, which extends in a carvernlike ledge over the water. The waves of the Pacific, rolling into the mouth of this cavern, drive the water upward through the Blow Hole with terrific force, spew-ing geysers twenty feet or more into the air. This spectacular act of nature creates a terrific force of water within the cavern that would pulverize any object thrown into it, such as a human body, and destroy all evidence of it in a matter of minutes.

It was apparently also a matter of minutes that prevented Mrs. Fortescue, Tommy Massie and the sailor, Lord, from reaching the place and getting rid of the body of Joseph Kahahawai—an act that might have effectively prevented criminal action against Tommy Massie or Mrs. Fortescue. Since Kahahawai's clothes were also found in the car, tied up in a bloody bundle, it is possible that the essen-tial evidence of guilt in the Massie-Fortescue case would have been disposed of, had the police not intervened.

The behavior of the three people as they stood or sat at the road-side, awaiting the arrival of additional police and the coroner, pre-sented some interesting sidelights. Radio Patrolman Percy Bond, who arrived with a third police car, later reported that when he walked over to Detective Harbottle and said, "Good work, kid!", young Massie, standing nearby, looked up and smiled, and then clasped his hands as if he were shaking hands with himself.

"Weren't you speaking to me?" he asked.

Bond shook his head.

Later, Bond said, Mrs. Fortescue approached him and spoke to him—the first words she had uttered since the police cars stopped them on the highway. "Haven't I met you somewhere?" she asked. He assured her they had not met. She smiled, and said, "I thought you came down from the coast about two months ago—the same time I did."

Perhaps the most bizarre description of the scene on the windswept bluff overlooking the Pacific, as the three people and the gathering forces of the police milled around the car in which the body of Joseph Kahahawai lay, was furnished by a reporter for the *Advertiser*. In describing Mrs. Fortescue's calmness, the reporter wrote:

> While waiting for the patrol car, she might have been waiting for the first race at Pimlico.[1]

Obviously impressed with his own simile, the reporter—Ray Coll, Jr.—went on to note that "the crowd around her might have been groups of strolling dignitaries on their way to see the horses in the paddock." While the ability of Thalia Massie's mother to remain calm under the stress of extremely trying circumstances certainly was not to be criticized, particularly in view of the fact that she undoubtedly believed the slain youth had criminally assaulted her daughter, the reaction of the *Advertiser's* reporter was almost incredible, and it had certain connotations.

This rather lyrical reporting of the event was perhaps the best illustration that can be offered of what was to become a tendency among the *haoles* of Honolulu in the next few weeks—perhaps more pronounced among the second tier of white people in Honolulu, whom Bill Pittman had sarcastically referred to as "servile sycophants . . . servants of an outmoded caste of people who rule Hawaii," than it was among the *haole* elite themselves. Here was a woman, caught red-handed in the act of driving a car in which the body of a man who had just been killed lay in the back, the corpse still warm in a blood-soaked roll of canvas—and she was compared with the patrons of a race track idly watching the horses coming out of the paddock at Pimlico!

The *Advertiser* story even noted that while Mrs. Fortescue, an obvious murder suspect, was walking back and forth along the coral fringe of the road, high over the sunswept beach of Hanauma Bay, "the police, feeling her dignity, addressed her respectfully as she strolled along the dusty road with all the grace of a woman walking across a ballroom at some brilliant social function."[2]

Mrs. Fortescue, a slender, handsome woman in her mid-fifties with graying hair, possessed an air of hauteur that may have been due partly to her family origin, and partly the result of suppressed emotional reactions. This contributed to the impression of superiority over the common run of criminals when she was later provided with the opportunity of a "news conference" at the Police Station. "I cannot see why we were not placed in the custody of the Navy," she said, "instead of being sent to a common jail where the scum of the town is brought."

For perhaps three quarters of an hour the three people who had been arrested in the car—Mrs. Fortescue, Massie and the sailor, Lord —remained at the scene of the arrest, waiting for enough police and other dignitaries to arrive to take soundings on the situation. Then they were bundled into a patrol car and driven into Honolulu.

Meanwhile the fourth member of the group that had participated in the kidnaping and killing of Joseph Kahahawai, Machinist's Mate Albert O. Jones, was picked up by police at the Massie house, where he said he was "standing guard." He was taken to the police station and searched, and a .32-caliber cartridge clip was found, wrapped in the fake summons which had been used to get Kahahawai into the car. An empty shell also was found in his pocket.

Jones was turned over to the Navy, in custody of Captain Ward K. Wortman, for "his own safety"; and subsequently the other three were also turned over to Navy custody. This aroused a storm of protest from the Honolulu authorities as well as from some local citizens; but on this matter the Navy Department in Washington took a firm stand. Secretary of the Navy Charles F. Adams wired Admiral Stirling ordering him to *refuse to deliver the four accused to Terri-*

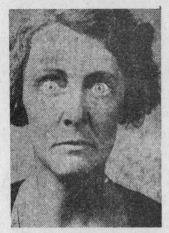

Left, a photograph of Mrs. Fortescue taken immediately after her arrest for murder. Right, Detective George Harbottle.

Police removing the body of Joseph Kahahawai from the murder car.

torial authorities, a step that would hardly have been taken in the case of a foreign government, let alone a Territory of the United States.

The general assumption by the *haoles* of Honolulu, as well as the Navy, that this was a special situation, requiring the most delicate handling by the police and all concerned, may have been justified in the minds of Mrs. Fortescue and Massie; and perhaps even in the thinking of the two sailors, Lord and Jones, who found themselves suddenly thrust into a mess that was not of their making.

However, it could hardly be justified in the public pronouncements of such men as Admiral Yates Stirling and the Chief of Naval Operations in Washington, Admiral William V. Pratt. What had happened was a clear-cut case of "lynch law," and would have been recognized as such west of the Pecos or south of the Mason-Dixon line. Yet Admiral Pratt came forth with this illuminating comment, in a message to Stirling at Pearl Harbor:

> Under such circumstances, and for this crime, they [American men] have taken the law into their own hands repeatedly when they felt the law had failed to do justice.[3]

The Admiral did not specify what kind of "American men" he was referring to; but his statement amounted to an outright acceptance, and by inference, approval of the practice of lynching whenever American men "felt the law had failed to do justice."

The *Advertiser* and the *Star-Bulletin*, sensing that things might be getting out of hand, came forth with words of caution, which by this time were a bit late. Under the heading, "We Must Keep Our Heads," the morning paper said editorially: "Vengeance which takes the form of execution cannot be condoned. No man or woman is justified in taking the law into his own hands and killing another."

The *Star-Bulletin* was slightly more forceful:

> People who take the law into their own hands usually make a mess of it.
>
> Especially is this true when the misguided ones are from the ranks of those sworn to uphold and protect the Constitution and the laws of our country . . .
>
> We have before us a horrible example of what hysteria and lack of balance will do.[4]

The newspapers on the Mainland, however, were not worried about "lack of balance." The New York *News,* in a headline on January 11, warned of a "Melting Pot Peril!" The New York *Times,* under a three-column headline on page one, referred to the "mongrel mixture of races in Hawaii" and decided this was the cause of the shooting of Joseph Kahahawai, an Hawaiian.

The Hearst newspapers, with characteristic restraint, unloosed a barrage all the way from New York. In a two-column editorial on the front page of the New York *American,* headed "Martial Law Needed to Make Hawaii Safe Place for Decent Women," this leading exponent of journalistic veracity said:

> The situation in Hawaii is deplorable. It is an unsafe place for white women outside the small cities and towns. The roads go through jungles and in these remote places bands of degenerate natives lie in wait for white women driving by.
>
> At least 40 cases of these outrages have occurred, and nobody has been punished.[5]

Whether Admiral Yates Stirling got his information from the New York *American,* or vice versa, was never made clear; but at almost the same time that this statistic was announced by the *American,* the Commandant at Pearl Harbor was authority for a statement, in a report to the Navy Department at Washington, that "40 cases of rape have occurred in Honolulu in the past year." When he was questioned as to the accuracy of this, the Admiral said: "I have not made a single statement that I cannot prove by documentary evidence."

The best documentary evidence that comes readily to hand is a Report to the Senate Committee on Insular Affairs, made by the Department of the Interior on January 16, 1932, in which the following statistics are listed as sex offenses in Hawaii for 1931: [6]

Rape	1
Assault with intent to rape	11
Total	12

In the City and County of Honolulu for the same period, there were listed:

Rape	1
Assault with intent to rape	4
Carnal abuse of a female under 12	2
Total	7

The New York *American*, in a further comment on the killing in
Hawaii, referred to the outcome of the Ala Moana assault case a
month earlier, noting: "The perpetrators of this crime against pure
womanhood, against society and against civilization, were freed on
bail after a disagreement of a jury of their kind."

The jurors of "their kind," as previously listed, included seven
white people, two Japanese, two Chinese and one Hawaiian. It
might be noted also that geographically, the "jungle" nearest Honolulu is the Puna Jungle, on the Island of Hawaii, some 250 miles
southeast of Oahu, in which there are practically no roads and very
few people.

The source of the general misinformation and hysteria, both in
Honolulu and on the Mainland, was varied and not easily identified;
but it is worth noting that some of those who previously had been
willing to accept the guilt of the five Ala Moana boys as proved
prima facie, without a trial, evinced a sudden disposition to proceed with caution. This may again be illustrated by an excerpt from
Walter Dillingham's "private memorandum":

> When the news swept through the town that Kahahawai had been
> kidnapped from the door of the courthouse there was the most
> intense excitement, and when this was followed within an hour
> or two by the word that his body had been found in the tonneau
> of a car out near a cliff by the ocean, and that in the car were
> Mrs. Fortescue, Lieutenant Massie and one enlisted man in the
> Navy, Honolulu was brought up standing, facing for the first time
> a lynching.
>
> Grave as had been considered the situation by many of our
> leading citizens, the full purport of the chain of events was only
> brought home when cables carried the stories and editorial com-
> ments on the tragedy as viewed by people on the mainland. The day
> after the news was flashed to the mainland of the killing of
> Kahahawai, newspapers here began to receive samples of what was
> being said of conditions in the islands, including comments on
> the attitude of the people of Hawaii, and threats of congressional
> action to take over the control of our affairs.[7]

It was the last possibility—"Congressional action to take over the control of our affairs"—that bit most deeply into the minds of the *haole* elite. It was one thing to knock the Hawaiian-Democrat voters sprawling with charges of "bungling" and maladministration of justice; it was quite another thing to expose Hawaii, which had been safely in the control of the Big Five and their fellow travelers for a half-century, to alien "control" from Washington.

The Chamber of Commerce promptly called a meeting of "leading citizens" and decided that a special session of the Territorial Legislature should be called. It was called, and a bill was passed creating a Police Commission in Honolulu with the power of appointing a Chief of Police. In Dillingham's "memorandum" he naïvely notes that "an excellent Police Commission was appointed. This Commission named Mr. Charles F. Weeber, who for ten years had been my confidential man and Secretary, as Chief of Police."

Walter Dillingham may have spoken for the *haole* elite, but he did not speak for the Hawaiians and Portuguese, or even for the Japanese and Chinese, who were not directly involved in these harsh happenings but were aligned in general with the sentiments of the Hawaiians. The feelings of the "man in the street" were expressed in gathering places along River Street, which ran through the slum areas of downtown Honolulu, and in beer shops on Kukui Street and in Kakaako. Hawaiians are not belligerent by nature; they are easygoing and friendly. But their anger was slowly rising. When white sailors and soldiers from Pearl Harbor and Schofield Barracks came into town, they usually gathered in the beer shops and similar places around the Aala Park area; and when one of them would remark, "Damned good for the black bastard! He got what was coming to him!" a burly Hawaiian would often move alongside him and mutter in guttural pidgin English: "You like to try it yourself, white meat? You like to get what's comin' to you?"

Usually the sailors, who traveled in groups, would close ranks, and there were few outright battles, in spite of lurid reports of race rioting that gained currency on the Mainland. But the bitterness was not on the surface; it was deep down in the racial consciousness of the Hawaiians, who seemed to be watching and waiting. Most young men of Hawaiian blood were proud of their physical abilities, but they seldom forced an issue. The result was a stalemate of mutterings, veiled threats of reprisal, but few confrontations.

Even the "beach boys," who had held a mass meeting shortly after the attack on Thalia Massie was first reported to disavow involvement in the affair, began to recognize the signs of the deepening chasm between them and their white-skinned brethren, with whom they used to mingle freely and with ostensible equality. Along Waikiki Beach the tourists found less amiable chit-chat and more stolid reserve on the part of the dark-skinned Hawaiians who taught them to swim and ride surfboards.

The deepening chasm was expressed at the funeral of Joseph Kahahawai. An old Hawaiian, David Kama, delivered the eulogy. David Kama's brother had been shot by a soldier several years earlier, and standing above Kahahawai's grave, he said:

"Poor Kahahawai! These *haoles* murdered you in cold blood. They did the same thing to my brother. They shoot and kill us Hawaiians. We do not shoot *haoles*, but they shoot us! Never mind—the truth will come out! Poor boy, God will keep you. We will do the rest . . ."

The seething temper of the populace—on both sides of the fence—was rising rapidly. The question whether the Navy or the Territorial courts should try Massie, his mother-in-law and the two sailors, was debated with complete disregard for the law itself, which required that the Territory assume jurisdiction in criminal cases. The New York *American,* again broadcasting from five thousand miles away, insisted editorially that the Navy should assume jurisdiction:

> Lieutenant Massie is wrong in not insisting that his case be submitted to a naval court. The whole Island should promptly be put under martial law and the perpetrators of such outrages upon white women should be promptly tried by a military court and executed. Until such action is taken, Hawaii will remain unsafe for decent white women.[8]

These events are cited not for their historical value, but because they provide an almost unbelievable illustration of the mass hysteria that followed these events of violence. Again, it may be worth while to ask at this point: What was the origin of this hysteria?

A Hawaiian boy had just been killed by four white people, who obviously had taken the law into their own hands in disregard of the basic concepts of civilized law and order. They may have felt they had provocation; and without doubt, the gray-haired lady from Kentucky, who had come late on the scene, did feel they had provocation. Whether Massie, who had been an eyewitness to the fiasco in Judge Steadman's court, still held to the conviction that Joseph Kahahawai was one of the boys who raped his wife, may have been problematical.

Yet in all the outpouring of hysterical anger from Mainland newspapers, and from high representatives of the Navy Department —and even from the "leading citizens" of Honolulu—hardly a word was expressed on the matter of the lynching. The full force of the attack was directed at the Ala Moana case! Neither Admiral Stirling, the Commandant at Pearl Harbor, nor Admiral Pratt, the Chief of Naval Operations, seemed to have a critical comment on the four white people—three of them Navy personnel—who had killed a Hawaiian boy!

Admiral Pratt actually announced at the Navy Department that this distinguished branch of the Government would "back up" Lieutenant Massie, and sent a cable to Admiral Stirling giving "full approval" for whatever actions he might take or statements he might make on behalf of the accused killers.

Even the representatives of civil government in Hawaii were stampeded by the hysteria.

Delegate-to-Congress Victor S. K. Houston, a former Navy officer, appeared before a hastily called meeting of the Naval Affairs Committee of the House of Representatives in Washington to "explain the Hawaiian situation." Shortly afterward he cabled Governor Lawrence Judd of Hawaii that the Committee was concerned because "in the past there have been frequent occurrences of the crime of rape resulting in the majority of cases in light sentences or acquittal."

Delegate Houston, whose job was to represent Hawaii—including the Hawaiians—told the Governor that "the general attitude of police officials in Honolulu toward the crime of rape has, in my opinion, been such as to lend encouragement to the perpetration of this offense."

What was the reason for all this criticism leveled at Hawaii and the Ala Moana rape case—and none of it directed at those who had invoked "lynch law"?

In all this welter of calumny and abuse heaped on Hawaii over the Ala Moana case and in the frantic efforts of the "leading citizens" of Honolulu to disengage themselves from responsibility for the whole mess, there was one sane voice raised publicly; and that, oddly enough, was in the Japanese-English newspaper, the *Hawaii Hochi*. In an editorial on January 12, it said:

> Kahahawai is dead, shot through the heart according to police theory, at the home of a woman of culture and social position. This woman, together with her son-in-law, a naval lieutenant, and two enlisted men, have been charged with murder in the first degree, the punishment for which, in Hawaii, is death on the gallows.
>
> The crime is the logical consequence of events that have gone before. With a certain type of character the influence of circumstances tends toward the wreaking of private vengeance. To this end, the local hysteria and impatience with "due process of law" contributed no small share.
>
> An innocent woman, the wife of one suspected avenger and daughter of another, was brutally ravished by local gangsters. The law is often slow; the evidence against the accused youths was not regarded by the jury as sufficient to justify a conviction, and a mistrial resulted. Preparations for another trial were under way when one defendant, Kahahawai, was removed from the jurisdiction of all earthly courts by an act of bloody violence.
>
> Whatever one may think of the guilt or innocence of Joseph Kahahawai, the fact remains that under American law he was entitled to a presumption of innocence until his guilt was finally determined by a competent tribunal—until he had been pronounced guilty by a jury of twelve men.
>
> The good name of the community has been blackened . . . all because we refused to be stampeded into an act of mob violence— or to railroad five defendants to prison. A little group of people apparently determined to take the law into their own hands . . . who are charged with this offense against law and order, are members of the Naval personnel of the United States. We cannot place the blame on the Navy or censure an entire organization

for a crime of a few of its members . . . But those who are in command, who are responsible for maintaining discipline, surely have something to answer for. Admiral Pettingill [Admiral George Pettingill, Commander of the Pearl Harbor Submarine Base] . . . told the world Hawaii was not a safe place for wives of Naval officers, because one woman was outraged . . . The Hawaiians are asking a question that perhaps Admiral Pettingill or Admiral Stirling can answer. They are asking whether Hawaii, their own homeland, is now safe for Hawaiians! [9]

The Arrival of Clarence Darrow

During all this turmoil and rising racial bitterness in Hawaii, there was an old man with graying hair, one stray lock characteristically hanging over his right eye, living most of the time in Chicago. He was at Lawrence, Kansas, delivering lectures to young law students, a few days after Joe Kahahawai was killed in Honolulu. His wise gray eyes, set wide apart in a grizzled face over high cheekbones that looked as if he might have some Indian origin, glanced over a telegram, the last line of which read:

"Will you accept this case at a retainer of $40,000."

This was Clarence Darrow, veteran of almost fifty years of courtroom battles, and perhaps America's greatest criminal lawyer of his day. He had been the champion of the underdog—the defender of John T. Scopes, the Tennessee schoolteacher, in the famous "monkey trial" a few years earlier when he debated William Jennings Bryan; of Eugene Debs after the Pullman riots in Chicago; of Big Bill Haywood, charged with murdering Governor Steunenberg of Idaho; and of the McNamara brothers in the Los Angeles *Times* bombing case. He was also the man who saved two wealthy young Chicagoans, Nathan Leopold and Richard Loeb, from death in 1924 for the killing of a nine-year-old boy.

Darrow had retired from active practice in 1928, and was taking trips around the country, lecturing to law students and others on the tricks and traps of the law. Now he was being asked to take a new kind of case—one that seemed to involve deep racial issues; and the locale was in faraway Hawaii. The wire was from Montgomery Winn, an attorney in Honolulu representing Mrs. Grace Fortescue, Thomas H. Massie, Albert O. Jones and Edmund J. Lord, accused of killing Joseph Kahahawai.

Darrow did not reply at once. He had several lectures and speeches to give, including one in Kansas City, in which he referred to the recent kidnaping of the Lindbergh baby. "Capital punishment is no cure for anything." he had said. "It will not stop murder or kidnaping. It simply adds another murder to the list." Capital punishment had just been suggested as a cure for rapists in Hawaii.

While Darrow was deciding whether to take the case, things were happening in Honolulu. The four accused of killing Joseph Kahahawai had finally been returned to the custody of the Honolulu police, after much confusion and exchanges of legal and quasi-legal opinions between the Attorney General of the Territory, Harry Hewitt, and Admiral Stirling and his faithful aide, Captain Wortman.

It was considered in the best interest of all concerned to let them remain at Pearl Harbor "for their personal safety"—and also their comfort—with a police guard from Honolulu. On January 20, Montgomery Winn, local attorney for the four accused people, announced that he would seek their release on *habeas corpus* proceedings unless the grand jury acted immediately.

The grand jury was not anxious to act. Whatever the jurors did would be wrong in the eyes of a substantial portion of the people of Honolulu. An indictment would assure the excoriation of the entire jury by most of the *haoles*—including the business community, the "leading citizens," and probably Walter Dillingham. On the other hand, failure to indict in the face of the rather obvious fact that one of them had killed Joseph Kahahawai, would involve some bitter words from the opposite side—the Hawaiians and other "nonwhites," as well as a few *haoles*, such as the white editor of the *Hawaii Hochi*, who had a particularly acid pen.

In the midst of this uncertainty, the grand jury met on January 22 to hear the evidence on the kidnaping and killing of Joseph

Kahahawai. Twenty-six witnesses paraded before the grand jurors during two days of testimony. On the afternoon of the second day, Judge Albert M. Cristy, before whom the case was docketed, called the grand jurors in and asked if they had reached a decision.

The foreman nodded. They had decided to return "no bill."

Judge Cristy was a small man, rather dapper, with a dark mustache and dark eyes. No one had ever accused him of being intimidated in matters of the law, by the *haole* elite or by anyone.

He leaned forward, his sharp glance boring into the eyes of the foreman.

"The grand jury," he said, "is not required to pass upon the guilt or innocence of those accused of a crime. You have two obligations and only two: One is to determine whether a crime has been committed, and the other is to determine whether in the circumstances any person or persons may have been involved in the commission of that crime to the extent that they should face trial."

He pointed out that the facts presented to the grand jury indicated fairly clearly that a man had been killed, and "under the laws of the Territory, no man may legally take the life of another except in legitimate self-defense or unless he is an officer of the law."

The fact that three people were caught with the body in the back of the car in which they were riding, the judge suggested, was sufficient ground to assume they were involved in the affair. He told the grand jury to report again at ten o'clock the following Tuesday, January 26, and dismissed them for the weekend. The following Tuesday the grand jury met again, and at noon they filed into Judge Cristy's courtroom. They had been unable to reach an agreement.

There was a small crowd in the courtroom, and there was evident tension in the air. Over the weekend there had been extensive discussions, particularly in such places as the Oahu Country Club and the Pacific Club, where the leading citizens gathered. Those who leaned to lynching as the best means of solving problems thought perhaps Judge Cristy should be taken away some place and disposed of and the whole case would be forgotten. Most of the *haoles* felt the "code of honor slaying" should be invoked, one way or another; but there was not much expert opinion as to how it should be done. The legal minds, more deliberate and mature, juggled the questions pro and con; and within the sum of their cerebral convolutions they came up with almost every solution except the correct one—which was for the grand jury to return an indictment, as it was required to do by law, and put the matter to trial.

There were other discussions in Aala Park and along the docks where the "wharf rats" gathered. Most of these were Hawaiian or part-Hawaiian. Their thoughts were not expressed in guarded legal terminology, as were those of the *haoles* at the Pacific Club. In substance, they said, "The Goddamned *haoles* will let them go! Maybe we should do to them what they did to poor Joe Kahahawai!"

In the beer places in Iewlei and on Kukui Street there was a more ominous confrontation—because these were the places where the sailors and local boys hung out, and they frequently settled their differences of opinion in a more direct way than merely talking about them. There were one or two scuffles, but no outright violence over the weekend. Honolulu waited tensely to see what the grand jury would do.

When Judge Cristy called them into his courtroom at noon on Tuesday, his manner had changed from one of mild anger to cold fury. His voice snapped.

"It has come to my attention," he said, "that some of you gentlemen on the grand jury have entered your sessions with your minds so fixed and determined on personal views of the law and the facts, that you are prepared to prevent any indictment in the matter now pending.

"I have instructed you that under the laws of this Territory no man may legally take the life of another except in self-defense or as an officer of the law. You will return to your chamber and consider this case on that basis, and within two hours I shall expect an indictment."

Within two hours he got one. The grand jurors, evidently aware by now that the law also fixed certain responsibilities on members of the grand jury itself—which, if disregarded, might involve contempt proceedings—voted a true bill.

The furor in the city was immediate and strident. The more extreme representatives of the *haole* groups, who had suggested getting rid of Judge Cristy, were more adamant than ever. "He should be impeached!" "The jury was coerced—it's a clear violation of the judicial code." "What kind of men are we—to let this thing happen, these people suffer?" Many Navy officers lived in Honolulu; and the *malihini haoles*—both Naval and local—seemed to coalesce into a solid ferment of indignation. People who had been friends or associates for years split on this matter, and refused to talk with each other. Women who were merely overheard suggesting that "maybe the dead boy wasn't guilty" were ostracized by their "better-informed" neighbors.

The "leading citizens" were casting about for some means of stalling things off until the emotional crisis should subside. Delegate Houston had cabled from Washington the suggestion that the death penalty for rape and mandatory sterilization for "lesser sex offenses" should be made part of the law. The Honolulu police force should be increased, the Sheriff's Office investigated and the Civil Service Commission given "power over the Chief of Police."

Admiral Stirling, who got more press in this affair than in all the rest of his career, chimed in with a suggestion that the grand jury be investigated. He reported to the Navy Department in Washington that the vote in the grand jury was twelve to nine for returning "no bill" until Judge Cristy intervened; and this report was published in the local papers in dispatches from Washington.

The *Hawaii Hochi* asked: "How did the Admiral know what took place in the secrecy of the grand jury room?" and noted that it was a criminal offense to pry into secrets of grand jury deliberations.

The trial date had been set for March 10; but Montgomery Winn came into court and demanded that the indictment be quashed on the ground that two "no bills" had been voted before Judge Cristy ordered the jury to meet again. Judge Cristy asked Winn how he knew what happened in the grand jury room; and when Winn refused to divulge the source of his information he was held in contempt.

Meanwhile a search had been going on for a Public Prosecutor to take over all prosecution of criminal cases for the City and County of Honolulu. The Legislature had passed a law at its special session, establishing a number of things, including the death penalty for rape and a Public Prosecutor for Honolulu. On February 10, John C. Kelley, an Irish lawyer with a reputation for toughness in the courtroom, was appointed to this post.

On March 3, Montgomery Winn—who had been purged of his contempt, presumably for divulging the source of his information from the grand jury room; or perhaps admitting he never had it —appeared in Judge Cristy's court and asked for a delay in the trial date. He said Clarence Darrow had accepted the case, but would not be able to reach Honolulu until March 24.

Pretrial Problems

The period of more than two months that intervened between the grand jury's indictment and the date finally set for the opening of what became known as the Massie-Fortescue trial, found the people of Honolulu—and of the country as a whole—ranging solidly on one side or another.

On the Mainland there was very little known about the actual state of affairs in Honolulu. Much of this was due to the uncertain and vacillating attitudes of those who represented Hawaii in Washington, and in particular, Victor Houston, the Delegate. On March 17, 1931, a Honolulu attorney who was a *haole*, and also an important political figure in Honolulu, wrote Houston:

Dear Victor:

I still regret what you have said as to the local situation, a situation that did not call for words of an exciting nature or those suggestive of bad conditions in Honolulu. A few days ago the local press carried items showing you had suggested vigilantes for patrolling our streets. If this is a fact, the proposal is worse than damn fool, for the reproduction of this stuff by the Mainland press serves to prove that the alarming stories published a few weeks ago were founded on fact and were justified . . . Vigilantes are akin to members of a lynching party; Governor Judd's tin soldiers patrolling the streets . . . Governor Judd hasn't the wisdom to carry out this role, or the guts to be a czar if he wishes to.

It is not pleasant to write as I have done, but these are the sentiments of,

Yours truly,
Harry T. Mills.[1]

Realization that the "alarming stories" being published on the Hawaiian situation were doing no good for Hawaii was coming slowly but surely to the attention of the "leading citizens"—the *haole* elite. The specter of a "Commission Government" for Hawaii had long been conjured up by the Big Five and the Republicans to frighten Hawaiian voters into backing away from almost every issue; but now it began to look, as the *Hawaii Hochi* said some time later, as if the "chickens were coming home to roost."

In his illuminating "private memorandum," Walter Dillingham expressed this note of sudden alarm:

> In mainland newspaper reports conditions were exaggerated and it was very evident that people there consider we were up against a race issue. As a matter of fact this is not true. The problem is a sex crime problem, and crimes of this character have taken place here in the past just as they have all over the world.
>
> The Hawaiians are a peace loving people, with true sporting instincts, and their sex relations have been more social than brutal. Court records here show that Hawaiians have been particularly free from the stigma of rape and because of this the charge that Hawaiians were guilty of the attack on Mrs. Massie caused many Whites, as well as Hawaiians, to question whether or not this crime had been committed by people of that race. Because of this, recent events have come nearer to causing a race issue between the Whites and the Hawaiians than at any time since the first white settlers came to these shores.[2]

It is noteworthy that Dillingham, in reducing the whole affair to a "sex crime problem," was able to overlook a half-century of growing racial tensions engendered by the gradual take-over of Hawaii by the descendants of the American missionaries and Yankee and English traders. In this connection one authority—perhaps less economically efficient than Dillingham in the affairs of Hawaii, but certainly more competent in the field of social analysis—may be quoted briefly. Lawrence A. Fuchs, who conducted a number of sociological studies on Hawaii in connection with the University of Hawaii, has this to say:

> Just as control was the major objective of the elite, the desire to maintain privilege was the major purpose of the lesser *haoles*. The censuses in 1920 and 1930 showed the *haoles* to be living in self-

segregated, high-prestige districts—the Upper Nuuanu Valley,
Manoa Valley, Waikiki, Kahala, Alewa Heights, Pacific Heights . . .

Racial tensions between the Hawaiians and *malihini haoles*,
including servicemen, were highest during the 1930's, first at the
time of the famous Ala Moana case, and later as relations between
Tokyo and Washington brought the two nations closer to war.[3]

The facts plainly indicated that regardless of Dillingham's efforts
to convert the tensions in Honolulu, after the killing of Joseph
Kahahawai, into a "sex crime problem," the conflict over the Massie
case was basically racial, and it was drawn along *haole* vs. Hawaiian
lines, not on the issue of the white people vs. the yellow races.
As an interesting sidelight on this point, the following excerpt
is taken from a letter sent to Delegate Victor Houston by a man who
was more or less a compatriot of the Hawaiians, although not from
Hawaii. This was Prince Haneta 'a Refareri, of Maupiti Island, in
the Society Group. Although Tahitian, not Hawaiian, the Prince
felt the kinship of Polynesian blood quite keenly, and he wrote to
the Delegate from Hawaii as follows:

Ever since Polynesia fell under European influence we, the Polynesian race, have been consistently held up to the world as a simple,
lazy, ignorant and sensual race of tawny savages with no sense of
moral restraint.

The result of this is that any attempt on our part to defend our
already much depressed peoples in a crisis is always met with offen-
sive insinuations which, by the way, never overlook the painful
reminder of our racial inferiority.

With reference to Lieutenant Massie, the letter went on:

I am exceedingly regretful of what is the act of an apparently molly-
coddle weakling who seemingly engaged in a dastardly murder,
presumably to avenge the attack on a white woman and [his] wife,
though many of our own women have been attacked under similar
circumstances and the only law used in these circumstances is the
washing of white lime so that it will glare under the tropical sun . . ."[4]

There was another source of information, made available in the
interim between the indictment of the Massie-Fortescue group and
their trial beginning early in April, 1932, and that was a report of
Assistant United States Attorney General Seth Richardson, who was

sent to the Islands to make an investigation of "sex crimes" in Hawaii shortly after the killing of Joseph Kahahawai.

In his report on the results of the investigation, Assistant Attorney General Richardson had this to say:

> We found in Hawaii no organized crime, no important criminal class, and no criminal rackets. We did not find substantial evidence that a crime-wave, so-called, was in existence in Honolulu, either disproportionate with the increase in population or in comparison with crime records in other cities of similar size on the Mainland.
>
> We found, however, ample evidence of extreme laxity in the administration of law enforcement agencies.
>
> We found a condition of inefficiency of the administration of justice which, in effect, constituted an invitation to the commission of crime and which largely destroyed the morale of law enforcement agencies.[5]

The Honolulu police force was described as "impotent, undisciplined, neglectful and unintelligent, with its chief concern political activity." The County Attorney, Jimmy Gilliland, who managed to disassociate himself personally from the embarrassment of trying the Ala Moana case, was referred to as "an inexperienced, inefficient County Attorney, immersed in politics, and his deputies appointed largely for political purposes."

Amidst the frantic efforts of the "leading citizens" to restore order out of the chaos they had been largely instrumental in creating, Clarence Darrow arrived in Honolulu. He promptly let loose a blast against the new Territorial laws making rape a capital offense. At a press conference, shortly after he reached the old Alexander Young Hotel, where he set up headquarters, Darrow said:

> A man committing rape will get the same punishment under this law that he would get for murder, so he might as well go the whole way and remove the evidence.[6]

The new law, which the Legislature had virtuously written into its records as a kind of token payment against its past sins and a promise to be good in the future, was described by Darrow as "opening the door for gold-diggers and blackmailers."

The *haoles* were taken a little aback by the great lawyer's forth-

Mrs. Fortescue with Clarence Darrow.

right remarks. Darrow, slightly stooped with the weight of more than seventy years on his shoulders, made it clear from the beginning that he was down there "to heal old wounds, not to make new ones." He told newspapermen—some of whom he had known in New York and Chicago—who were in Honolulu to cover the trial, that he had no intention of "carrying on a crusade for the white people in Hawaii."

"I'm down here to defend four people who have been accused of a crime that I do not believe was a crime," he said.

With this cryptic introduction, the trial opened at the Territorial courthouse before Judge Charles Skinner Davis on April 4, 1932.

The Strange Story of "Tahiti"

There was one question that had filtered into pretrial discussions and street-corner debates on the merits of the approaching trial. The two *haole* dailies—the *Advertiser* and the *Star-Bulletin* —had more or less disregarded this question, in the excitement of the killing of Joseph Kahahawai and the arrival of Clarence Darrow; and yet it struck more deeply into the heart of the whole affair than almost anything else. The question being asked on the streets, in beer shops and even in the clubhouses of the *haole* elite, was this: If Joseph Kahahawai and the four other defendants in the Ala Moana trial were not Mrs. Massie's attackers—*who did attack her?*

There was no question whatever that Thalia Massie had been beaten severely. Whether she was actually raped was still a moot point, with little likelihood of its ever being resolved. But there could be no doubt that she had been attacked. Who did it? And under what circumstances?

There were evil rumors floating about, none of them verified. Yet the question was bound to intrude itself into the trial of the four white people, in spite of Clarence Darrow's strenuous efforts to prevent this. He had hardly gotten off the boat when he told several newspapermen—Russ Owens of the New York *Times*; Bill Ewing of the Associated Press; Danny Campbell of the United Press; and the writer—that the real issue was not whether Joseph Kahahawai was guilty or innocent.

"The real point to consider," he said, in a low, drawling voice, as he sat in his suite at the Young Hotel, "is that these people *believed* he attacked her. We are not and will not retry the Ala Moana case. We are trying four people for a crime that we contend was not a crime in their eyes."

Shortly before Darrow arrived, a strange story crept into the assortment of rumors, unconfirmed reports and mysterious allusions by the local *cognoscenti*, that were traveling the rounds in Honolulu.

It will be recalled that on the night of September 12, Joe Freitas, the doorman at the Ala Wai Inn, had seen the "girl in the green dress" standing in the doorway of the Inn about midnight. A dark-skinned youth had passed her, and she turned and said, "Hello, Sammy." Joe Freitas had recognized the man as a young fellow who hung around with the music boys at the Ala Wai Inn, with his friend, "Tahiti."

Tahiti's real named was Philip Kemp. He was part Tahitian and part French, and about twenty-two years old when these events occurred. He had no particular job in Honolulu, traveling around with a group of boys that included, among others, his friend "Sammy," who was also reputed to be part Tahitian.

Word had trickled into the police station that Tahiti knew something about the Ala Moana case; and during the time the Ala Moana trial was in progress Detective Lucian Machado had brought him in for questioning. The story told by Tahiti was not very clear, even in his own mind. He said his friend "Sammy" had shown him a gun while they were talking in a hotel room one night, explaining that he was "afraid some boys would beat him up." The reason for this, Tahiti said, was that his friend "knew too much about the case they were trying—the attack on the white woman."

Machado made a report of this to his superiors, but the vagueness of the story—plus the fact that it would have been poor strategy to have given public attention to such a tale, with the County Attorney's office committed to the theory that the five boys on trial were guilty of the attack—caused it to be dropped in the limbo of nonessential information. However, Tahiti had mentioned several things in his story that interested Machado and some of the other police officers who were later excoriated by Griffith Wight, the

Deputy County Attorney, as being "disloyal" to the Police Department.

Among these details were the names of the three youths who had been mentioned by Tahiti. One of these was a big Hawaiian called "Bull"; another was a Japanese known as "Shorty"; and a third was a Filipino-Hawaiian who was not further identified. Some of this information fell into the hands of a reporter for the *Hawaii Hochi,* a redheaded Irishman, Leo Crowley, who printed a story that there was a possible alternate gang of assailants of Thalia Massie. The members of this gang, the story said, had left the Islands for Los Angeles.

This was in February of 1932, more than a month after the killing of Joseph Kahahawai. Honolulu was seething with controversy over the question whether the killing should be regarded as an "honor slaying" or outright murder. Since the possibility of an alternative explanation of the attack on Thalia Massie was somewhat germane to this situation, Attorney General Harry Hewitt decided to investigate the report.

Philip Kemp was in jail at the time, on a charge of vagrancy. He was taken up to Hewitt's office and questioned for hours. Assistant Attorney General Harold Kay was placed in charge of the investigation, which was reported in detail by the *Hochi* but not by the *Advertiser* or *Star-Bulletin.*

Philip Kemp still did not have all the facts very clear in his mind. He described again the events he said happened: his friend "Sammy" had showed him a gun; "Sammy's" fear of some kind of reprisal because he "knew too much about the attack on that *haole* woman." The story did not hang together very well, but Hewitt took it seriously enough to send to Los Angeles for information about "Sammy" and his three friends. Philip Kemp had described one of "Sammy's" friends as having "two gold teeth" and when the Los Angeles Police traced the group, they found this to be true. They had located the four boys through reports of a fight between them and another group of Hawaiians.

Hewitt asked the Los Angeles Police to send "Sammy" to Honolulu and when he arrived, he was taken to Hewitt's office and confronted with his former friend, Tahiti—or Philip Kemp. "Sammy" denied any knowledge of Kemp's rambling story, including his possession of a gun; and as a result, the matter was dropped.

Jack Kelley was in Hewitt's office during the interrogation of "Sammy" and Kemp. He had the latter's statement that "Sammy" had admitted picking up "the *haole* woman" and the further statement that "Sammy" and his three friends had left for the Coast during the Ala Moana trial because the case was "getting hot."

The *Hawaii Hochi*, in an effort to stir up some action in the matter, published a story containing the text of an affidavit it was reported to have obtained from Kemp covering his story. The two *haole* newspapers continued studiously to ignore the matter, however, and it had little public currency.

The importance of the Philip Kemp story to Jack Kelley was not its validity as proof of anything; the part-Tahitian youth was too vague and rambling in his account to offer anything in the way of verifiable evidence. But the fact that the story had not been seriously investigated—by the Honolulu Police or by Attorney General Hewitt—left an open possibility. If it were proved to be true, it would be *prima facie* evidence that Thalia Massie had identified the wrong boys—and Tommy Massie, his mother-in-law and the two sailors had killed an innocent man.

This would erase any claim of "honor slaying" in the defense of the four white people who killed Kahahawai; and it was upon this issue that Jack Kelley threw down the gauntlet to Clarence Darrow almost at the moment the trial opened.

The Massie-Fortescue Trial

They sat only a few feet apart, at separate tables facing the bench, the graying veteran of nearly a half century before the bar, and the young Irish lawyer from Honolulu. They were quite a contrast, these two. Clarence Darrow had the wisdom and wiles of many famous legal battles in his keen gray eyes. Jack Kelley, with sharp blue eyes and a bald head that shone like a skinned coconut, was forty years Darrow's junior and had no particular legal history except in the community in which he lived.

Nevertheless, Kelley was in no way awed by the reputation of the great Clarence Darrow. Almost the first question he asked of one of the prospective jurors, sitting in the jury box to their left, was a challenge to the issue Darrow raised with newspapermen before the trial.

"Would you be willing to render a verdict of guilty in this case even if you feel that the defendants believed it was right to commit murder—under the circumstances? That is, even if they believed the man they killed was guilty of rape?"

Darrow held up his hand. The courtroom, filled with people who had waited for hours in line to find seats, seemed to sense the importance of every word. There was a faint stir, a rustling of women's dresses, as they leaned forward.

"Just a minute, please," Darrow said to the venireman. "I shall object to any line of questioning that seeks to bring in any trials or crimes or alleged crimes that are not part of this case."

Kelley stood up.

"Your Honor," he said to Judge Davis, "I want to know whether these jurors are going to be influenced by what they think of the guilt or innocence of Joseph Kahahawai. We have a right to know that in order to know whether they can reach a fair verdict."

Barry Ulrich, a tall young man who had been assigned to assist Kelley, also stood up. It was quite apparent to everyone that in the first few minutes of the trial, the underlying issue was to be squarely joined. Charles Skinner Davis, the judge, knew it, too. The issue was: Did Tommy Massie and the three other defendants believe Joseph Kahahawai had assaulted Thalia Massie; and if so, was the killing, in the course of an effort to obtain a confession from him, justifiable on the grounds of an undefined "code of honor"?

Barry Ulrich thumbed through a law book, and said to Judge Davis:

"We are entitled to know whether this juror will try the case under the law, and only under the law, in arriving at a decision."

"It isn't the law!" Darrow's voice rang out. "That point was settled in our earlier discussion of this case with Your Honor—and we will argue it any time. It isn't the law!"

Judge Davis, anxious to avoid issues that would impede the selection of a jury, told Ulrich and Kelley they might ask the jurors if they would try the case under the law, but they could not go beyond that, involving other matters, or previous trials.

Kelley then fired the next question—which outlined the next basic issue.

"If it appears that all four defendants were present and took part in this affair, even if only one of them fired the shot, or even if none of them is proved to have fired the shot but was a party to this case, will you be willing to render a verdict of guilty if the Court instructs you that this is the law?"

It had been indicated in newspaper stories and remarks of the lawyers that the defense would rely on a theory of temporary insanity—if Tommy Massie fired the fatal shot; or even if Mrs. Fortescue fired the shot. Shadford Waterhouse was the venireman under questioning; and he was a member of a missionary family, one of the *haole* elite and an accredited member of the best families of Hawaii.

Kelley literally bored into Waterhouse. He demanded, in effect, that he cast aside his inherited prejudices and agree to render a verdict against the white defendants, if this were justified under the law and the evidence. Waterhouse looked at Kelley, and nodded. "I will," he said.

In another instance, Kelley asked a Swedish employee of the Oahu Railway and Land Company, Olaf Sorenson, if he knew Walter Dillingham—whose family owned the company. Sorenson said he did; but he denied that this would affect his determination of the guilt or innocence of the accused.

It should have been evident to Clarence Darrow that the line was being drawn on basic racial issues; but apparently he chose to ignore this warning. As the examination of veniremen continued, it became apparent even to those newspapermen who came from distant parts—but were sufficiently sophisticated to understand the underlying issues—that Darrow was making several major miscalculations. The first of these was one that was endemic among the class of people with whom Darrow was thrown into contact. This was the theory, voiced by Walter Dillingham, that the "race issue" was not involved in this case. Darrow had been exposed only to the viewpoints and opinions of these people, like Dillingham, who lionized him at elaborate dinners at their homes on Diamond Head or Pacific Heights, or at luncheons at the Pacific Club. They still clung to the theory that the attackers of Thalia Massie must be the five boys she had identified; otherwise, why would she have identified them? As a consequence of this rather naïve assumption, it was assumed further that the killing of one of the "friends" was therefore entirely justifiable.

This miscalculation led to the further assumption that in view of the general belief that the Ala Moana defendants were guilty, all that was really needed to defend the killers of Joseph Kahahawai was to establish some kind of *pro forma* and reasonably acceptable explanation of the affair, and the four white people would be set free. This was the genesis of the theory of "temporary insanity" discreetly promulgated by Clarence Darrow.

What Darrow—as well as Walter Dillingham—failed to recognize was that a large and angry segment of the people of Honolulu did not accept this presumption as valid. They did not believe that failure to convict in the first Ala Moana trial was mere bungling, but rather that the inept performance of the prosecution in that case was due to its inability to construct a convincing case simply because there was no case.

Darrow's second miscalculation was his assumption that the spell of his oratory, with its deeply humanistic theme, would move the Oriental mind. In the evenings, after court sessions, he frequently gathered with newspapermen assigned to the trial, and his old crony from Chicago, Charles Eugene Banks, to talk over the day's happenings. One night he asked a question.

"You newspaper fellows down here know the way these people think. How do you figure them out? How do you measure the mentality of Chinese—or part-Hawaiians? I can figure out pretty well what the white people are thinking, but I can't tell anything about what these fellows think from their expression, because they don't seem to have any expression."

His listeners laughed. Russ Owen of the New York *Times*, who was not a Honoluluan, but had known Darrow for many years, spoke up:

"I don't think you can use the same tactics you usually use, Judge." Darrow had never been a judge; but newspapermen at the trial, out of deference and respect for the old man, usually addressed him as "judge." "What you've got to do is assume what they will do in a given situation. In this case, the given situation is that a man has been shot, and if Judge Davis tells them shooting a man is against the law and they find these people did the shooting, that's all there is to it. They'll find them guilty."

Darrow nodded.

"That's the damned trouble with trials," he said. "Everybody thinks about the law and nobody thinks about people. It's what is in people's minds that makes them do things—not what the law says." He leaned forward, his loose jowls trembling, his voice suddenly sharper. "It's what these people thought that made them do what they did. Damn it—they thought Kahahawai was guilty of raping that woman, and whether he was or not isn't the point! They *thought* he was."

This was perhaps the first crack in the old man's own armor of thought. As the fantasy of many races passed before him, it was evident that he was losing command of the situation. During the courtroom sessions, he had raised points haltingly at times, and at other times he simply sat and stared, while George Leisure, the New York lawyer who had come out to join the battery of defense attorneys, conducted the questioning. The parade of different faces was wearing on the old warrior's nerves—the change from sturdy plantation Scot with honesty and forthrightness written all over his face, to an impassive Chinese countenance with nothing written on his face, and then to the stolid men of Hawaiian blood, who seemed almost indifferent to his questions—all this was beginning to confuse Darrow.

At one time, Barry Ulrich, assisting Kelley, said to a prospective juror:

"Regrettable as it is that one of these defendants is a lady of culture and refinement—to whom you would ordinarily extend every courtesy—and painful as it might be, would you find her guilty of murder if the evidence and the instructions of the court indicate she is guilty?"

The venireman to whom he addressed the question was Kam Tai Lee, working for a cold storage company in Honolulu; he had previously said he was a graduate of the University of Hawaii.

Darrow had been watching him keenly; and after Ulrich finished, he leaned forward.

"You are a graduate of the University here?"

Lee nodded. Darrow suddenly smiled, and Lee smiled back.

"You understand the seriousness of these charges, Mr. Lee? If these defendants are not proven guilty—you'll give them the benefit of a reasonable doubt?"

Lee said he would. Darrow leaned back and sighed. The old man still did not know what to think about the Oriental mind. Lee was not challenged by either side, and remained in the jury box.

As the days wore on, and the crowd of onlookers became more restive—they had come to witness a performance, not an exchange of psychological subtleties between lawyers and the men in the jury box—the character of the jury became more definite. Even Walter Dillingham, in his "private memorandum," admitted that "an exceptionally fine jury was empaneled." But it was not an "acquitting" or a "convicting" jury. It was what Judge Davis later described as "an ideal jury—a jury that waits for the evidence and weighs it, and listens to the instructions of the court as to the law."

In one instance, Darrow was quite obviously puzzled by strange currents and conflicts of viewpoints that were inherent in the entire situation—the old background that emerged inevitably from the Ala Moana trial, which he had sought desperately to avoid. This became evident in the questioning of Clarence Hao, a relative of the Deputy Sheriff of Honolulu, David Hao.

Hao, a dark, solidly built Hawaiian, told Darrow under questioning that he was a member of the Naval Reserve.

"You are a Navy man?"

"Oh, yes."

"And you are related to the Deputy Sheriff?"

"Oh, yes."

Darrow shook his head. He consulted for a moment with Montgomery Winn, the Honolulu member of the battery of defense attorneys which included not only Darrow and Leisure—the latter a partner of General "Wild Bill" Donovan who became creator and head of the Office of Strategic Services during World War II ten years later—but also Lt. L. H. C. Johnson, of the United States Navy, who was assigned as a matter of Navy regulations to protect the interests of the two enlisted men, Lord and Jones.

Winn shook his head. Whether Clarence Hao would lean toward the defendants from the Navy—Massie, Lord and Jones—or on the side of the Territory, which in a sense represented the dead Hawaiian, Joseph Kahahawai, was too tough a problem to solve. Hao was excused.

By the time the jury was finally selected it consisted of seven men of Caucasian blood, one Portuguese; two Chinese and three who were of Hawaiian blood, two of them only part-Hawaiian. They were sworn in by Judge Davis and the trial was adjourned until Monday morning, April 11.

Ropes and Bullets

The second major miscalculation which Darrow made was Jack Kelley. It is quite possible that the great legal warrior, known to the world as the champion of the downtrodden, had hoped to run roughshod over the local side, hammering home his magic weapons of tolerance, understanding, mercy for the accused, against a slightly awed home-town lawyer. If so, he was mistaken.

Jack Kelley was far younger than Darrow, as has been noted. He was not widely known beyond the confines of the Territory, where he had practiced law for several years until he was selected for the newly created post of Public Prosecutor for Honolulu. But he did not seem intimidated by Clarence Darrow.

Kelley was a fairly large, squarely built man with broad shoulders. He sat hunched forward at the prosecution's table, his bald head, fringed with a monkish crown of red hair, gleaming like the setting sun against the dark background of Judge Davis' bench. He was quick-witted and incisive, with Irish pugnacity and sharpness of tongue. And he knew Hawaii and the Hawaiians, as Darrow did not.

It was quite evident the Territory would depend upon circumstantial evidence. No one except the four accused could say who killed Joseph Kahahawai. No one else had been there. In the charged air of a courtroom in which there was almost dead silence, Kelley quietly and precisely outlined the case for the prosecution.

He described the scene at the courthouse, just outside the room in which the trial was being held; the queer document used to lure Joseph Kahahawai into the car, the misspelled word "Teritory" and the strange lettering pasted on the fake summons.

He described the house in upper Manoa Valley, on Kalawalo Avenue, where Kahahawai was killed. It was a dingy bungalow, set back among a few trees with hedges along the side. There were only four rooms—a living room, a kitchen, and two small bedrooms. The house was dusty and looked as if it had not been lived in—except for the remains of two fried eggs in a skillet on the kitchen stove. The house, Kelley said, had been rented by Mrs. Grace Fortescue when she arrived in Honolulu in October. There were no pictures on the walls; no phonograph or radio. At the breakfast table in the kitchen, there were places set for two when the police, led by Inspector John McIntosh, arrived that morning in January.

The bedroom was apparently the place where the shooting took place. There were bloodstains on the floor, Kelley said; and a torn strip of white undershirt was lying on the floor—which matched the undershirt rolled in a bundle with the other clothes of the dead man. The bathtub was clean, he said; but they would produce evidence that the drainpipe under the tub was filled with blood.

Joseph Kahahawai had been killed with a .32-caliber pistol, he said. It was known that there were two pistols involved in the case —a .32-caliber Colt and an Iver-Johnson revolver of the same caliber. He did not say which gun was used to shoot Kahahawai. The bullet had cut through the pulmonary artery, having been shot somewhat downward across his body. An inch either way and Kahahawai might have lived. As it was, he bled to death. A broken watch on his wrist showed that death had occurred at 9:45 A.M.

At one point in his outline, Kelley suddenly changed the pitch of his voice. He had told of Joseph Kahahawai and his cousin, Eddie Ulii, arriving at the courthouse; Kahahawai reporting to the Probation Officer, William Dixon, and then leaving the courthouse with his cousin while a woman and a man watched him, and the woman suddenly pointed at him.

Kelley turned suddenly from the jury and faced Mrs. Fortescue, sitting rigidly behind the defense counsel's table. She straightened slightly when he pointed at her.

"There, as he stood under the shadow of Kamehameha, under the outstretched arm of the great Hawaiian who brought law and order to Hawaii, the finger of doom was pointed at this youthful descendant of the King's people," Kelley said, his voice ringing out in the hushed courtroom. "We will prove that it was the finger and hand of Mrs. Grace Fortescue that pointed to that doom—that in the vernacular of today, it was Grace Fortescue who 'put the finger' on Joseph Kahahawai!"

There was hardly a sound as he spoke, except for a slight sigh, apparently from the Hawaiians or their sympathizers in the crowd. But it was quite evident that Jack Kelley meant to tread openly upon the ground that Clarence Darrow had tried to declare "out of bounds"—the ground of racial dissension and bitterness in Hawaii that had grown out of the Ala Moana case.

Once again, while he was describing what was found in the little bungalow on Kalawalo Avenue, Kelley's calm, matter-of-fact voice rose to a dramatic pitch. He was told of the finding of a .45-caliber automatic pistol shoved behind a cushion in one of the chairs; and then of finding pictures of the five Ala Moana defendants in a purse left in the living room . . . "the pictures so placed in the purse that the picture of Joseph Kahahawai was uppermost . . . so that every time you opened the purse, the first picture you would see was that of Joseph Kahahawai!"

His voice rising suddenly, Kelley said:

"And the police found two other things . . . a torn piece of an undershirt and a coil of rope. A rope with a purple thread running through it, exactly like the rope that bound a white sheet around the body of Joseph Kahahawai! It had that one distinctive mark, ladies and gentlemen of the jury—a purple thread that ran through the rope. We will show that there is only one place on Oahu where that kind of rope can be found—at the Naval Station at Pearl Harbor, where it is now in use at the Submarine Base where the three male defendants in this case are stationed!"

A minute later, Kelley said in a much lower voice:

"We will show from physical evidence in the bedroom of Mrs. Fortescue's house that Joseph Kahahawai was shot as he sat there, and that he was taken into the bathroom, where he strangled and bled to death." He added, in sharper tones: "There was no struggle in this room that can be shown from physical evidence—no struggle that would enable these people to claim self-defense for shooting Joseph Kahahawai!"

As Kelley put his witnesses on the stand—first, Edward Ulii, the dead man's cousin, who told of the events that took place near the courthouse the morning Kahahawai was taken into the Buick car, driven by Mrs. Fortescue; and then the testimony of the policemen who arrested three of the defendants on the bluff overlooking Hanauma Bay—it became evident that the prosecution was laying the grounds for its own defense, anticipating the claim of the defense lawyers that the "state of mind" of the four people would be their defense.

Johnny Cluney, the detective who had first arrested Horace Ida on the night Thalia Massie was attacked, was called to the stand. He had been present when Tommy Massie was first taken in custody, after the discovery of the body of Joseph Kahahawai in the car in which he was riding. On cross-examination, Montgomery Winn asked Cluney:

Q. Do you recall making a statement to me when I asked you to describe Massie, in which you said, "Massie was very stern, sitting straight up, never saying a word—just looked straight up." Do you recall that?
A. Yes, I do.
Q. And Lord was sitting in the car, very firm, and not saying a word?
A. Yes.[1]

On redirect examination, Kelley asked: "They were just as firm as they are now, sitting in this courtroom, weren't they?" Cluney said yes, they were.

The police officers who were at the scene of the capture, on the saddleback of Koko Head overlooking Hanauma Bay, were questioned closely—by Darrow as well as Kelley—as to the demeanor of the three people as they sat on rocks or walked along the side of the road. Detective George Harbottle, in the radio patrol car that had overtaken the Buick with the dead man, was asked at one point to identify Mrs. Fortescue.

He rose from the witness chair and walked across the intervening distance between the witness stand and the bench where the defense lawyers and the defendants sat. The thin-faced woman from Kentucky seemed to recoil as he reached out and touched her shoulder.

Leisure cross-examined Harbottle, and again it was evident the defense was seeking to establish a "state of mind" of the defendants.

Q. [By Leisure] Did you talk to Lieutenant Massie?
A. No.
Q. Did you carry on a conversation with any of the men?
A. Lord. I asked him whose car it was.
Q. What was Mrs. Fortescue doing at that time?
A. She was sitting on a rock alongside the road.[2]

Harbottle, on redirect questioning by Kelley, told of the incident in which Radio Patrolman Percy Bond had walked over to him and said, "Good work, kid!" and Massie, standing nearby, had smiled and clasped his hands as if shaking hands with himself.

During the three days in which the prosecution presented its case, the exchanges between Kelley and Darrow became sharper and sharper; and the tension in the courtroom seemed to increase as the courtroom battle became rougher.

Darrow, in cross-examining witnesses, sought to establish an atmosphere of sympathy for the defendants—of understanding of their motives, of the searing hatred that had grown in Massie's mind at the attackers of his wife, and the emotional tension of Thalia Massie's mother, who had come to Honolulu to see that her daughter was protected from insults and slander.

In the face of this, Jack Kelley was forging an iron ring of facts. On one occasion, when he sought to introduce a picture of the Buick sedan in which the slain youth had been abducted, Darrow objected on the ground that it was not important or relevant.

"We will concede that is the car," he snapped.

Judge Davis intervened mildly.

"There doesn't seem to be any dispute about that car," he said.

"Not yet," Kelley said. "But there will be."

This came when a Japanese, Chris Omura, from the Rosecrans Garage, from which the car was rented, was put on the stand to identify the car rental contract. Kelley asked him if he "recognized the defendant, Thomas Massie."

Kelley had stated, in explaining the use of the witness to Judge Davis, that "this evidence shows the preparation of plans by the defendants—that it was premeditated. It was the same car that was seen in front of Mrs. Fortescue's house on Kalawela Avenue at 7:30 o'clock the next morning."

On cross-examination, Attorney Winn asked Omura if the testimony that he had recognized Massie was "the same testimony you gave before the grand jury."

Kelley jumped to his feet.

"Do I understand that Counsel is asking that question based on a known fact?" It will be recalled that Winn was held in contempt of court by Judge Christy when he professed to know the vote in the grand jury room for returning a "no bill" against the Massie-Fortescue defendants.

Winn said he would change the question.

"Have you a transcript of the grand jury's evidence before you?" Kelley demanded. Winn said, "I wish I had," and sat down, smiling. But Kelley's face was flushed with anger.

During the examination of Dr. Robert B. Faus, the City and County Physician, Kelley began to develop the theory that Kahahawai was shot by a bullet that had coursed downward diagonally from the right side of his chest through the region of the heart. This was significant, because it might indicate the point from which the shot was fired—and thus establish who actually fired the shot. It might also indicate that Kahahawai was lunging forward when he was shot—in defense, rather than in blind anger.

Darrow and Kelley began to wrangle furiously over every point— whether or not there were bloodstains on the floor; where the coil of rope with a purple thread came from; the description of the bungalow where Kahahawai was shot; whether it was surrounded by hedges or trees, and so on.

In the last phases of the prosecution's case, Kelley produced a row of glittering bullets and cartridge shells, playing with them like metallic toys before the jurors. He showed the steel-jacketed .32-caliber bullet taken from the body of Joseph Kahahawai, and then picked up an empty shell. He handed them to the jurors.

The shell was taken from Albert Jones's pocket when he was brought down to the police station on January 8, the morning of the killing. A cartridge clip containing the same kind of bullets was found wrapped in the fake "summons," which Jones had under his shirt. Kelley also produced testimony showing that a box of thirty-three additional shells of the same type were found in Jones's locker at the Army and Navy Y.M.C.A.

The final bit of drama in connection with all this physical paraphernalia, which Kelley manipulated on the table like a magician about to make something disappear, was in the testimony of Vasca Rosa, a clerk in a hardware store, who said he sold two pistols to Jones and Mrs. Fortescue—a .32 Colt automatic and a .32 Iver-Johnson. The clerk sat in the witness chair, holding one of the shells and the bullet dug out of Kahahawai's body. Kelley asked him to put the shell into the cartridge. Rosa twisted the tiny bit of metal into the empty shell, looked up at Kelley, and said:

"It fits."

The final witness for the Territory aroused the bitterest resentment Darrow had displayed. This was Mrs. Esther Anito, the mother of Joseph Kahahawai.

Chief Inspector John McIntosh had wound up the Territory's basic case in a plain and forceful way—more so, indeed, than his testimony for the Territory at the Ala Moana trial, when he shied away from every question that he could not answer on a basis of fact. In this case, he described clearly all that he had seen, or that had been reported—including the fact that Jones "acted drunk" when he was picked up at the Fortescue bungalow in Manoa, but was quite sober when he was questioned at the police station.

At one point, Darrow himself opened a line of questioning that gave Kelley an opportunity to establish one item of evidence that seemed otherwise unobtainable. McIntosh had described the departure of Thalia Massie from the police station to Pearl Harbor, where her mother and the three men were taken shortly after they were arrested. He asked her facetiously if she "carried a purse."

Kelley leaped at the opening. On cross-examination he said:

"Was the purse large enough to have concealed a .32-caliber automatic Colt pistol?" Up to that point the death weapon had been missing; and as Kelley later said, "This was the only possible chance I had of getting it into the record."

During this exchange, Mrs. Anito—who had been married formerly to Joseph Kahahawai, Sr., the slain man's father, and with whom young Kahahawai had been living before he was killed—remained quietly in a chair behind the table where Kelley and Ulrich sat. This was on the morning of April 14, the day the Territory closed its case.

She was a slender woman, of medium height; her dark face was concealed for the most part by a handkerchief which she pressed to her eyes. When she was called to the stand, and stood up, Darrow immediately arose and stood between her and the witness stand.

"We will concede everything this witness has to say," he said "We will stipulate she is the mother of Joseph Kahahawai—that she saw him that morning when he left—anything . . ."

Kelley stood up.

"There are two mothers in this courtroom," he said, his voice low and biting. "One is a defendant, and the other has no defense. Her son is dead. We think both should be permitted to testify."

Darrow sat down and slowly shook his head. The old warrior was not defeated; but in a legal sense, he was being mortally hurt.

Esther Anito sat in the witness chair, talking in a low voice, now and then pressing the handkerchief to her face. Her eyes were filled with tears as she told, in a halting voice, how she had been summoned by the police to go to the funeral parlor and identify the body of her son.

When she finished her testimony, there were a few others in the room who were weeping. Darrow looked back at the people in the seats behind the rail that separated the court from the onlookers. He shook his head again and scowled. Later he said to newsmen:

"I guess we had it coming. The sympathy can't all be on one side."

Darrow was beginning at this point to have the appearance of a weakened old bull in a bull ring; his heart still beat fiercely, but his aging body no longer stood up to the rigors of courtroom battle.

The Case for "Honor Slaying"

The first witness put on by the defense was Tommy Massie. He was dressed in a dark blue suit, with a light tan tie. His face was still set in the hard lines that seemed to have become fixed on his features since the beginning of the trial. He was tight-lipped, tense, short in his answers. He seemed to consider carefully every question Darrow put to him, before he spoke.

Darrow led him gently through the early years of his life—in Winchester, Kentucky, where he was born; at the two military schools he attended before matriculating at Annapolis; his life at the Naval Academy; and his marriage to Thalia Hubbard Fortescue, on the day he graduated, when she was a girl of sixteen.

This was in 1927. He had first been assigned to the airplane carrier *USS Lexington* and later was transferred to the Submarine Base at New London, Conn. He was attached to the submarine S-34, which was later stationed in Hawaii; and he had lived in the Islands for two years with his wife.

At this point, Darrow asked:

"Do you remember an incident last September, going to a dance—?"

Massie passed his hand across his eyes.

"I could never forget it," he said.

He explained that he had gone to the Ala Wai Inn that night with two fellow officers—Lieutenant Jerry Branson and Lieutenant Tom Brown, and their wives.

"Mrs. Massie didn't care about going at first—but she finally agreed," he said.

Kelley got to his feet, and walked over in front of the lawyer's tables.

"I do not intend to interrupt with objections," he told Judge Davis. "But I feel that at this point we are entitled to know the relevance of this testimony. It is a matter which counsel has sought quite strenuously to avoid in this case—and I want to know the reason." He turned to Darrow. "Is it your intention to go into the Ala Moana case?"

"I am going to make this brief," Darrow said. "But I do intend to go into that case—yes."

"Then the prosecution should be informed at this time if one of the defendants will make an insanity plea," Kelly said. "If insanity is to be the plea, we will not oppose any objections to this testimony."

Darrow walked back and talked with George Leisure and Montgomery Winn. Then he returned and stood before the witness.

"We do intend to raise the question of insanity—in the last part of this tragedy," he said. "That is, the one who fired the pistol."

Kelley said he would object to further testimony of the witness, Tommy Massie, "along these lines, unless the prosection is informed that the plea of insanity is to be made in his behalf."

Darrow said he didn't see "how that is necessary at this time." Kelley said it was "known that certain well-known psychiatrists are here, in Honolulu, to testify." He added:

"We have the right to examine this witness through alienists if it is claimed that this defendant was insane at the time of the murder was committed."

It was common knowledge in Honolulu that Dr. Edward H. Williams and Dr. Thomas H. Orbison, two prominent psychiatrists from the Mainland, had arrived from the Coast a few days earlier. Newspaper reporters had questioned them, but they had not given any reason for their trip.

Darrow grumbled a bit, but finally said if the prosecution wished to have "certain doctors come and listen to the testimony, we will not object to that, but we may not see fit to submit the defendant or defendants for whom insanity will be claimed to the examination of any physicians."

Kelley's objection was overruled by Judge Davis, and Massie went on with his story. He told of his search for his wife after she disappeared from the Ala Wai Inn; how he had gone with Branson to the Rigby house in Manoa Valley; and finally his telephone call to his home, which Thalia Massie had answered with the distracted cry:

"Come home! Something awful has happened . . ."

Massie went on:

"As I ran up the steps, I could hear her crying. She ran to the doorway and collapsed in my arms. There was blood coming from her nose, her lips were bruised and bleeding—and there was a large bruise on the right side of her face. I thought at first a truck had run over her!"

Massie stopped for a moment, holding his face in his hands.

Under Darrow's gentle prodding, he continued his story. He had asked Thalia what had happened, and she sobbed, "It's too terrible!" She kept sobbing, he said, and finally told him that some men had dragged her into a car, beaten her, taken her to a place a little way off the road, and ravished her.

"I said, 'Oh, my God, no!'" Massie said, his voice dropping so that his words were almost inaudible. For several seconds he sat, saying nothing, and staring at Mrs. Fortescue, who set a few feet away behind the lawyer's table.

Finally, Massie went on. He said he was in a daze for some minutes, and Thalia kept crying, "I want to die! I hope I die!"

He said he tried to comfort her, and asked her if she had taken precautions to prevent "conception or disease," and she replied, according to his story: "Yes, I've done everything I can."

Massie said he finally called the police, and asked them to take her to a hospital. "They kept on asking her questions," he said. "I told them to stop asking questions and find the men who attacked her."

Later, at the police station, one of the detectives asked him if he thought her attacker might have been Lieutenant Branson, who was at the station under arrest, after having been picked up by Officer William Simerson a short distance from the Massie home.

"I told the police not to waste their time with him—that he was with me all evening," Massie said. "I told them to go on with the investigation."

He said he finally drove his wife back home, and she kept asking, "Why didn't they kill me?"

"You didn't sleep that night?" Darrow asked.

"How could I?"

Massie said the next day he cabled Mrs. Fortescue, Thalia's mother, and then returned to the Queen's Hospital, where she had been taken, and "stayed there until the nurses made me leave."

Massie's lips began twisting as he told of the several times the police brought suspects before her—at home and in the hospital—and she identified four of them. Darrow asked Massie if she "knew any of the four assailants."

Kelley said, "Your Honor, I object to the use of the word 'assailants.'"

Darrow looked at Kelley, and then said: "Let's call them alleged assailants. Or suppose we call them four men."

"The four people," Massie said, his face twisted in a grimace, "were brought before her. She said, 'They are the ones.' Then she called me to her side and said, 'Please, darling, don't let there be any doubt in your mind, because you know what it means. Don't you know if there was any doubt in my mind, I could never draw an easy breath?'"

Massie stopped, and so did Darrow. This excessive burst of emotional feeling possibly had not been expected by him. He turned and walked back to the table, his finger pressed against his temple. It was fairly well known in Honolulu that Mrs. Fortescue's brother, Robert Bell, a nephew of Alexander Graham Bell, was with the Massie-Fortescue party at Pearl Harbor. He was a young man known to be experienced in "little theater" productions; and it was suspected by Jack Kelley, among others, that he had rehearsed the witnesses in the dramatic effects that might be achieved in the course of their testimony. But it is doubtful if even Clarence Darrow expected anything quite as spectacular as Massie's testimony.

Kelley watched sharply. The introduction of this unnecessary and overemphasized testimony reflecting Thalia Massie's possible doubt as to the identity of the boys she had accused and identified—in the form of her protest to the contrary—as, as Kelley later phrased it, "an unexpected windfall." Yet it set the stage for the most dramatic turn of the trial.

Massie had continued, after a brief pause, to describe the events that followed on the night of the attack. He told of the examination of his wife by Lieutenant Commander John E. Porter, the Navy physician, and Dr. Paul Withington of Honolulu; the discovery of her broken jaw. With raw harshness, he told of the surgical operations performed, the wiring of her jaw, the extraction of a tooth from the swollen and broken jaw to make healing possible. "They made me hold her hand," he said. "I saw the whole thing. They

233

had to cut away her gums, and I thought she was asleep. But suddenly she screamed."

Kelley's other "windfall" came almost accidentally. Massie had described in detail his wife's account of what happened after she left the Ala Wai Inn "around 12 o'clock" to go for a walk and get some air. He described how she was beaten in the car, noting that he had asked her "which one beat her the most and she said one was Chang and the other was Kahahawai—but Kahahawai had beaten her more than any!"

He told how she had suffered during the nights, after the jaw surgery; and at one time he said she awakened screaming: "Don't let them get me!"

"I comforted her," Massie said. "I told her there was no one there but myself, but she said, 'Yes, Kahahawai was here!'"

All this, Massie said, was wearing on his nerves. He went back to the Submarine Base at Pearl Harbor and reported for duty, but during the nights "the whole thing would come back to me and I would get up at night and pace the floor . . . and then I would see a picture of her . . . her crushed face."

"Ever get that out of your mind?" Darrow asked.

"Never."

It was at this point in Massie's testimony that he mentioned the matter of pregnancy. "The danger of this preyed on my mind," he said. "After Mrs. Massie's mother came, we knew an operation was necessary to prevent pregnancy.

"Did you know she was pregnant?" Darrow asked.

"There couldn't be any doubt about it," Massie replied.

Kelley knew this was a major flaw in Massie's testimony. He had in his briefcase, on the table, a copy of an official report of Thalia Massie's operation at the Kapiolani Maternity Home, signed by her physician, Dr. Paul Withington. She was admitted to the Kapiolani hospital on October 13, 1931, and placed in room No. 2. The signed report of her case follows:

Patient has not menstruated since being assaulted on September 13, 1931, and in view of circumstances it is deemed advisable to currette her. Consultant, Dr. Porter. [Lieutenant, Commander John E. Porter]

Postoperative diagnosis: Amenorrhea.
Condition of patient: Good.
Anaesthetic: Ethylene 25 minutes.
Findings: Cervix old bilateral tear. *Contents of uterus negative.*
   No enlargement. [Italics added]
What was done: D. & C. [Dilation and curetage]
Surgeon: Paul Withington.[3]

Whether Clarence Darrow knew of this report at this time is problematical; but certainly Tommy Massie knew the results of the dilation and curetage operation performed on his wife at the Kapiolani Maternity Hospital, which gave currency to the rumors she was pregnant, and which definitely proved she was not pregnant. And Jack Kelley knew about it, because he had the report.

The effort to introduce this proof that Thalia Massie had become pregnant as a result of the supposed assault on the Ala Moana Road was not contested by Kelley; nor was any effort made to impeach Massie's evidence. Nevertheless, Tommy Massie's testimony left no doubts in Kelley's mind as to the honesty of his testimony, or the integrity of the defense case. In effect, this set Kelley's course for the most dramatic dénouement of the trial.

The closing phases of the defense were marked by two events which, in retrospect, must be considered the major blunders of Clarence Darrow's handling of the case. The first was the introduction of psychiatric testimony.

Darrow was quite ill on Friday, and the trial sessions were adjourned until Saturday morning. Tommy Massie completed his story, explaining that he had "blanked out" as they questioned Joseph Kahahawai in the bedroom of Mrs. Fortescue's rented bungalow.

He told of taking the big Hawaiian into the house, threatening him with a gun and demanding a confession. According to Massie, Kahahawai finally blurted out:

"Yes, we done it."

At this point, Massie said, he lost all track of what happened. As Darrow defined it, Massie "held the gun" that shot Joseph Kahahawai. Beyond that, Massie remembered nothing.

Darrow announced at the beginning of Saturday's session:

"There has been some misunderstanding on this point. We believe a plea of 'not guilty' does not require that it be stated who fired the shot. But we are willing to say that the evidence shows that the defendant, Massie, now on the stand, held the gun when the shot was fired."

Kelley hammered away at the young Navy officer's story, but Massie sat grim-faced and apparently unmoved by Kelley's questions, replying to them briefly and without any change in his story. At one point, Kelley asked Massie where they put the remainder of the rope used to tie up the body of the dead Kahahawai. Massie hesitated an instant, started to speak, and then stopped. Finally he said: "I don't remember."

At another point, in his cross-questioning, Kelley had asked Massie why he went along on the trip to Koko Head with the body of the slain youth, presumably to dispose of it in the Blow Hole. Massie shook his head; later, as Kelley continued his questioning, Massie suddenly said: "I know why I went now. Jones told Mrs. Fortescue to take me along to get some fresh air. I remember him saying that."

Prosecuting Attorney John C. Kelley examining evidence in the Massie-Fortescue trial.

236

An Error in Judgment

It is quite possible that if Clarence Darrow had known more about the undercurrents of racial feelings and the bitter hatreds brewed by the Ala Moana case in Honolulu, he would not have introduced "temporary insanity" and psychiatric testimony into the Massie-Fortescue trial. He would have relied on the theory of "an honor slaying"—the code of honor that might justify a husband's killing a man who had criminally assaulted his wife.

Certainly, if he had understood the processes of the Oriental mind—and there were three Chinese on the jury—he would not have relied on the *pro forma* defense that Tommy Massie was suddenly insane at the moment Joseph Kahahawai purportedly confessed.

But as has been noted, Darrow was getting along in years, and although he had not lost the fighting character of his earlier trials, he must have lost some of the mental agility which had made him the greatest criminal lawyer of his time. In any event, he missed what Jack Kelley thoroughly understood: that a pair of psychiatrists, considered among the rank and file of Honolulu to be little more or less than "witch doctors," would not be the means of saving his clients.

The two defense alienists, Dr. Williams and Dr. Orbison, pondered hypothetical questions for two days and came up with the same results on all questions; Dr. Orbison described the hypothetical situation which he had gleaned from examining young Massie as "shock amnesia"—a "mental bomb" that exploded in Massie's mind when Kahahawai is supposed to have said, "Yes, we done it."

Dr. Orbison opened his testimony by taking a few pot shots at "psychologists" as opposed to "psychiatrists," apparently in anticipation of the possibility that Dr. Stanley D. Porteus, professor of clinical psychology at the University of Hawaii, might be called by the prosecution.

Then he launched into a vivid description of what must have gone on in Massie's mind when Kahahawai supposedly "confessed." Under some rather pointed cross-examining by Barry Ulrich, who noted that "amnesia" was not a legal insanity defense, the Mainland doctor changed his terminology to "an uncontrollable impulse" which presumably took possession of the young Naval officer when he was confronted with what he regarded as "direct and final proof that this was the man that assaulted his wife."

Dr. Williams contributed much the same opinion, except that he called it "somnambulistic ambulatory automatism" and described it as "a walking daze, in which a person may move about but is not aware what is happening." Darrow, leading him through the maze of complex terminology, asked if "this disease is curable" and Dr. Williams quickly assured him it was. He even went into the glandular conditions that contributed to this state of mind, or lack of it, and wound up by stating:

"In my opinion, he became insane the moment he heard the words of Kahahawai."

Ulrich battered away at Dr. Williams for a while, but since neither Ulrich nor the jury seemed to understand what the doctor had said, and there was some possibility the doctor didn't, either, the whole thing went down in the records under the baseball nomenclature of "no hits, no runs, no errors"—except, perhaps, for the general error of having introduced this testimony in the first place.

However, it became necessary, in Kelley's view, to counterattack; and by the end of the week he had two psychiatrists of his own on the ground. These were Dr. Joseph Catton of Stanford University and Dr. Paul Bowers of Los Angeles. They were not due to arrive, however, until the weekend.

Ulrich, in his cross-examination of Dr. Orbison, had asked one searching question:

"Your testimony, Dr. Orbison, is based solely on one assumption —the truth of Lieutenant Massie's story, that is that he believed Joseph Kahahawai was the man who attacked his wife, isn't that so? If those facts fail, your story fails, and your testimony is value-less. Isn't that so?"

Dr. Orbison pondered a moment, and then said this was correct. Darrow stared at the tall, dignified Honolulu lawyer, as if he would try to read Ulrich's mind. There seemed to be a moment of un-certainty in the old lawyer's eyes, as if he were not sure whether or not the prosecution was getting ready to challenge the basic posi-tion of the defense—that is, that Tommy Massie believed Kahahawai was guilty of attacking his wife at the time he shot him.

Ulrich quickly veered away from this point, however.

"Would you say that it is impossible that Massie could be telling a lie—that is malingering in his testimony? Isn't it usual in cases of this sort for the defendant to simulate insanity and then hire expert witnesses who can testify in support of this pose?"

This aroused Dr. Orbison's ire to the extent that he appealed to Judge Davis, saying that Ulrich was asking questions "so mean that I cannot answer him." The two exchanged invectives for several minutes, the purport of which seemed to be a question of which profession was more subject to the enticement of money in rendering professional judgments—a lawyer or a psychiatrist. Judge Davis finally asked them to continue with the testimony, and Ulrich fired his parting shot:

"You think Massie is quite sane at present?"

Dr. Orbison said, "Yes, of course."

"Just a one-killing man," Ulrich said. "That's all."

A Question of Privilege

On Wednesday, April 20, Thalia Massie was called to the stand. In many ways she was the most important witness for the defense of her husband and mother and the two sailors accused of the "honor slaying" in her behalf. It was she who had suffered most—except for the slain Hawaiian boy; and as she took the witness stand, her pallid face showed the scars of surgery on her jaw and the emotional ravages of the past six months. She turned and looked squarely at the lawyers ranged in front of her.

The courtroom was filled—as it had been for most of the trial. In the forefront was the assembly of local white women, who paid daily tribute to the accused, sighing sorrowfully, almost in a body, as the defendants paraded up the aisle to take seats behind the lawyers' table. Many of these onlookers had hired stand-ins to hold seats for them, so that they might arrive at the courthouse at their leisure. Others stood in line in the corridor and scrambled for seats as soon as the courtroom doors were opened at 9 o'clock in the morning.

Thalia Massie took the stand at 10:53 A.M. on Wednesday. She was dressed in a dark suit, and had removed her hat, so that her fawn-colored hair, drawn tightly around her head, set off her pale features. Her blue-gray eyes, more prominent than ever in her drawn face, stared almost defiantly at the lawyers and the others before her.

Below, behind the lawyers' table, her mother sat rigidly in her chair, beside Thalia's husband. The two enlisted men, Lord and Jones, sat near Lieutenant Johnson at the lawyers' table. Massie sat for the most part with his head bowed, sometimes holding his face in his hands.

Several days before this session of the trial, a professor from the University of Hawaii, Dr. E. Lowell Kelley, had dropped in at Jack Kelley's office at City Hall and showed him some papers. They were records of an examination taken in a course in psychology at the summer session of the University the previous summer. One of the examination papers was that of Thalia Massie.

Kelley looked them over and laughed slightly. He put the papers in his drawer, and except for showing them to a couple of newspapermen, he had not attached any particular importance to the matter. They merely reflected Thalia Massie's answers to certain questions of psychology. One set of questions had to do with marriage; the questions were: "Are you married? If so, are you happily married?" The answers required were merely "yes" or "no"; but on this subject Thalia Massie had written some rather extensive answers, covering the margins and the back of the paper. Kelley shoved them in his briefcase, however, on the morning Thalia Massie was to testify.

When Thalia had identified herself and taken an oath to "tell the truth, the whole truth, and nothing but the truth," she sat down. Darrow had gotten up and walked part way down the aisle to meet her; now he stood at one side of the witness chair.

Darrow led her gently through a series of questions, most of which concerned the night at the Ala Wai Inn. Kelley got to his feet several times, and objected to Darrow's "retrying the Ala Moana case."

Darrow nodded agreeably. A master of courtroom technique, he had no intention of letting Jack Kelley break into the drama of his presentation. At Judge Davis' suggestion, he said he would confine his questions to "what Massie told her and what she told Massie."

"When did you next see Tommy—after you left the inn?" he asked.

Thalia Massie's figure stiffened suddenly, and her eyes filled with tears. She was trembling visibly. "As soon as I heard his voice on the telephone I asked him to please come home—something terrible had happened."

At that point she broke down completely, holding her face in her hands and sobbing audibly. Darrow stood beside her, looking at her closely. Mrs. Fortescue, who had been watching with bright eyes, suddenly stood up and took a glass of water from the table, which she handed to George Leisure. He took it up to the girl on the stand.

Thalia Massie finally straightened up and dabbed at her eyes. Then, twisting her handkerchief in her hands, she said:

"He asked me what happened. I didn't want to tell him because it was so terrible. I finally told him . . . that they had beaten me and raped me."

The women in the front rows—most of them middle-aged—sighed in a gusty exhalation. Some of them were weeping, patting their eyes with handkerchiefs. Kelley, hunched at the prosecution table, watched impassively as she continued in a halting voice to describe what happened. Once or twice he half stood up, as if to object; and then he sat down again.

She continued to describe the events of that night. "Chang got out of the car first," she said. "He said, 'Come on, baby—you're going for a ride!' They drove me down the Ala Moana . . . out into the bushes. Chang and Kahahawai dragged me out. I tried to hold back, and Kahahawai hit me." She dropped her head for a moment.

"Did you tell him [Lieutenant Massie] what they did?" Darrow asked, gently.

"Yes—I said they had raped me. That Kahahawai had broken my jaw. He wouldn't even let me pray," she suddenly said, in a harsh voice. Her hands were clenched and her words rang out sharply in the courtroom. "I told him he'd knocked my teeth out. He said, 'What do I care—shut up!' I said, 'Please don't hit me any more,' and he swore at me . . ."

Kelley finally arose from his chair. His neck was becoming red and his bald head was glowing like a sunset.

"I don't want to be interjecting objections," he said. "But she is only entitled to say what she told her husband."

Darrow turned sharply toward the prosecutor.

"This is hardly the time to be making objections," he said. His voice was low, but pitched in a hard, penetrating key.

"I haven't been making enough of them," Kelley snapped.

At this point, Thalia Massie broke down again and began sobbing. After a moment she continued, telling how she had identified her attackers at the hospital. She said when Kahahawai was there she had told Tommy Massie that he was the one who had hit her most.

"Tommy was there," she said, half sobbing. "Tommy asked me if I was sure, and I said, 'Yes—I'd never say he was if I was not positive.'"

She told of Massie's care for her during the time she was recovering.

"He took such good care of me . . . He was kind and attentive, and never minded how much I woke him up at night." Darrow

Thomas and Thalia Massie.

asked for a recess, and led her down to a chair beside her mother and Tommy Massie. When she resumed the stand, she told of the "rumors and stories" that were going around town.

"Tommy worried about them—I told him not to worry, but he kept on." She said he once told her it would be "wonderful" if they could get one of the Ala Moana boys to confess. Then, on the day Joseph Kahahawai was killed, she said Albert Jones, the sailor, came to her house in the morning and seemed "pale and trembling." He handed her a gun and said, "Here, take this."

She asked him what had happened, she said, and Jones replied: "Kahahawai has been killed!"

She said later a reporter from the Honolulu *Advertiser* talked with her, and she told him, "I'm sorry he has been shot, but it is no more than he deserved."

When Kelley arose from his chair to cross-examine Thalia Massie, there was little question in the mind of anyone who knew him that he was fighting mad. He asked several questions in sharp, clipped tones, about what happened when Jones arrived that morning; and in particular he wanted to know whether she had instructed her maid, Beatrice Nakamura, to say that Jones arrived at 8:30 A.M. She looked at Kelley for a few seconds, and then said sharply:

"No, that isn't so."

"Didn't you instruct her to say that Jones was there when she came?"

"Yes, but that isn't the same thing. She was there."

Kelley asked her if she remembered a telephone call by Jones to Lieutenant Leo L. Pace, commander of the *S-34,* the submarine on which Massie was stationed at Pearl Harbor, telling him: "Lee, cover him up—cover them all up."

"He wouldn't call a lieutenant he didn't even know by his first name."

"He called your husband 'Massie' at the police station," Kelley said.

She looked at him, her eyes glittering.

"He would never have done it in my presence!"

Kelley said:

"You have testified, Mrs. Massie, that your husband was always

244

kind and considerate to you—that there were never any quarrels. Is that correct?"

She nodded. "Yes, that is so."

Kelley walked back to the table. His face was red with anger; and he pulled out of his briefcase the paper Dr. Lowell Kelley had given him. He walked back to the witness chair, and handed it to Thalia Massie.

"Is that your handwriting, Mrs. Massie?"

She glanced over the paper, and then stared at the prosecutor.

"Where did you get this? You realize, of course, that this is a private and confidential matter?"

Kelley said, coldly:

"I'm asking questions—not answering them, Mrs. Massie. Is that your handwriting?"

She half rose from her chair, her voice suddenly quite shrill.

"I refuse to answer. This is a private matter between a patient and physician, and you have no right to bring it into open court like this!"

"Is this man a doctor?" Kelley demanded.

She said yes—he was.

She began to tear the document. Kelley watched her, without speaking. Suddenly the courtroom burst into applause, and some of the ladies in the front row stood up and cheered. Judge Davis banged his gavel so hard on the bench he broke the handle. The bailiff, Moses Kaululau, stood beside the jury box, his mouth open, staring at the girl on the witness stand.

Thalia Massie arose from the chair and walked down toward the place where her mother and husband were sitting. She ran the last few steps, clutching the torn strips of paper, and fell into Massie's arms. Kelley stared after her.

"Thank you, Mrs. Massie, for at last appearing in your true colors," he said, and walked over to the prosecution table and sat down. Darrow also got up from his chair. He asked that Kelley's remark be stricken from the record.

Judge Davis said it would be. He glared at the crowd, many of whom were still standing, applauding the girl who had just torn up the paper.

"There will be no further demonstrations in this court," he said sharply. "If there are, the court will be cleared!" He looked at Kelley. "Do you have any further questions, Mr. Kelley?"

Kelley shrugged, and shook his head. Thalia Massie was in her husband's arms, sobbing. "What right has he got to say I don't love you? Everybody knows I love you!"

Darrow looked over at Kelley, and then at the witness.

"The defense rests," he said.

The Morning After

The conclusion of Thalia Massie's testimony in the trial of her husband and mother had several repercussions. In the gathering places of Honolulu the opinions were varied. Racial problems take subtle forms; and there was no one, including Clarence Darrow and Walter Dillingham, that did not have to admit at this point that it was a racial problem.

When Thalia Massie tore up the document that seemed to allude to her personal life with her husband, it raised numerous specters. The most immediate reaction of the *haole* community was an attitude of praise. The white people who cheered for her in the courtroom still cheered for her; the *malihini haoles* in particular were filled with admiration for what she had done. Many of them wanted to know how a "confidential document" such as a psychology test at the University of Hawaii had found its way into the hands of the Public Prosecutor. But the dark-skinned people—Hawaiians and part-Hawaiians—wondered why she tore it up.

The Honolulu Medical Association had a different reaction. Dr. Joseph E. Strode, president of that august body, called a meeting for the following Friday night to find out whether a "privileged communication" had been, in fact, divulged to the public. As a matter of record, the meeting debated the matter and wound up by defining the word "doctor." A resolution was passed noting that no medical doctor had violated the oath of secrecy between physician and patient, and suggested that the difference between a medical doctor and an ordinary doctor, like Lowell Kelley, be more clearly defined in the law.

Attorney General Harry Hewitt was prevailed upon to rule on the matter, and he made public a statement that the document torn up by Thalia Massie on the witness stand "was not a privileged communication," and in fact it could have been subpoenaed by Kelley from the records of the University of Hawaii if he had so wished, providing the University kept records of examinations. A few people thought Dr. Stanley Porteus, director of clinical psychology at the University, was responsible for the whole business, and probably instigated it. A reporter for the *Advertiser* asked him about it and was told to "go to hell."

Jack Kelley was frankly nonplussed by the whole situation. As he explained to reporters, "I got mad when she tried to pull that lovey-dovey stuff, and so I showed her that paper. Maybe I shouldn't have done it."

The man who most clearly realized what had happened was Clarence Darrow. He knew the damage had been done. The jury empaneled to try the case was, as Walter Dillingham had said, "an exceptionally fine jury." The question an unbiased juror was going to ask himself was: Why did Thalia Massie tear up that document? What was she trying to hide? There had been ugly suspicions and rumors circulating around the town after the Ala Moana trial; reports of fabricated evidence, lying by witnesses. And there was the unvarnished fact that only two of Thalia Massie's friends from the Navy—Lieutenant Tom Brown and his wife—had appeared to testify for her. There were many angles to the case that had never been explained.

The furor and fanfare might go on among the townsfolk, pro and con; but in the quiet seclusion of the jury room, each juror would remember that she had destroyed a piece of evidence, and would wonder why she had done it.

The two psychiatrists that Kelley had brought down from the coast—Dr. Catton and Dr. Bowers—were due to testify Saturday in rebuttal. There had been a brief court session Friday, in which Kelley asked that it be made a matter of record that the document torn up by Thalia Massie was "not a privileged communication."

Kelley turned to Darrow, who sat morosely in his chair.

"I think Counsel will agree," he said.

Darrow nodded. "I don't think it was privileged under the laws," he said, and the trial was then held over until Saturday morning.

At this point another issue was arising that obsessed the curb-stone lawyers of Honolulu: If Tommy Massie, named as the killer of Joseph Kahahawai, was declared "temporarily insane," what would happen to the other three defendants? Would they be guilty of a crime, or would they be exonerated?

Defense counsel had prepared an instruction, to be submitted to Judge Davis, covering this point. "If Massie was insane," Mont-gomery Winn had pointed out to newspapermen, "no crime was committed. If there was no crime, how can anyone be held as an accomplice or accessory?"

The instruction they submitted said: "One cannot be convicted as an aider or abettor if a person charged as a principal was not crim-inally responsible for his acts, because of his lack of mental capacity or extreme youth."

After considerable digging into law books, it was discovered that there was no precedent for this situation under Territorial court decisions or the law. The issue therfore was likely to resolve itself into the matter of the kidnaping of Kahahawai, which was a felony, or forcible detention, which was a misdemeanor. After this was kicked around the clubs and street corners for a day or so, it seemed possible that the "mystery law"—or lack of it—covering the relations of Massie's three accomplices to the killing, might prove the determining factor in the jury's final verdict.

Darrow and Leisure had refused to permit the two prosecution psychiatrists, Drs. Catton and Bowers, to examine Massie. Their contention was that it would be of no value to examine him at this time, since no one claimed he was insane three months after the killing of Joseph Kahahawai. Kelley replied with considerable sar-casm that "if that sort of testimony has no value for the alienists we have here to testify, why does it have value for the defense psychiatrists—who never talked with Massie until long after the killing?"

Dr. Joseph Catton was expected to be the big seige gun of the prosecution. He had acquired considerable fame as a "debunker" of psychiatric testimony; and since the defense now relied wholly on the theory that Massie was "temporarily insane" when Kahahawai was killed, Darrow marshalled all his artillery against the Stanford expert.

This was, in a sense, the old warrior's last stand. It was, in fact, Clarence Darrow's last criminal trial; he never took another case and he died a few years after the Massie-Fortescue trial. Prior to the two psychiatrists' appearance, Kelley brought in Mapuana Peters, a stenographer at the City Hall and the daughter of former Chief Justice E. C. Peters of Hawaii. She was a quiet, intelligent girl; and her testimony was impressive. She had been present at the interrogation of Tommy Massie immediately after his arrest, and had taken down his statement.

Chief Inspector John McIntosh had asked Massie if he had been at Pearl Harbor that morning, prior to the kidnaping of Kahahawai —presumably to get the coil of rope.

"I have no statement to make," Massie said.

"Any statements about your actions or movements?"

"None whatever."

Kelley then asked Mapuana Peters to describe Massie's apparent state of mind at this time—12:10 P.M., on January 8, about two hours after the killing at which he was presumed by the defense to have gone "temporarily insane."

"He was quite calm," she said. "He seemed to know exactly what he was talking about. He spoke in a calm, level voice."

Dr. Bowers contributed more or less theoretical comments on Massie's state of mind at the time of the shooting; he said he had to rely on witnesses, such as Miss Peters, since he had been denied an opportunity to examine Massie himself. But he had dug into his background, however, and he began to bring the focus of plain understanding into what had been a confused picture.

He said there was nothing particularly abnormal in Massie's early history. He grew up in military surroundings, attended the Naval Academy, "where any fundamental traits of character, neurotic or psychotic tendencies" would probably have been observed.

"Nothing in his record would indicate that he was subject to states of delirium or loss of memory," he said. "In my opinion, he was not insane."

At only one point did Darrow try to interrupt Dr. Bowers' testimony. That was when the psychiatrist started to say: "He had information that his wife suffered from"—

Darrow jumped up and tried to stop him, but Dr. Bowers went on:

—"suffered from a dreadful experience." Darrow sat down.

"Doesn't this go to the heart of your case?" Barry Ulrich asked Darrow. The old man nodded. "I have no objection," he said. Ulrich turned to Dr. Bowers.

"If it is your testimony that Thomas Massie thought the law had failed, is it also your testimony that he must have been insane to act as he did?"

Dr. Bowers shook his head. Darrow started to rise again, but sat down. It seemed that he had let the door open, and now he could not close it. Dr. Bowers then said: "The killing of an individual was part of a plan. He held a gun on this man, and had knowledge of the possible consequences of his act. He took deliberate and premeditated steps to gain his ends. I believe he weighed the probable consequences of his acts. He even wore goggles and gloves, to give the appearance of a chauffeur. He secured the automobile and made preparations for his act. After having committed the act— after having shot the man—he took steps to cover up his traces. At no time do I find any indication of insanity, or symptoms of insanity, in this sort of conduct."

Barry Ulrich had moved over to the end of the rail in front of the jury box. It happened that the three Chinese members of the jury were sitting at that end. Ulrich knew the psychology of Chinese people; they were coldly logical. Dr. Bowers' words, probably the clearest and most understandable language that had been offered on the complex subject of Massie's state of mind at the time Kahahawai was shot, were aimed directly at the three Chinese jurors sitting behind Ulrich.

Dr. Bowers concluded his testimony, and Darrow asked only one question:

"I assume you were paid—or expect to be paid—for coming down here?"

"Yes," Dr. Bowers said. "I do."

As the trial neared its end—Judge Davis said on Saturday he

hoped all the testimony would be in by then, but agreed to adjourn the trial until Monday to permit Dr. Catton to testify—it was apparent that Clarence Darrow was girding himself for a final effort to demolish the chain of facts and logic which Jack Kelley was forging around the four defendants.

He rose frequently from his chair while Dr. Catton was testifying; at times he paced back and forth in front of the jury box like an angry lion, shaking his head so that the unruly gray locks flipped from one side of his broad forehead to the other. For two hours he fought bitterly to discredit the cool logic of the psychiatrist from Stanford University. At the end, he seemed physically exhausted.

Dr. Catton's analysis of the case under direct examination was brief. He said Lieutenant Massie, steeped in the traditions of the Navy and the section of the country from which he came—the bluegrass lands of Kentucky—was suddenly confronted by the tragedy of the Ala Moana case, the attack on his young wife. "The horror of this," Dr. Catton said, "fixed in his mind ideas that any normal and sane young man would have under the circumstances."

When Massie lost confidence in the ability of legal machinery of the Territory to satisfy his need for justification of his own desires and vindication of his wife's honor, "he determined to take into his own hands the means of obtaining that justification." After kidnaping Kahahawai, holding a gun pointed at him, and shooting him—"for whatever reason"—young Massie had "behaved as any normal man would act" in seeking to "cover up traces of his act."

At one point Darrow rose and objected, his voice ringing out in the courtroom, to Dr. Catton's use of the words "alleged assailants" in referring to Kahahawai and the other four Ala Moana defendants.

"Don't you believe that story—of the rape?" Darrow thundered.

"I haven't had an opportunity to talk with your client," Dr. Catton said, in a quiet voice. He was a tall man, with a low, well-controlled voice, and he spoke with an attitude of authority that seemed to infuriate Darrow. "If you wish, I will refer to the men Massie believed had attacked his wife."

While Dr. Catton recited in slow, measured words his summary of the plan which he said Massie had laid out at "two meetings the night before, and a meeting the next morning," Darrow raged before the jury box, demanding that Dr. Catton be restrained from "summarizing this whole case." At this point, the gray-haired mother of Thalia Massie, who sat sternly throughout the previous days of trial, suddenly leaned over, her face in her hands, and began to sob. It was the first—and only—time during the trial that Mrs. Fortescue seemed to give way to her emotions.

When Dr. Catton reached the point where he was describing the scene at the Fortescue bungalow where Kahahawai was shot—taking his information from records of the trial itself—it was evident the jury was paying closer attention to his testimony than at any time during the previous assortment of monologues on the psychiatric aspects of the case. The men in the jury box leaned forward, listening intently. Darrow was not unaware of this; he kept glancing at the jurors, and at times jumped up and offered objections, usually couched in sarcastic terms, to break the flow of Dr. Catton's narrative.

When the psychiatrist referred to a "conflict of beliefs—the belief Massie held that Kahahawai had beaten and assaulted his wife, the belief of the populace—as indicated by the rumors he had heard—and the belief of the jurors who tried the case," Darrow arose and stood trembling before the jury box, wagging his large head back and forth, and roared his objection to "testimony that assumes a conflict—there was no conflict!"

"This California doctor doesn't know any more about what the populace thought than if he was in Australia," he said to Judge Davis. "He only knows what these lawyers"—he waved disparagingly at Kelley and Ulrich—"have told him!"

After some altercation with Kelley, Darrow sat down and Dr. Catton started to resume his testimony.

"Now you wait!" Darrow shouted, jumping up again. Then he sat down.

Dr. Catton continued calmly: "He [Massie] believed that some people believed his wife was not assaulted—that he, Massie, had beaten her up—that it was the result of her being with another Naval officer. We find him acting as a sane, normal, rational man in desiring justification against these rumors. I believe that he believed he could not depend upon the forces of law and order to work out his case—and he made the first step away from depending on legal and orderly processes."

This rather precise summary of the logic of lynching appeared to impress the jury quite as much as it disturbed Clarence Darrow. By the time Dr. Catton had concluded his statement of the case, describing the "normal fear-flight mechanism" in the acts which followed the shooting of Kahahawai, the case of "somnambulistic ambulatory automatism" and whatnot, propounded by the two defense doctors, seemed to have been completely demolished along with the theory of "temporary insanity."

Darrow sought for an hour of savage cross-questioning to break down Dr. Catton's story. At one point he asked Dr. Catton if he remembered the verdict in a case in which he had testified that the accused killer was insane.

"It was eight or nine years ago," the doctor said.

"You can't remember the verdict?"

"I think it was manslaughter."

"Do you have amnesia?" Darrow asked, with heavy sarcasm.

"I can't remember what I had for breakfast last Thursday, either," Dr. Catton said evenly. "I'm amnesic about that."

The Verdict—and the Penalty

The closing hours of the Massie-Fortescue trial were in many ways among the bitterest in the history of Hawaii. They laid bare gaping wounds of racial hatreds which Clarence Darrow had hoped to heal. To the people of Honolulu it was akin to the horrible experience of discovering insanity in the family.

Darrow planned to close for the defense; but George Leisure, the New York lawyer—who had few illusions about sentiment in a murder trial—was chosen to summarize the case for "honor slaying." Without once referring to it, and even specifically denying that the defense relied upon it, he nevertheless made plain that the fundamental issue for the defense was the right of a man to kill to protect his wife's honor.

He spoke of "the shame of a living death—the shame that has no compensation and no end," that would hound a man for life who failed to act in such a crisis. Leaning forward over the jury rail, as if he would project his ideas forcibly into their minds, Leisure said the jury "must decide whether a husband whose wife had been ravished—and who kills the man that did it—shall spend his life behind dark prison walls, all because the shock proved too great for his mind."

Leisure trimmed his sails carefully in order to remain in legal waters. He conceded that the law made killing a legal offense; but he insisted the law also covered a situation where a "compelling need" would force a man to an act that he would not have considered under normal circumstances. Fighting for one's life, he said, was one such need recognized by the law. Was not "fighting for a man's wife—fighting for her honor," an equal need?

Barry Ulrich, who led off for the prosecution, struck with equal vigor and equal knowledge of the law. He agreed that there were cases in which the law permitted the taking of life—such as self-defense.

Then his voice suddenly rose, almost for the first time during the trial.

"But you cannot make Hawaii safe against rape by licensing murder," he thundered. "You cannot use a plea of insanity as a peg on which to hang this verdict!" And he then took a shot which probably penetrated more deeply than anything any of the alienists had said.

"You jurors—the judge of this court—the people of Hawaii, all of us, are on trial. We have been charged with not being able to govern ourselves. You twelve people have the responsibility of answering that charge. Will you vote for the irresponsible acts of 'lynch law'—or will you vote for law and order?"

The bitterness that lay behind the Territory's experiences of the past few months—and which was to beset them not only in the months but in the years to come—probably was not understood by Darrow and Leisure. Their contacts in Honolulu, as had been noted, were with the *haole* elite, the "leading citizens" and the *malihini haoles* from the Navy. It is doubtful if the underlayer of public sentiment that had festered like a closed wound since the Ala Moana trial was thoroughly understood by any of the battery of defense counsel—any more than it was understood by Admiral Stirling.

But Kelley and Ulrich understood it; and so did the members of the jury, who were all citizens of Honolulu. It was on this point that the original miscalculation by Darrow had its most damaging effect. He had failed to take into account what was perhaps the most important single factor in the whole case—the racial conflicts that had grown out of the Ala Moana case.

Leisure, for example, discussed the Ala Moana case as if it were a *fait accompli*—and yet a jury in Honolulu had failed to agree on a verdict. The four remaining defendants were still free on bail, with a legal presumption of innocence. Even Walter Dillingham, in his memorable "memorandum," published privately a few weeks later, had written:

> There is still in the minds of a great many people of all nationalities, a feeling of doubt as to the guilt of the accused [in the Ala Moana case].[1]

Clarence Darrow obviously sensed this situation, but he did now know to deal with it. At a gathering of newspapermen in his room one evening, during the trial, he had repeated what he had said earlier: "The important point is not whether these five boys were guilty of attacking Massie's wife; the important point is that Massie *believed* they were guilty."

Leisure said further, in his summation:

"We are making no plea under the unwritten law. We are making no plea that a man can go and kill. This man waited three months before he acted—and then why did he act? To get a confession—the one thing in the world that would have helped his case."

Had Leisure understood better the temper and feelings of the "populace" in Honolulu, he probably would never have made this point. As Dillingham noted in his "memorandum": "The feeling of the town after Kahahawai was killed was obviously divided. Many expressed satisfaction over his having been slain while others wished that he had been killed when he was first identified by Mrs. Massie. From the Oriental and Hawaiian quarter there was a strong feeling of resentment over the killing by lynch law."

The great industrialist did not explain why there was a "strong" opinion on the matter of "lynch law" in the "Oriental and Hawaiian quarter" as opposed to the *haole* segments of the population, where disagreement with lynching might have been expected to have the most widespread support. Perhaps he knew the *haole* elite better than most people, and had reasons for the inference. In any event, the defense appeared to have overlooked what might easily be the determining factor: Honolulans were by no means united on the *haole* assessment of the Ala Moana case.

There appears to be little doubt, in retrospect, that the outcome of the Massie-Fortescue trial—the legal fate of the four defendants— was decided in those last few days of the trial, culminating in the final clash between Clarence Darrow and Jack Kelley.

Darrow's Last Stand

Barry Ulrich had warned the jurors that if they "followed their feelings" in reaching a verdict—if they permitted sympathy, stirred by Thalia Massie's appearance as a witness, to color their judgment—they would destroy the administration of justice in Hawaii. "All of them have suffered terribly," he said. "But you will be told by the court that no man may take the law into his own hands —that no amount of prior suffering caused by another can justify taking the life of the man who caused it. It is your duty to reach a verdict on the facts—not to estimate the worth of the law."

There was a brief recess, and then Darrow arose from his chair and walked over to the jury box rail, where he stood for perhaps half a minute, looking at them and saying nothing. His face was drawn and almost gray. The steel-gray eyes which had ranged over the faces of the jurors hour after hour for three weeks now seemed weary. He finally said in a low, conversational tone:

"We are getting close to the end of this case, and probably all of you will be glad when it is over." He smiled, and several jurors smiled back.

It had become clear from the testimony of the last few days— particularly from Darrow's reaction to Dr. Catton's testimony that Massie's actions had been "normal and sane"—that the final argument between Darrow and Kelley would be on a basic difference in their interpretation of law and order. That was the unbridgeable chasm that divided them: their diverse concepts of law and justice. Darrow believed in "humanity" and all it stood for, in court and out of court. Kelley stood for the law. One would plead for understanding, sympathy, human tolerance; the other would ring down the

257

iron bars of the law and demand punishment for those who defied the law. Darrow made this clear in his first words.

". . . This case illustrates the mysterious workings of man and human destiny, illustrates the effect that grief and sorrow has upon human minds and upon human lives. It shows us how weak and powerless human beings can be in the hands of relentless circumstances."

The old man spoke at times with the ringing words of a prophet of old, calling upon the inescapable power of the human conscience. At times his voice was scathing in denunciation of "man-made laws" and those who would place these before the human needs of man. At other times he spoke as a friend, a neighbor or a minister might speak, talking of human destiny and the ills that befall men and women.

He traced the background of the defendants, Tommy Massie and Mrs. Fortescue, and of Thalia Massie—even though she was not one of the accused. "Eight months ago, Mrs. Fortescue lived in Washington, respected, known, moving along her way . . . Eight months ago Thomas Massie . . . was a lieutenant in the Navy, respected by his friends, intelligent, courageous, belonging to the most dangerous branch of the service. Eight months ago his young wife, handsome, attractive, intelligent, was known, respected and admired by the whole community. What has befallen this family in this short space of time? They are here today in the criminal court. The jury is asked to send them to prison for life.

"What has happened in this long series of events, beginning plainly at a certain time and ending—no one knows where?"

He looked at the faces of the jurors, as if to implant the words in their minds by the sheer force of his eyes. Then he shook his head.

"This is the hardest story in human history. In this case you see the fate of the whole family—their life, their future, their name—bound up in a criminal act committed by someone else in which they had no part."

He had spoken quietly and compassionately at first; but now he turned toward Kelley and Dr. Catton, who sat at the prosecution lawyers' table. His voice rang with scorn and anger.

"I listened to Dr. Catton spinning his story out of his head, and telling what the mind could do and what it couldn't do, like a spider sitting in his web, seeking to devour someone . . . What does he know about it? What does anyone else know about it? What do we all know about the workings of our minds, the small part we have of the workings of the human mind, and of all the forces that come together to make a human mind?"

Striding back and forth, his voice seldom raised except to direct a bitter blast at Kelley or Catton, the old man began to weave his magic spell of human understanding upon the twelve men in the jury box. For the most part they sat quietly, listening gravely and intently. Three of the jurors were Chinese, and they sat with impassive faces and inscrutable eyes. They had listened carefully throughout the trial; but as Darrow said frankly, after the trial, he doubted if he "ever got through to those Chinese fellows."

George Leisure had addressed his argument to a simple effort to find a legal pretext upon which the four could be set free under the "unwritten law." But Darrow directed his appeal to their hearts, not their minds or sense of logic. He began to dig deeply into "natural law" and the "forces of nature"—man's right to defend and protect the honor of his wife, and the laws of nature which cause a mother to protect her young.

"We contend in this case that for months Massie's mind had been affected by all that was borne upon him," he said. "Grief, sorrow, trouble, day after day, week after week, month after month."

He told of Thalia Massie walking out of the doorway of the Ala Wai Inn, bored with the party, as she had testified, "intending to go down the street and come back and join her husband again at the dance." The old man shook an admonishing finger, and his voice rang sharply.

"What did Massie learn from her a few hours later?" He turned and faced Thalia Massie. "An unbelievable story!" The girl looked at him, her heart-shaped face showing little expression. She seemed to have been drained of emotional reactions. Darrow, still looking at her, traced the story of the kidnaping and assault, as Thalia Massie told it on the stand in the Ala Moana trial. It was this story he had sought to keep out of testimony or argument in the trial, until he could introduce it with his own witnesses, under his skilled direction.

Now he described it with full effect.

"She was left on that lonely road," he said, "in pain and agony and suffering . . . the greatest humiliation a woman can suffer at the hands of man!" He described Massie's effort to find his wife, until he reached her by telephone and she sobbed: "Please come home! Something awful has happened!"

". . . A story as terrible, as cruel, as any story I have ever heard," Darrow said. " 'Hurry home—something terrible has happened to me!' You would think, on the presentation of a portion of this case, the efforts of the prosecution"—he waved at Kelley—"to send this family to prison, that she had done something, or that they had done something, instead of being harmless and subject to the cruel fate which overhangs them!"

Darrow traced the story detail by detail, describing her hurt face, her broken jaw, the weeks of suffering. At this point, for the first time in his summation, he spoke of "the other stories"—the "vile stories that spread over Honolulu."

"No one raised even a doubt about her story," he said, "except for the originators of a few vile slanders that were carried from tongue to tongue. Has anybody placed a finger upon a single fact to contradict the saddest tale that was ever brought to a husband? If they have, they have kept this tale for eight long months and possibly it was necessary to save their own freedom."

Kelley glanced up from his note pad, on which he had been scribbling; and for the first time since Darrow started speaking, Kelley's sharp blue eyes displayed a thoughtful interest. Why had Darrow raised this point? Whether he had studied the record of the Ala Moana case with care, or whether he had chosen simply to disregard the "alibi testimony" produced by the defense in that trial, was problematical. He never, to the writer's knowledge, discussed this aspect of the case with newspapermen, during or after the trial, except to point out that the issue was not the guilt or innocence of Joseph Kahahawai, but the fact that Massie *thought* he was guilty.

Nevertheless, this unexpected reference to those who may have remained silent because "it was necessary to save their own freedom" came as a surprise to Kelley. If Darrow believed there were suspects other than the Ala Moana defendants, he made no effort to reconcile this with his remark that there was not "a single fact" to contradict Thalia Massie's story. Did Darrow actually believe there might be others—that Thalia Massie had identified the wrong suspects? If not, why did he refer to those who remained silent?

This may have been a critical point in the case; but Darrow chose to ignore the issue. His only reference to any other story was his effort to justify the defense contention that Tommy Massie had been driven to the brink of insanity and was "temporarily insane" when he killed Kahahawai.

"Out of the clear air, with nothing on which to rest, strange, slanderous stories were spread over these Islands about Lieutenant Massie and his ravished wife. Stories that she had never been raped . . . stories that this husband of hers, whose faithfulness has been been plainly evident to every person who sat in this courtroom during these long, trying days—that this husband broke his wife's jaw!"

Darrow turned from Massie to the gray-haired lady from Kentucky, Mrs. Grace Fortescue. She had remained in her chair, stiff and silent in unbending dignity throughout the ordeal of the trial, breaking into low sobs only once—when Dr. Joseph Catton of Stanford was testifying, reviewing the story Thalia Massie had told her husband.

"Gentlemen," Darrow said in a low voice, "I wonder what fate has against this family, anyhow? I wonder when it will get through taking its toll and leave them to go in peace? . . . Here is the mother." He pointed to Mrs. Fortescue. "What about her?"

He told how Massie had cabled his mother-in-law after the assault on Thalia Massie. "And she came," Darrow said. "Five thousand miles over land and sea." He spoke of eulogies that had been written about mothers, and then, his voice almost inaudible to all except the jurors, he said:

"I don't want to bring forth further eulogies. . . . I want to call your attention to something more primitive. . . . It is not a case of the greatness of a mother. It is the case of what nature has done. I don't care whether it is a human mother, or the mother of beasts or birds in the air. They are all alike. To them there is one all-important thing and that is a child they carried in their womb, and without that feeling there would be no life preserved upon this earth."

He stood squarely for a moment in front of the jurors, his feet spread slightly apart, part of his hair falling over his eyes.

"There she is—that mother—in this courtroom! She is waiting to go to the penitentiary. All right, gentlemen—go to it! Let me say this. If this husband and this mother go to the penitentiary, it won't be the first time a penitentiary has been sanctified by its inmates . . . When people come to your beautiful Island, one of the first places they will want to see is the prison where this mother and this husband are confined.

"Men will wonder how it happened and will marvel at the injustice and cruelty of men, and will pity the inmates and blame fate for this cruelty, the persecution and the sorrow that has followed this family!"

With his great head thrust forward, his shaggy locks of unruly hair still hanging over his forehead, Darrow seemed to glare at the jurors. Then he turned and walked back and forth for a few seconds, still shaking his head.

"Gentlemen," he said, turning toward them again, "you are asked to send these people to the penitentiary. Do you suppose if you—and you—and you"—he stretched out his hands, as if he would lay the message of mercy physically upon their heads—"if you had been caught in the hands of fate, do you suppose you would have done differently?

"Life comes from the devotion of mothers, of husbands, of the love of man and women . . . When this dies in the human heart, then this world will be desolate and cold and the earth will take its lonely course around the sun, without a human heartbeat, with nothing except thin air . . ."

Darrow turned and shook his finger at Kelley, who was sitting hunched over the prosecution table, watching Darrow with implacable blue eyes.

"Every instinct that moves human beings, every feeling that moves the mother of an animal, is with us in this case. You can't fight against it! If you do, you will fight against nature! . . . What a theory!"

It was at this point that Darrow seemed to have reached the highest moment of drama in his supreme appeal to the "natural law" of mother-love. But what he must have forgotten—and Jack Kelley did not—was that every man and woman of Hawaiian blood in the courtroom knew there was another mother there. That was the mother of Joseph Kahahawai.

"Let me say to you," Darrow continued, wagging his finger at the jurors like an angry schoolmaster, "that if on top of all else that has been heaped upon the devoted heads of this family, if they should be sent to prison, it would place a blot on the fair name of these Islands that all the Pacific seas would never wash away!"

He spoke of "something deep in the instincts of man, a yearning for justice, of what is right and wrong, of what is fair between man and man, that came before the first law was written and will abide after the last law is dead." Again and again he turned from the letter of the law to man's inherent need for human justice. "How much would you, and you, and you"—again pointing to the jurors, one by one—"how much can any human mind stand? Some men have gone insane by a word, by fear, by fright . . . others by slow degree."

He described Massie's long nights of suffering as he watched over his wife. "He began to think of vindicating his wife. She had been lied about." At one point he turned and pointed directly at Kelley. He had just told of some evidence presented by the Territory, which concerned an incident years before in Sayville, New York, where the Fortescues had lived. Young Massie and Thalia—then Thalia Fortescue—had taken a baby carriage with a small baby in it, and pushed it up the street; and when the frightened mother overtook them, they were arrested. "The police court the next morning dismissed the case! My God—what are you thinking of? Mrs. Massie was then seventeen—stealing a new-born baby? And yet that prank was introduced into this court—where they are trying to land Massie and Mrs. Fortescue in prison. There are some things that even a prosecutor should not do . . ."

He turned back to the jury.

"Gentlemen, why should it be? Why should any one man in this world want to accomplish the destruction of someone else? I don't believe you could find any twelve men in the world who would want to accomplish this wicked design."

Kelley, scribbling notes on his pad, smiled and shook his head.

Darrow referred only briefly to the two sailors, Albert Jones and Edmund Lord. "Are Jones and Lord, two common seamen, bad? Jones was faithful, he was loyal when a shipmate asked for help. Was this bad? There are so many ways to measure goodness and badness. They went along in case they were needed. There isn't a single thing these two boys did that should bring censure."

In dwelling mainly on the human factors, the sufferings and the instincts of those most concerned—Thalia Massie's husband and her mother—Darrow made little mention of the facts in the case, the iron chain of evidence which Kelley had forged. And at only one point did he touch upon the issue which perhaps most deeply concerned the people of Hawaii—the racial issue. In its simplest terms, this issue was the growing feeling among Hawaiians and other non-whites that there was one law for the dark-skinned people in the Territory, and another for the whites.

Near the close of his four-hour summation, Darrow stood at the rail, his hands resting on it, and said softly:

"Let me say one last word. I should be sorry to leave this beautiful land with the thought that I had made anyone's life harder . . . that I had compared any one class against another class. I have all the sympathy and understanding to make these Islands happier instead of creating more pain. I never knew what it was in my life to have any feeling of prejudice against any race on earth." He turned and again looked directly at Jack Kelley. "And I defy anyone to find a single word of mine or a line I have written that would contradict what I say."

Darrow's last remarks were the valedictory of an old warrior who had defended men of all degrees of guilt and innocence, and all stations in life, because—as he once said to the writer—"if a human life is worth anything, it is worth saving."

"There it is," he said finally to the jury. "Take it, gentlemen. Take these poor, suffering people—not in anger, but in cool judgment, in pity and understanding . . . I have no feeling on account of race against the four or five men who assaulted Mrs. Massie—and my clients knew that when I took the case.

"Take it broadly . . . take it humanly. You have in your hands not only the fate, but the life of these poor people. What is there for them if you pronounce a sentence of doom upon them? You are in a position to heal, not to destroy . . . to bind up wounds. This case is in your hands, and I ask you to be kind and understanding and considerate, both to the living and to the dead."

Darrow walked over to his chair and sat down. He seemed utterly spent, and for a time he sat at the table, his face in his hands. Judge Davis ordered a brief recess—from 2:23 to 2:37 P.M.—and then Jack Kelley arose and walked over, holding a roll of notes in his hand.

It was evident from the first words of the young Irish prosecutor that he intended to take up the challenge exactly as Darrow laid it down. The old man had preached a sermon on human pity; Kelley intended to preach one on the law.

"I stand before you for the law," he said, "opposed to those who have violated the law and those who ask you to violate the law."

He turned and regarded Darrow thoughtfully for a moment. Then his voice rang harshly in the courtroom. "Are you going to decide this case on the plea of a man who for fifty years has stood before the bar of justice which he belittles today, or are you going to decide this case on the law?"

He aimed a finger at Tommy Massie, sitting beside his wife, his thin-featured face almost ashen from the strain of the four weeks of trial.

"They ask you why Massie should take upon himself the blame for shooting Kahahawai. I'll tell you why. Because he couldn't hide behind the skirts of his mother-in-law. He couldn't blame those two men whom he had inveigled into this case. I am going to paint a picture of a conceited, vain, egotistical individual who is responsible for what happened since September 12—the selfishness of the man who insisted that his wife go to a party she didn't want to go to. Clarence Darrow tells you he is a brave, frank witness."

Kelley seemed almost to snort as he spoke. In contrast with Darrow, who had rested his aging body on the rail of the jury box most of the time, Kelley stood squarely on his feet, his white suit gleaming against the dark panels of the old courtroom.

"I can show you evasion after evasion in this witness," Kelley thundered. "His actions are the basis of everything that happened, and his actions caused the death of Joseph Kahahawai. That is the clear issue in this case—not sympathy or insanity."

Kelley turned directly toward Darrow.

"The defense counsel, headed by a man who has distinguished himself during his entire career by disparaging the law, has been hedging and whipsawing back and forth, proceeding on one theory and then another. It was only after the greatest pressure that they reluctantly admitted that Thomas Massie fired the shot that killed Joseph Kahahawai.

"The great Darrow told you it didn't make any difference who fired the shot. That was the story they relied upon. Then he asks you to believe that Massie fired the shot—because he couldn't hide behind the skirts of his mother-in-law! He couldn't put the blame on the two enlisted men. So Massie took the blame—and it is labeled temporary insanity."

Kelley turned and pounded his fist on the rail before the jurors.

"Since the case of Harry Thaw, that defense has been the sheet-anchor for the rich and influential, so they can hire liars as experts and put on a defense of insanity. That was what was done in this case. This defense is not insanity; it is sympathy."

He turned toward the white-haired Hawaiian woman—Esther Anito, the mother of the dead Kahahawai—who was sitting quietly behind the lawyers' table.

"They tried to keep that poor mother off the stand—because they said it was an appeal to sympathy. But Massie was willing to sacrifice that girl"—he pointed to Thalia Massie, sitting beside her husband—"he was willing to sacrifice her on the altar of his own ego, to put her on the stand and make a Roman holiday for this claque that came to cheer for her"—he waved at the phalanx of middle-aged women, mostly white, who still sat in the front row of seats—"so that a demonstration could be staged that was a disgrace to this court and the whole territory!"

Kelley had been standing on the edge of the platform, facing the crowd of onlookers. There were some gasps of astonishment, but Judge Davis rapped his gavel and the noises subsided. The Prosecutor turned back to the jurors.

"Let us suppose," he said quietly, "that this defense they offer is an honest defense. Let us suppose they entered into a plan to get a confession, and that Massie went insane? Where were Massie's brave comrades at the Submarine Base—the officers, Pace, Wortman, Brown and Branson—who knew his mind and had followed his sufferings? Where were they when he made his plans? Why did he have to get enlisted men to carry out his plan? Was it solely to get a confession?"

Kelley began to trace Massie's own testimony at the trial. Referring to Clarence Darrow's statement that Massie had told a "straight story," Kelley asked:

"Was it straight?" He walked back to the lawyers' table and picked up a heavy sheaf of papers. It was the transcript of testimony. "He slipped twice," he said, holding the transcript before the jury. "Once I asked him if he put the coil of rope under the davenport. He started to say he was positive he did, and then he caught himself. He said he did not remember."

Kelley waved the transcript again.

"Well, the next time he didn't catch himself." He flipped over the pages of the transcript and read from page 478 a series of questions he had asked Massie. At one point Massie was asked why he had gone in the automobile that took away Kahahawai's body, and he said he did not remember.

Kelley, reading from the transcript, followed the questioning for several lines, and then he quoted Massie as suddenly saying:

"I know why I went now. Jones told Mrs. Fortescue to take me along to get some fresh air. I remember his saying that."

Kelley laid the transcript on the table, and turned to the jury.

"If he remembers that," he said, "he remembers everything that happened—and the insanity defense flies out the window like a little dove of peace."

Kelley—who lived in Honolulu and knew the speech habits of Hawaiians—struck at another point in Massie's story. He had testified that Joseph Kahahawai had said, "Yes—we done it!" and then Massie said he blanked out.

"No Hawaiian would ever say, 'We done it'," Kelley said. "He would have said 'We do it' or 'We been do it.' That is the Hawaiian vernacular. There is no past tense in the Hawaiian language and they don't use that vernacular, which is common on the mainland."

Darrow had talked for four hours; and Kelley had talked less than an hour when he finally turned to the jury.

"You have the most vital duty to perform of any twelve men who ever sat on a jury box under the American flag. Do not pay any attention to what the admirals say [He had previously referred to threats of military rule in Hawaii]. With General Butler [Smedley Butler, former commandant of the United States Marines], I say, 'To hell with the Admirals!' If you do it, you will have nothing to fear. . . . I put this case in your hands. . . . I pray that there will be no racial lines."

Then, turning again toward Mrs. Anito, who was still sitting quietly behind the lawyers' table, Kelley stood for a moment, looking at her. The courtroom was still. Kelley looked first at the gray-haired Hawaiian woman, wearing a long white "Mother Hubbard," or *holoku*—the type of garment the missionaries had introduced in Hawaii a century before. It looked like a shroud on the frail, dark-skinned woman, leaning forward, her head bowed and now and then holding a handkerchief to her eyes. Then he turned toward Mrs. Fortescue.

"Mr. Darrow has spoken of mother-love," he said, his voice low and biting. "He has spoken of 'the mother' in this courtroom. Well"—his tone sharpened—"there is another mother in this courtroom. Has Mrs. Fortescue lost her daughter? Has Massie lost his wife?" He turned, his finger pointing across the room at the Hawaiian woman, who was now weeping. Kelley's words rang out like a clap of thunder. "But where is Joseph Kahahawai?"

The courtroom was absolutely still.

Clarence Darrow may have felt the lash of Kelley's scorn. He leaned back and drew his hand across his forehead, as if to mop his brow. Mrs. Anito's sobbing was the only sound in the courtroom. Mrs. Fortescue, sitting only a few feet away, did not permit herself a glance at "the other mother." She stared stonily ahead.

Kelley ended his summation at 3:35 P.M., two minutes less than an hour after he began. Judge Davis delivered his instructions to the jury, and at 5 o'clock on Wednesday, April 27, the case was given to the jury. At 5:30 P.M. on Friday, after almost fifty hours of deliberation, the foreman of the jury, John Stone, advised the clerk of the court, Milnor Wond, that the jury had reached a verdict.

Aftermath of Justice

In his summation to the jury, George Leisure had said: "When a jury returns a verdict, that *is* law and order." He made the remark in support of a plea for acquittal; and it is interesting, in the light of this concept of "law and order," to see how it was carried out.

When the jury filed into the courtroom, Foreman Stone handed a slip to Court Clerk Milnor Wond. The defendants, Mrs. Fortescue, Tommy Massie, Albert Jones and Edmund Lord, were asked to stand. Thalia Massie stood beside her husband.

Wond read the verdict. All four defendants were found guilty of manslaughter—a lesser offense than the second-degree-murder charges on which they had been tried. The jury recommended leniency. The penalty under Hawaiian law for manslaughter was a maximum of ten years' imprisonment at hard labor.

Thalia Massie leaned against her husband, and began to sob. The others stared stoically at Judge Davis. There were about thirty people in the courtroom, gathered by that curious grapevine communication that tells people when a jury has reached a verdict. There was not a sound from any of them.

Montgomery Winn asked that the defendants remain in custody of the Navy "according to the arrangement now in effect." Kelley looked at Winn, and said, "I don't know what arrangements are in effect, but it will be satisfactory if the Naval authorities give assurance the defendants will be present."

Captain Ward Wortman, of the Submarine Base, turned to Kelley and said sharply: "You know what those arrangements were."

"I do not know," Kelley snapped.

"You know damned little!" Wortman shouted; and Judge Davis rapped his gavel. Winn then said a motion would be made for a new trial, and Judge Davis set the sentencing for nine o'clock the following Friday morning, May 6th.

The jury had been questioned only once by Judge Davis as to whether they could reach a verdict. That was about two hours before the verdict was announced. He had called them in and Foreman Stone said he thought a verdict was possible.

Word had spread magically through the city. Fred Lowery, the new Police Commissioner, and Chief of Police Weeber—Walter Dillingham's former "confidential man"—were on hand, and police were deployed at trouble spots around Honolulu, such as Aala Park. Admiral Yates Stirling was in the courtroom when the verdict was announced, and he promptly went into whispered conference with Winn, Darrow and Leisure. After a few minutes the whole group left, under Naval escort, returning to the U.S.S. *Alden* at Pearl Harbor, where they had remained throughout their period of custody.

Darrow told newsmen later that he was "stunned by the verdict," but it became apparent that he was not too stunned. He knew at the time exactly what was transpiring at Pearl Harbor, at the Governor's office, and in Washington.

The Honolulu *Advertiser* reported on Saturday, the day after the verdict was announced, that it was "freely stated in Naval circles that 'they won't serve time.'" This report was pretty well confirmed around town. Cables began to pour into Honolulu from Washington.

Meanwhile, a petition had been prepared which was to be delivered to Governor Lawrence Judd immediately after sentencing. It read:

We, the undersigned defendants in the matter of the Territory vs. Grace Fortescue et al., and their attorneys, do hereby respectfully pray Your Excellency in the exercise of power in you vested of executive clemency, and in view of the recommendation of the jury in said matter, to commute the sentence heretofore pronounced in said matter.[2]

The sentence "heretofore pronounced" was at ten o'clock in the morning of May 4. Judge Davis had advanced the date of sentencing two days and hastily summoned the convicted defendants into court. Under Hawaiian law, the ten-year sentence was mandatory, with reduction in the term served to be at the discretion of the prison parole board. Judge Davis asked each of the defendants in turn if they had any statement to make, and each replied they had none. They were sentenced individually to "ten years at hard labor in Oahu prison."

It was only after the sentencing that it was disclosed by the defendants—who had been "sworn to secrecy"—that arrangements had already been made for a "commutation of sentence" from ten years at hard labor to one hour at the Governor's office! There was almost a gala atmosphere in the courtroom while the defendants awaited the arrival of Major Gordon Ross, commander of the Hawaii National Guard and at that time the High Sheriff of Honolulu, who took them in custody and led them across the street to the Governor's suite in Iolani Palace, where they were destined to serve their sentence.

Governor Judd welcomed them with broad smiles, and shook hands all around. He handed each of them a document indicating their individual sentences were commuted to "one hour." The hour passed pleasantly, amid the chit-chat usually incident to a cocktail party; and by noon all four defendants walked forth as free people once more.

It was disclosed that a good many cables had passed back and forth between Honolulu and Washington. On the Tuesday before sentence was to be passed, Governor Judd had received a particularly important message from the Hawaiian Delegate-to-Congress, Victor Houston, which said in part:

> Since justice seems to have been served by the recent findings, may I as an individual urge you to exercise your pardoning powers at the appropriate time. Also may I recommend allowing the present defendants to remain in the custody of the Navy until the matter is finally disposed of.

The Massie-Fortescue trial defendants immediately after serving their one-hour sentences at Iolani Palace. From the left: Clarence Darrow; E. J. Lord; A. O. Jones; High Sheriff Gordon C. Ross; Mrs. Grace Fortescue; Mrs. Thalia Massie; Lt. Thomas H. Massie; and defense counsel George S. Leisure.

I am convinced Hawaii's interest will best be served by the suggested action.[3]

Hawaii's "interests" had been more specifically delineated in a telegram Houston sent to Princess Abbe Kawananakoa, the last royal descendent of the Kings of Hawaii, who was a power among the Hawaiian people. The message, dated May 5, 1932—the day after the commutation of sentence—said:

MESSAGE TO GOVERNOR CONTAINED FOLLOWING ON PARDON QUOTE CRISP [Rep. Charles R. Crisp, Dem., Georgia] YESTERDAY INTRODUCED BILL PROVIDING FOR CONGRESSIONAL PARDON OF MASSIE FORTESCUE DEFENDANTS. DELANEY INTRODUCED RESOLUTION REQUESTING PRESIDENT TO PARDON. CONGRESSMAN THATCHER CIRCULATING PETITION URGING YOU TO PARDON. CONSIDERABLE INTEREST AROUSED BY REASON OF PRIOR TRIAL THESE DEFENDANTS AHEAD OF RETRIAL ALA MOANA CASE. UNQUOTE.[4]

The *Advertiser* revealed that a petition signed by "106 Congressmen" had also been sent to Governor Judd, urging him to pardon the Massie-Fortescue defendants. The message said:

We, as members of Congress, deeply concerned with the welfare of Hawaii, believe that the prompt and unconditional pardon of Lieutenant Massie and his associates will serve that welfare and the ends of substantial justice. We therefore earnestly request that such a pardon be granted.[5]

Thus did those who were "deeply concerned with the welfare of Hawaii" seek to persuade the Governor to undo the work of a Territorial jury that had heard this case in every aspect, listened to the evidence and testimony, deliberated upon it for nearly fifty hours, and reached what Judge Davis described as a "fair and reasonable decision."

Darrow was elated at the release of his clients. "I am very much gratified," he said. "This is the way it should be, and I approve of what the Governor has done. . . . This case has gone before a jury of a hundred million people. That jury has rendered its verdict, unhampered by foolish and absurd rules of law."

It remained for the jury of twelve in Honolulu, and their fellow citizens, to find out during the next few months just what the "jury of a hundred million people" had done to law enforcement in Hawaii.

The Finale

        The curtain had rung down on the great Clarence Darrow's last performance in a courtroom; but there was still a final act in the tragedy of the Massie case as far as Hawaii was concerned. The retrial of the Ala Moana case had not taken place; and there were mixed feelings in Honolulu as to whether it should take place.

The Massie-Fortescue trial had ended only one phase of the Islands' ordeal—and it left open wounds. The first indication of this was a clamor raised in Honolulu and in Washington concerning the commutation of sentences. This reduction in sentence from ten years to one hour did not exonerate the four defendants from the verdict returned by the jury. It merely shortened the time they served. This gave rise to questions of citizenship: manslaughter was a felony in Hawaii, and conviction removed certain privileges of citizenship.

At first there was considerable disposition among the higher officials in the Territory—such as Governor Lawrence Judd and Attorney General Harry Hewitt—to drop the whole matter. As Hewitt expressed it to newspapermen, "Let's forget the damned thing and go about our business!" Even Clarence Darrow said it was a good solution to the case. "A commutation is not theoretically a pardon," he said. "They have served their time. I believe Congress will act to restore Lieutenant Massie's position in the Navy, providing there is any change in status."

There were others, however, who felt a full pardon should have been granted. The *Advertiser* was quite definite on this point; on the morning of May 5—the day after the sentences were commuted —it said editorially:

> In view of the recommendation of the jury in the Massie case, together with the request of Delegate Houston and more than a hundred Congressmen that he issue a full pardon, the *Advertiser* feels that Governor Judd, in giving them a mere commutation of sentence, has evaded the issue and again placed Hawaii in an awkward light before the nation.
>
> The Governor's action has the effect of a grudging acquiescence to a powerful public sentiment, whereas by granting a pardon he would have gracefully complied with that sentiment.[1]

The *Star-Bulletin* was less inclined to advocate this "graceful" compliance with what many regarded as blackjacking the Territory into an act which contravened its laws and the verdict of a trial jury. On May 3, before the sentencing, the afternoon paper commented:

> Unless our whole structure of Government, the foundations of our liberties and our civilization, are to be set aside, there was only one method of dealing with the killing of Joseph Kahahawai. That was the method followed.[2]

On the afternoon the sentence was passed, and the subsequent commutation was ordered by Governor Judd, the *Star-Bulletin* said:

> The people of Honolulu have sustained their reputation as law-abiding citizens, possessed of self-control . . . Only the passage of time will determine the ultimate wisdom of these developments.[3]

The *Hawaii Hochi*, a perpetual gadfly for the *haole* elite, was not so sanguine as the *Star-Bulletin* about this state of affairs. On May 10, the Japanese-English newspaper, whose white editor was perhaps the most articulate spokesman for the Hawaiian-Democrat voters, let loose a blast at the Republican party for its role in the Massie-Fortescue affair:

> More harm has been done the cause of Americanization by recent events than can be remedied in many years . . . [Our] Republican leadership has been discredited, and many of the most powerful people in public life stand branded as traitors to Hawaii in the eyes of the common people.

> The Republican party stands accused of selling Hawaii's birthright for a miserable mess of pottage. The voters are saying that Republican inefficiency made the Ala Moana case possible; that chicanery of officials bungled the first trial and sought to railroad certain suspects without sufficient evidence; that their cowardice prevented adequate defense of Hawaii's honor when it was attacked on the Mainland following the killing of Joseph Kahahawai; that acquiescence of these leaders in the reign of terror and intimidation was climaxed by the surrender of the principle of self-government. . . .

> Unless we take a stand and fight every inch of the way, there will be nothing left to distinguish Hawaii from an Indian reservation!" [4]

Escape from Paradise

One official of Honolulu who proposed to take a stand on the matter was Jack Kelley, the Public Prosecutor. Having disposed of Clarence Darrow in the trial of the Massie-Fortescue defendants, he lost no time in getting the legal wheels rolling for a retrial of the Ala Moana case.

On May 6, Kelley went before Judge Albert Cristy and obtained a summons for Thalia Massie to appear as the complaining witness in the new trial of the four remaining Ala Moana boys. Kelley also asked that a trial date be set for May 25.

Clarence Darrow had advised Thalia Massie not to appear again in any court in the Territory. The reasons for this were not disclosed. Kelley asked Darrow and Leisure if the "agreement" under which the four defendants in the Massie-Fortescue trial had been released included Thalia Massie's appearance as a witness in the Ala Moana retrial.

Leisure told Kelley there were no plans for any of the defendants to remain in Hawaii. At this point the last act of the tragedy began to take on the character of a Mack Sennett comedy. The *S.S. Malolo* was scheduled to depart for San Francisco on Sunday, May 8—four days after the sentencing and subsequent freeing of the Massie-Fortescue defendants.

Kelley had Police Officer Dewey Mookini stationed at the gangplank to serve a summons on Thalia Massie requiring her to appear as a witness in the Ala Moana retrial. Meanwhile, unknown to those on the Aloha pier, where the *Malolo* was docked, the *USS Alden*, the naval vessel on which the Massie-Fortescue troupe had been held in "protective custody," or some similar arrangement, drew up on the offshore side of the *Malolo*. Thalia Massie, Mrs. Fortescue, Lieutenant Massie, the two sailors and Mrs. Fortescue's brother and sister, Robert Bell and Mrs. Helen Ripley, were transferred to the liner.

Another police officer, Detective Lono McCullum, had been posted on the bridge in anticipation of this maneuver, and he signalled Mookini. The Hawaiian policeman raced up the gangway and down the corridor where he understood the staterooms of the departing defendants were located.

He collided with the ubiquitous Captain Ward Wortman of the submarine base, who stood in the corridor. Wortman flung his arms around Mookini and began to yell, "He's attacking me! He's attacking me!"

Mookini was not as big as Wortman, but he was tough. He used his elbows to get loose and started after Thalia Massie, who was scuttling toward her stateroom. Wortman, who had played football at Annapolis, threw a rolling shoulder block on Mookini, and the two went down in the passageway.

The astonished deckhands of the *Malolo* gazed at this strange way the *haoles* had of taking their departure from the Islands. A few, recognizing that Mookini was Hawaiian, were cheering him on, as the police officer struggled to free himself in order to tap Thalia Massie with the summons. She was tugging at the door of her cabin, and Mookini was yelling, "I serve you! I serve you!"

Wortman, his arms wrapped firmly around Mookini's legs, bellowed, "Take your hands off me!"

When they finally got up, and Wortman had brushed off his uniform and to some extent recovered his composure, he said, "I shall report this to your superior officer!"

"Go ahead, Captain," Mookini said. "It's Judge Cristy."

"And don't you ever lay hands on me again!" Wortman shouted.

"You can't give me orders!" Mookini shouted back. "I'm doing what I'm ordered to do."

"Say 'Sir' when you address me!" Wortman yelled. 'I'm an officer of the Navy."

"So am I—of the Honolulu police," Mookini replied. "You say 'Sir' to me. I'm entitled to as much respect as you are."

While the two were debating these matters of protocol, Darrow and Leisure came down the hallway; and Leisure finally arranged for Mookini to serve Thalia Massie with the subpoena five minutes before the ship was due to leave. This seemed to be a satisfactory solution, and Wortman and Mookini were persuaded to shake hands, while the cameras of the news photographers, who had caught up with the parties, registered the event on film.

This was the last time Thalia Massie, her husband and her mother were seen in Hawaii, but it was not the last time they were heard from.

When the *Malolo* arrived in San Francisco, Mrs. Fortescue was prevailed upon by the press to utter some opinions on Hawaii. The San Francisco *Examiner* of May 13, 1932, quoted her as saying:

Unless the United States takes quick action to hold and preserve what it has in Hawaii, Japan will take over the Islands.[5]

She expressed the hope that Honolulu might become "safe for decent women." In connection with the attack on her daughter, she added: "Whether Honolulu has been made safe for women as a result of our trouble I do not know. But the better citizens there are demanding a return to lawfulness."

Thalia Massie, however, was less circumspect. After she returned to her home in Lansdowne, Pennsylvania, she issued a statement to the Associated Press, and the dispatch subsequently was published in Honolulu. The story quoted her as saying she had "made a deal with the authorities in Honolulu" to leave the Islands so that the prosecution of the Ala Moana case might be dropped. Her quoted statement was:

> I was not to appear against these men, and consequently no evidence against them could be presented. The indictment against them would have been quashed immediately afterwards.[6]

Thalia Massie referred to certain "suppressed evidence" which she said was "in the hands of the prosecution," including witnesses who had seen the abduction and would have been able to identify her attackers. "There are two witnesses to identify them who have never been brought into the case," she said.

When this statement appeared in the Honolulu newspapers, on October 3, 1932, it was confirmed by Captain F. J. Horne, Chief of Staff at the Naval Base at Pearl Harbor. He said the names of these witnesses had been "given to the police, who did nothing about it."

It is interesting, in view of the official Navy pronouncement, to "look at the record," as the late Al Smith used to say. In a report dated May 23, 1932, by Captain Omar T. Pfeiffer, district legal officer, U. S. Marine Corps, addressed to the Commandant, 14th Naval District, Pearl Harbor, Hawaii, the following statement appears:

> On a Saturday night in September, 1931, H. J. Bouquette, E. J. Watkins and H. A. Patrick, all seamen first class, U. S. Navy, went joyriding in a ship's service store truck from the Submarine Base. Late in the evening, around 11 o'clock, they drove on Kalakaua Avenue . . . While driving on Kalakaua Avenue towards town, they passed a Ford touring car containing a number of men. The Navy men were in white uniforms and were easily recognized as belonging to the Navy. The men in the Ford called the Navy men some names, the name "dog face" being particularly remembered. The Ford continued on and the three Navy men decided to follow to have further conversation with these men and find out if they wanted to defend their words by combat . . .

> The Ford was seen to turn into John Ena Road. When the truck following [sic] into John Ena Road, the rear light of a car was noticed just around a bend in the road. The truck came abreast of the car . . . It was the same car in which the men had shouted

names while passing the Navy truck on Kalakaua Avenue. Two of the Navy men noticed a white woman in a peculiar position in the rear of the car. There were two men in the front seat and three in the rear seat with the woman at this time.[7]

The account then reports that the Ford turned right into the Ala Moana, heading toward town, while the Navy truck veered off to the left toward Fort De Russy. The report said the "Navy men read accounts in the newspapers of what happened in this vicinity on September 12, which was the same night they observed these things." Since they had taken an official Navy truck for a joy ride that night, they decided to say nothing about it. However, one of the men finally told Seaman Albert Jones, one of the Massie-Fortescue defendants, and Jones repeated the story to an officer.

Captain Pfeiffer said he reported the matter to Assistant Attorney General Harold Kay "about one month ago" and since he had "received no word from him, I interrogated these men on May 21, 1932." The time element is of some interest; the report apparently was not made until about a month prior to May 23, which would have been before the closing of the Massie-Fortescue trial, and six months after the Ala Moana trial.

During the period immediately following the Massie-Fortescue trial, an investigation was started by Governor Judd. In the course of this investigation, the Pinkerton Detective Agency operative, John C. Fraser, following up the Marine captain's report, interviewed Seaman Bouquette on August 25, 1932—some six weeks before Thalia Massie gave her information to the Associated Press.

Following is an excerpt from the official report of the Pinkerton Agency, quoting Bouquette:

On the night of September 12, 1931, I was with E. J. Watkins and H. A. Patrick. We were riding around in a Chevrolet bus which was obtained from Ships Service at the Submarine Base. We had taken the bus without permission and were driving from Kapiolani Park towards Honolulu, when we met another car, I am not sure, but I think it was a model A Ford touring car *painted a light grey, and with the top down.* [Italics added]. . . .

There were two men in front, and three men seated in the back. I saw no woman in the car. This car passed us and as they passed they hollered at us, I forget what they called us. After we thought it over we started back after this car. When we caught up with them it was right behind Waikiki Park on John Ena Road . . . I was driving our car . . . We drove slowly alongside of them to see if they would pass any more remarks, but they said nothing. At this time I observed there was a woman in the back seat of this other car. I am sure this was a white woman. There was not room for four in the back seat so one of the men sort of propped himself on the back of the seat where the top comes down, and the woman was between the other two men. . . . I heard no one scream. The dance had not let out yet [at Waikiki Park] . . . because there were plenty of cars there and I could hear the music. . . .

I got a good look at the male occupants of the car and would say they were Kanakas. . . . We noticed that the Ford car turned right onto the Ala Moana Road. About ten or fifteen minutes we drove back past Waikiki Park and noticed the dance was still in progress.[8]

The accounts of the other two men were generally similar, except that Seaman Patrick thought the top was up, not down; and Seaman Watkins did not see a woman in the car.

The details of the reports are interesting for two reasons: First, the time element would indicate that the event took place well before the end of the dance at Waikiki Park, which was 11:55 P.M.; and second, there was no indication of force or violence being used on the woman. It is also noteworthy that the sailors in the bus apparently followed the Ford car closely, and no one reported that it stopped anywhere.

Had this supposedly "suppressed evidence"—which was not available, according to the record, until eight months after the attack on Thalia Massie—been introduced, it could have accomplished only one thing: It would have indicated that the five men Thalia Massie identified as her abductors could not have been involved in the affair. They were in Waikiki Park at the time.

The Boomerang

Meanwhile the situation in Honolulu was—to use a diplomatic term—"worsening." In Congress a bill had been introduced by Representative Fred A. Britten (Rep., Illinois), Chairman of the House Naval Affairs Committee, to place Hawaii under the rule of the War and Navy Departments, with an Army general or Navy admiral in command of the Territory. The distinguished statesman from Illinois said:

"We cannot allow such an important possession as Hawaii [Hawaii was then a Territory of the United States, not a "possession"] to be completely dominated by the native population."

Under Britten's bill, all executive and judicial functions in the Territory would be vested in a Military Governor appointed by the Secretaries of War and Navy. Al Castle, one of the leading members of the Big Five, whose brother was William R. Castle, Jr., an Under-Secretary of State in Washington, returned from the States with "a stern warning" that the folks on the Mainland were "not pleased by the way things are going on in Honolulu." This presumably referred both to the verdict of the jury in the Massie-Fortescue case, and the failure of Governor Judd to nullify that action by granting a full pardon for the defendants.

By this time the shoe of the *haole* elite was beginning to pinch. It was one thing to have threatened the Hawaiians from time to time with a "Commission Government," as the Republicans had been doing for thirty years; it was quite another to have a General or an Admiral sitting over affairs in the Islands, controlling appointments and acts of Government—and possibly not as amenable to the wishes of the Big Five as the politically appointed Governors of Hawaii had been.

Congressman Britten, warming up to his task of saving the "possessions" of the United States from control by their own citizens, issued a denunciation of Governor Judd's commutation and demanded a full pardon for the killers of Kahahawai. "The native population in Hawaii," he said, "will go against anything American!"

Walter Dillingham was not insensible to these influences that were moving in a direction that might be dangerous to the suzerainty of the *haole* elite in the Islands. It was about this time he wrote and published his famous "private memorandum," dated May 17, 1932. In a letter to Delegate Houston on June 2, he explained his reasons for this remarkable document:

Dear Victor,

Now that the storm has blown over and there is no news value in the tragic history of recent events, I have prepared a memorandum in answer to many questions that have been asked me by correspondents all over the world. This memorandum is for private circulation. I hope you will find time to read it and that you will get what others will, which is a constructive thought that Hawaii, in spite of her mistakes, is better able to manage her affairs than to have them under the control of a dictator, politically or otherwise, appointed by Washington . . . [9]

In other words, Dillingham and his fellow members of the *haole* elite wanted to be sure who was doing the dictating. For many years the Big Five had lived under the comfortable assumption that they were doing it. The prospect of having an alien element in the "Paradise of the Pacific"—and particularly persons who may have been oriented to doing things the military way rather than by political persuasion—was disquieting.

This "private memorandum," which has been quoted in several earlier chapters, gave a rambling coverage of the events that led up to the Ala Moana and Massie-Fortescue trials; but one of its most revealing passages, which disclosed Dillingham's "constructive thought" on the situation, was in the latter part of the document, reviewing the second trial:

The impression made by Mrs. Massie and by Lieutenant Massie was most favorable, and many who attended the sessions with some doubt in mind as to the guilt of Kahahawai were entirely satisfied *from the evidence produced* that the gangsters were guilty. [Italics added] [10]

There was, of course, no evidence produced in the Massie-Fortescue trial that indicated one way or another whether "the gangsters were guilty" in the Ala Moana case. Clarence Darrow had been careful to keep any such evidence out of the testimony, except that which indicated Tommy Massie *believed* the Ala Moana boys were guilty.

Dillingham continued with what was perhaps the most remarkable expression of "constructive thought" in the entire document:

The attempt to establish the fact that Lieutenant Massie was insane when the shot was fired was not successful, but in the minds of a great many this attempt was unnecessary as there was *ample provocation for the shooting.* [Italics added] [11]

It is doubtful if Titus Oates, in his goriest day in the "Bloody Assizes," could have stated his attitude on the subject of judicial ruthlessness more explicitly. Regardless of whether Dillingham himself was one of the "great many" to whom this thought occurred, it amounts to an open and unequivocal acceptance of the principle of lynch law, despite avowals to the contrary.

There is some question, of course, as to whether Walter Dillingham and his fellow travelers among the *haole* elite were thinking very clearly in these times. The *Hawaii Hochi* expressed this possibility in a forthright editorial under date of May 20, 1932, entitled "Boomerang!" It said in part:

> For years our local leaders in politics and industry have been trying to frighten the people of Hawaii with threats of a "Commission form of Government." To serve their own selfish ends and whip reluctant citizens into line, they have painted a terrifying picture of this bogey-man . . .
>
> Now the chickens have come home to roost!
>
> The imaginary "bogey" has materialized into a very vigorous and menacing reality.
>
> The amusing feature of the present situation—if there is anything amusing about it—is that the threat is directed against the very ones who have been using it so long as a means of frightening the people of the Territory into doing their bidding.
>
> The latest measure introduced in Congress by Rep. Britten of Illinois is quite different from the "Commission government" idea . . . What is proposed is not a change in our status but a change in the method of selecting our Chief Executive. This solution would not deprive the people of Hawaii of their civil rights . . . But it would absolutely prevent the dictation of appointments by the local coterie of "big interests" . . . It would strike a fatal blow at the domination of the local government by our "captains of industry" . . .
>
> Thus does the club with which this little group has always threatened the people of Hawaii return as a boomerang to smite them on the head! [12]

The Ala Moana Question

Jack Kelley had moved quickly at the close of the Massie-Fortescue trial to bring this harrowing chapter in the history of Hawaii to a speedy end, as far as was possible within judicial processes. Two items were left: to conduct a thorough investigation into the Ala Moana case in all its aspects, including the work of the police and the Detective Bureau; and to bring the remaining four defendants to trial.

When Thalia Massie left on the *Malolo* on May 8, Kelley was without a complaining witness. He called in newspapermen and announced that he would retry the case anyway.

"I believe there are legal precedents," he said, "that will permit us to present the testimony of the complaining witness in the form of a transcript of the testimony in the first trial." His sharp blue eyes took on a savage glint. "We will put Thalia Massie on the stand in effigy."

This plan aroused an immediate storm of protest from several quarters—particularly in the Attorney General's Office, where Harry Hewitt and Harold Kay were perhaps more privy to the undisclosed elements of the Ala Moana case than, for example, Walter Dillingham. Hewitt at first refused outright to sanction Kelley's plans; but finally agreed to take the matter to Governor Judd.

The Governor was having his own pangs of conscience, and suffering from conflicting emotions.

The commutation of sentence and subsequent refusal to give the Massie-Fortescue defendants a full pardon pleased no one, including Governor Judd. The first act antagonized the non-*haole* groups and the Hawaiian-Democratic voting group; and although Governor Judd, a political appointee, was not exposed to ordinary reprisals for political mistakes, his fellow-Republicans who were in elective offices *were* quite vulnerable. The failure to go the whole route and pardon the defendants, on the other hand, had offended Washington, and this represented a direct danger to Governor Judd, an appointee of the President, Herbert Hoover.

Kelley, who had little or no political sensitivity, had already decided on his course of action. The first requirement was a thorough investigation of the Ala Moana affair; and the next was to bring the remaining four defendants to trial. The most critical question in Kelley's mind, as far as the investigation was concerned, was whether or not Thalia Massie had identified the wrong suspects. If she had, what was her motive?

Kelley held an impromptu news conference with Dan Campbell, of the United Press, and the writer. He said it was his plan to try the Ala Moana case again—with or without Thalia Massie. Campbell asked him bluntly how he hoped to justify putting Thalia Massie's testimony in the record—without Thalia—if he was not sure she told the truth in the earlier trial.

Kelley sat back and rubbed his bald pate. His sharp blue eyes had a way of following a questioner with deep interest, yet betraying nothing of his own thoughts.

"I haven't said I don't believe she told the truth," he said. "Nobody but Thalia Massie can answer that one—and she isn't here to answer it. But I have an obligation under the law—not just to Thalia Massie, but to the four boys she accused. They are covered by the law as well as she is."

Campbell was a short, swarthy man, with a small black mustache and dark eyes. He had a newspaperman's professional curiosity.

"You mean you've got the guts to put her on the stand—that is, put her testimony into the record—when you don't believe it?" He shook his head. "Do you think she lied, Jack? If she did—why?"

This apparently was the question Kelley wanted to bring out; but he wanted someone else to ask it. He began to trace the testimony in the earlier trial. The "alibi witnesses," Tuts Matsumoto and Robert Vierra, saw the Ala Moana boys at the Park just before midnight. Others had also seen them—William Asing, Tom Murada and Charles Kalani—at about the same time.

"Somebody was not giving the right story," Kelley said. "If Mrs. Massie was telling the truth, every one of these other people had to be wrong—or lying."

"Why would she lie?" he was asked. "What was her motive?"

Kelley smiled, and again rubbed his hand over his head. "Look at it this way. She left the party because she was sore—at Stogsdall, or Massie, or maybe everybody. She may have intended to go somewhere—to a bootleg joint, maybe, for a drink. She may have intended to meet someone there. Possibly she got mixed up with the wrong people and didn't necessarily want to admit all the circumstances. So when they brought in some boys, she identified them. It was the

286

easiest way out. After that she was stuck with her story. It isn't a very admirable explanation, but it's logical."

There was no question but that the testimony of the "alibi witnesses" at the Ala Moana trial created a situation in which it would have been impossible for the five boys accused of the rape to have picked up Thalia Massie at the time she said they did, driven her to the old quarantine station site, raped her six or seven times and have been able to reach King and Liliha Streets by the circuitous route indicated by Matsumoto and Vierra, and yet arrive there by 12:37 A.M.

This discrepancy placed Kelley in the unusual position of trying four boys who probably were not guilty. This brought up the second question: If the four remaining defendants in the Ala Moana case did not assault her, who did? At this point Kelley had retained his own investigator, Cornealous W. Gibbs. He had instructed Gibbs to trace every aspect of the Ala Moana case.

Gibbs needed answers to certain very specific questions:

First, if Thalia Massie was attacked—and there seemed every indication she had been assaulted in some way—and if the five Ala Moana defendants were not her assailants, who did attack her?

Second, who was "the white man who followed the white woman" down John Ena Road at about 12:15 on the night of the assault? Bill Pittman had said, in his address to the jury in the Ala Moana trial, that there "can be no question but what the white man who followed the white woman on John Ena Road that night knows what happened . . . Why wasn't he found?"

Third, if this "white man" was one of Tommy Massie's friends, as had been broadly hinted in the rumors and gossip at the time of the trial—why did he fail to testify? If his purpose had been to persuade Thalia Massie to return to the party, and in view of the fact that the honor of a fellow officer's wife was at stake, why was he not brought into court to tell what he knew of the affair?

Fourth, in a more general way, why was it that none of the Navy officers at the party—including Massie himself—failed to take the stand and testify under oath as to what had happened at the Ala Wai Inn before Thalia Massie took her fateful walk? With the exception of Lieutenant Tom Brown and his wife, Mary Anne Brown, who offered the innocuous testimony that she had gone upstairs about 11:35 P.M. and failed to find Thalia Massie, not one member of the Navy party came forward to tell what he or she knew. Why?

Fifth, and perhaps most important of all, from the standpoint of the killing of Joseph Kahahawai—was there any evidence or information that would indicate that Tommy Massie did *not* believe his wife's story? The fact that he had not testified in the Ala Moana trial might support this possibility; but it was merely negative and entirely inferential.

There was one other question in Kelley's mind, which he discussed freely with newspapermen and which seemed to bear on the entire Massie case; yet it had no real answer. That was the question of whether she was actually raped.

Kelley had access to all the reports of the Emergency Hospital, the Queen's Hospital and the Kapiolani Maternity Hospital, where she had been taken several weeks after the attack, presumably to find out whether she was pregnant and to remove the results of pregnancy, if she was. The diagnosis was negative. Thalia Massie was not pregnant.

In her statement to Chief Inspector McIntosh early in the morning after the attack, she had been asked:

Q. Will you relate what happened to you tonight?
A. I was assaulted six or seven times.
Q. You mean they raped you?
A. Yes.[13]

The physical requirements of raping a woman of the size and apparent physical condition of Thalia Massie, Kelley pointed out, were considerable.

"She said they hit her in the jaw and face several times. She obviously must have been fighting them off. The men were young and strong. While the law does not require that there be any physical evidence of such a struggle, the rule of common sense would indicate that there must have been some evidence. Yet there was none—except for the bruises on her face and the cut lip observed by the Bellingers and Clarks when they picked her up on the Ala Moana. She later was reported to have had a broken jaw, but this was not observed by the Clark boy, who looked at her very closely; nor by Dr. Liu. It could have happened later.

"The important point in the question of criminal assault is the negative aspect. Her clothes were not torn, and there was no sign of seminal matter on any of her garments. She had douched when she got home, and there was no indication from a medical examination that she had been raped."

It is interesting to note, in connection with this aspect of the case, the only official comment that was ever made on the matter. This was in the Pinkerton Report made to Governor Judd more than a year after the attack on Thalia Massie.

Governor Judd had met in San Francisco on June 9, 1932, with representatives of the Pinkerton Detective Agency and secretly retained them to conduct a thorough investigation of the entire affair. The results of this investigation are in the official files of the Attorney General of Hawaii. It includes interviews with Dr. David Liu, the Emergency Hospital physician who treated Thalia Massie and examined her within two hours of the alleged rape. Dr. Liu refused to be pinned down as to whether he thought she had or had not been criminally assaulted. He said he saw no sign of such an attack, but when he was asked if "this woman could have had four men and not show any marks?" he replied:

"Yes . . . One reason is because she had been a married woman."

Agnes Fawcett, the nurse who prepared Thalia Massie for identification, had a more positive view.

"She was clean as a new pin," she told the Pinkerton operative. In the report to Governor Judd, the Pinkerton Agency said:

Although the purpose of a group of men or boys kidnaping a strange woman late at night and violently removing her to an isolated and unfrequented spot may be obvious, and marks on her body would tend to support the woman's narrative that the purpose of the kidnaping had been rape, yet if rape had been committed and was to be established there are certain ingredients of the offense which are required to be proved.

We have found nothing in the record of this case nor have we through our own efforts been able to find what in our estimation would be sufficient corroboration of the statements of Mrs. Massie to establish the occurrence of rape upon her. There is a preponderance of evidence Mrs. Massie did in some manner suffer numerous bruises about the head and body but *definite proof of actual rape has not in our opinion been found.* [Italics added][14]

The question whether Thalia Massie was actually raped was not merely an academic question to Jack Kelley.

"Everything ties into that one question," he said a few days after the close of the trial and the departure of Thalia Massie, her mother and her husband for the Mainland. The Public Prosecutor was holding an informal press conference; but he was actually reviewing the case in his own mind.

"There is always the question of motive," he said. "There are two possible explanations why she got into that car—if she did get into it. The first is that she was dragged in, as she said she was. The second is that for one reason or another, she got in more or less voluntarily. If the latter reason is assumed, then she must have known who the boys were. They could have been young fellows she knew casually on the beach. This would not be unusual, or wrong in any way. Or they could have been music boys.

"This would explain the testimony of those who saw a girl in a green dress on John Ena Road, with a white man following her and a couple of fellows either pulling her along or helping her along. Who was this white man—and why was he there? Was he one of the fellows picking her up, or a member of the party at the Ala Wai Inn who followed her to try to get her to come back? This would also explain why she was willing to identify any boys *other than the ones who picked her up.* She may have figured that since the boys she identified were not involved, they would never be convicted. Or she may not have thought about that aspect at all. She may have just wanted to get out of trouble. When she got deeper into trouble, it's entirely possible that her own psychological reactions and deep emotional involvement might have temporarily erased the actual facts from her mind."

Kelley stopped talking for a moment; then he said:

"The only thing we have to go on now is a theory—since Mrs. Massie had left the Islands. The theory that fits the story told by Mrs. Massie at the Ala Moana trial doesn't fit any of the essential facts in this case. The theory I have indicated fits all of them."

The specter of a nightmarish miscalculation—that Thalia Massie had left the Navy party at the Ala Wai Inn to go for a ride with some friends from the beach, and found the ride rougher than she expected—was one of the rumors that had circulated through Honolulu, with no foundation in fact, but with unusual persistence.

"That would certainly explain why nobody from the Navy testified in support of her story," Kelley said. "It also indicates something else. If someone she knew had followed her, trying to get her to come back, then it follows that Massie knew the real story. And he knew it when he shot Kahahawai."

Kelley then told of a curious incident that had been reported to him. A man who apparently had wanted to obtain the reward of five thousand dollars offered by the Chamber of Commerce for evidence leading to the solution of the attack on Thalia Massie had come to Kelley with an unverified story of having listened outside the Massie home one night and heard Massie say to his wife: "You've got to go through with it—it means my job in the Navy if you don't!"

This apocryphal report had received a faint corroboration during the trial. Massie had testified, in support of the defense theory of temporary insanity, that he heard a noise outside his house one night and grabbed his gun and ran outside to see what it was.

"I heard the footsteps outside the house," Massie had testified. "I ran out with a gun, but I couldn't see anyone. But I know someone was there."

According to Kelley's amateur detective, he had been lying close against the wall, listening to the talk inside, when he accidentally kicked over a glass jar beside the house. When Massie appeared on the porch with a gun in his hand, the man flattened himself against the ground, and finally Massie walked back into the house.

"He told me that story before Massie testified at the trial," Kelley said. "But there was no way of backing up that kind of evidence, and I dropped it."

The Tahiti Story Again

Cornealous Gibbs did not drop it, however. He was a methodical, thorough worker; quiet and effective. He had tracked down the amateur detective, who had apparently learned the techniques of criminal investigation from a correspondence school; and the man's story convinced Gibbs that by a freak of detective work, he had stumbled on an important point: If Tommy Massie had made the remark the man supposedly overheard, it would indicate that he was aware of certain flaws in his wife's story, even before the Ala Moana trial. He would hardly have insisted that she "go through with it" unless there was a possibility of some disastrous consequence to him if she failed to take the stand.

As Gibbs reasoned the matter, this would imply that Massie's career in the Navy would be in jeopardy if his wife had to make any retraction in her story. This, in turn, seemed to indicate some extremely significant error, or an outright misstatement. Gibbs began to track down the elements of this possible "error."

His first step was to secure a copy of Thalia Massie's original statement to McIntosh, written in the Chief Inspector's handwriting. This was taken from a desk in the police station one night, photographed, and returned the same night. The photostatic copy of the statement, as previously noted, is partly reproduced in this book.

This puzzled Gibbs at first. If Thalia Massie left the Ala Wai Inn "around 12:30" she could not very well have been the "girl in the green dress" seen on John Ena Road at 12:15 A.M. However, Gibbs picked up some additional information which seemed to bear on this point. He looked up young George Clark, who rode in the Bellinger car that picked up Thalia Massie on the Ala Moana. The previously estimated time of picking her up was 12:50 A.M.; but George Clark said he had looked at his watch and it was ten minutes past one! He had not testified at the Ala Moana trial, for either the prosecution or the defense; so the previously estimated time of 12:50 A.M. had been accepted.

This added twenty minutes to the elapsed time from Thalia Massie's departure from the Ala Wai Inn—whether it was 11:35 P.M., around midnight or around 12:30 A.M. It also suggested something to Gibbs. Was there a period of time Thalia Massie did not want to account for—and if so, why? If she left the Ala Wai Inn at 11:35 P.M., as she testified, it would leave an hour and 35 minutes before she was picked up—and her own story made it necessary to assume she could have been gone only about 35 or 40 minutes, in order for the five Ala Moana boys to have kidnaped her, assaulted her, and arrived at King and Liliha at 12:37 A.M.

Gibbs next looked up the doorkeeper at the Ala Wai Inn, Joe Freitas. He had not been interviewed previously by anyone; but he talked quite readily. He told Gibbs he remembered the "girl in the green dress" because "when her party came in it was the first big party to arrive, and she walked ahead of the others, with her head bent forward. I thought maybe she was mad at someone, or maybe drunk."

He said he recalled seeing her standing in the doorway about midnight—after the music at Waikiki Park had stopped; and he thought she spoke to a young fellow named "Sammy" who passed through the doorway.

Gibbs began to fit the pieces together; and this led to the story told by Philip Kemp—the boy called "Tahiti"; and from Kemp to "Sammy," who frequently came to the Ala Wai Inn to meet some of his friends in the orchestra. They often cruised around town with friends or stopped at small "bootleg joints" after the dancing ended, singing and playing *ukuleles.* Gibbs had some information concerning the "music boys" who hung around the Ala Wai Inn. There was a group known as "Joe Crawford's boys," who played on the island of Maui and often came out to the Ala Wai to listen to the music when they were in Honolulu. A girl named Rose Hao, who was a sister-in-law of Ike Hao, one of the boys in the Crawford band, was reported to have circulated a story around Honolulu that these boys "knew about the attack on the *haole* woman." "Sammy" often was with this group.

Gibbs had traced this information as well as he could, but the events were old and it was difficult to determine if the information was factual or merely gleaned from published reports of the Ala Moana affair, or was a baseless rumor. He had talked with Philip Kemp, who was then serving a term in Oahu Prison, but the story of the part-Tahitian boy was much the same as that printed in the *Hawaii Hochi* some months before.

Philip Kemp was a frail, almost effeminate-looking youth, one of the derelicts that often drifted into Honolulu from the "low Islands" to the South. He told Gibbs of the gun his friend "Sammy" had shown him; he also described "Sammy's" fear that "sailors would beat him up," which didn't make much sense, since "Sammy" was not publicly associated with the Ala Moana case at the time. He said "Sammy" and his friends, "Bull"—the Hawaiian with the gold teeth—Shorty and the Filipino-Hawaiian, whose name he did not remember, left for Los Angeles when the Ala Moana case "got hot."

After "Sammy" returned to Honolulu early in March, Kemp said, he "begged him" to tell the same story he had supposedly told Kemp; but "Sammy" insisted at the confrontation with Kemp in Harold Kay's office that he knew nothing about it, and suggested that his friend Tahiti was "a little nutty."

Kelley had told Gibbs: "Either this boy 'Sammy' doesn't know anything, or he knows that as long as he keeps his mouth shut nothing will happen to him."

"Sammy's" alibi was that he had gone to a wedding the night Thalia Massie was attacked. Gibbs began to work on this alibi. He talked with Harold Godfrey, the manager of Waikiki Park, who knew "Sammy"; and through Godfrey he located Godfrey's sister-in-law, a girl named Maria Marques, who also knew "Sammy." The trail led to a man named Blackburn and a young companion of "Sammy's" named Roderigues. The latter had been at "Sammy's" home for dinner the night of September 12. About 7 o'clock they left for Kaimuki, looking for a young fellow named Eddie Kea; Roderigues drove, with "Sammy" and a girl named Vivian Freitas in the front seat and a man named Lewis in the back seat. Eddie Kea, who lived on Third Avenue in Kaimuki, was not home, so they drove back and picked up Blackburn.

At this point Gibbs struck a small amount of pay dirt; Roderigues said he left the group because he had to "drive out to Kahuku the next day to a wedding." Kahuku is across the Island of Oahu from Honolulu; and this was evidently the wedding "Sammy" said he attended the day of the attack on Thalia Massie. It was on Sunday, not Saturday.

Blackburn was next contacted; and he said he had driven his own car back to Eddie Kea's place, with "Sammy" in another car.

The party apparently broke up around 11 o'clock. Lewis said he went home early because he had to drive out to the country the next morning. He said "Sammy" took his car.

"Was 'Sammy' with you?" Gibbs asked Lewis.

Lewis shook his head. "No—just my wife."

The story of "Sammy's" movements that night began to take shape, in a vague and disconnected way. At first Gibbs was told that Vivian Freitas, one of the girls who had been with "Sammy" that night, had left with him after Roderigues, Lewis and Blackburn left; but when Gibbs talked with her, she said she left when Blackburn did. Thus the upshot of Gibbs' inquiry was that no one remembered seeing "Sammy" after 11 o'clock that night.

Gibbs spent several weeks tracking down friends of "Sammy," and finally brought "Sammy" himself into the City Hall one night and grilled him for five hours. "Sammy" said he knew nothing about the Ala Moana case.

The only results the investigator for Jack Kelley obtained were negative: he traced every movement of "Sammy" the night of the assault and found that he had no alibi from about 11:30 P.M. Saturday until 3 A.M. Sunday. He had not gone to a wedding in the country on Saturday, as he told Hewitt; the wedding was on Sunday.

The nearest to a positive clue Gibbs ever got was from a mechanic in a downtown garage, who had been with "Sammy" earlier the night of September 12. One of the girls who had also been with him came into the garage late in February 1932—after the killing of Kahahawai, and after "Sammy" returned from Los Angeles—and said:

" 'Sammy' is in real trouble."

The man asked her why, and she said:

"I was with him. I can prove it."

The End of the Trail

By the end of August 1932—some five months after the Massie-Fortescue trial and almost a year from the date of the attack on Thalia Massie—Kelley was in possession of about all the information he would ever have that might solve the mystery of what really happened to Thalia Massie on the night of September 12, 1931.

He faced a strange dilemma: If the five boys accused of assaulting Thalia Massie were not, in fact, her attackers, he would be in the position of prosecuting the remaining four even though he was certain they were not guilty.

If he failed to press the Ala Moana case for retrial, the entire matter would dissolve into the oblivion of "unsolved cases"—a notion that not only was repugnant to a Public Prosecutor, charged with enforcement of law, but violated the basic concept of justice which governs civilized people.

The questions that confronted Kelley at the beginning of the investigation, which he considered necessary for a retrial of the Ala Moana case, had been answered to some extent, and the answers were largely negative.

The report of the Pinkerton Agency was partially completed, and it was made available to Kelley. John C. Fraser, the Pinkerton operative in Honolulu, had come to the conclusion that the five Ala Moana defendants could not have been Thalia Massie's attackers, in spite of her positive identification of four of them. His report said:

Although there has been found no corroboration of the statement of Mrs. Massie that the alleged kidnaping and rape occurred at the times and places and with all the circumstances described by Mrs. Massie, neither has it been proved that the kidnaping and rape did not occur.

We believe, however, that it has been shown that the five accused did not have the opportunity to commit the kidnaping and rape as described by Mrs. Massie between the time she says she left Ala Wai Inn at 11:35 P.M., September 12, 1931, and the time she was picked up by the Bellingers and Clarks on Ala Moana Road, at 12:50 A.M., September 13, 1931.

That other persons would have had opportunity to commit the offense as related by Mrs. Massie there is no doubt, but a check up nine months after the alleged offenses of all persons who may have had the opportunity to be at places and at times described by Mrs. Massie in her narrative is impossible.[15]

This rather ambiguous conclusion left Kelley with the problem of determining whom to prosecute—if the five defendants in the earlier trial were not guilty, or at least were cleared of the possibility of guilt within the time limits established by Thalia Massie herself.

The identity of the "white man" who followed the "girl in the green dress" down John Ena Road was still unsettled, and it nagged at Kelley. The movements of the Navy officers who had been at the party at the Ala Wai Inn had been traced by Gibbs and by the Pinkerton operatives, with only negative results. Lieutenant Brown had left with his wife about 11:35 P.M. The members of the Miller party left about the same time, with the exception of the Stogsdalls, after the incident in which Thalia Massie slapped Stogsdall. Mrs. Stogsdall "thought they left at 12:10" because she had noticed the time when they got home; but she changed the story she first told Inspector McIntosh to conform with the others, stating that they "might have left earlier."

Lieutenant Branson was definitely seen at 11:55 when he took off his shoes and danced in front of the orchestra; and he was later seen with Massie at 1 o'clock or shortly afterward when Massie tried to phone his wife. The Pinkerton Report stated:

> Branson was there, according to witnesses, between 11:30 or a little later, and 11:55 P.M. When Massie returned he announced the time, saying, "Jerry, it's 11:55 P.M. and the last dance is announced." It was at this time that Branson took off his shoes and did some tap dancing.
>
> Instead of the dance closing at midnight it continued until 1 A.M. or a little after . . . At 1:15 A.M. Lieutenant Branson and Massie were at the telephone at the Inn, with Lieutenant Massie trying to get someone on the phone.[16]

There was an obvious gap between midnight and 1 A.M., during which it would have been possible for someone to have followed Thalia Massie when she left the inn, possibly in the hope of persuading her to return. This possibility would fit the testimony of witnesses who saw the "girl in the green dress" walking down John Ena Road about 12:15 A.M., followed by a white man. Eugenio Batungbacal had said in his testimony:

I saw the girl walking with the men the first time. I thought they go together—just go with the party. The girl is just like drunk, you know. I don't think the mens were . . . She looked as if she was drunk because two mens held this arm and she tried to get away. This is what make me believe she is drunk.[17]

The theory Kelly had been developing was based on the possibility that Thalia Massie may have left the Ala Wai Inn intending to meet someone, possibly to go to one of the small "bootleg joints" in the Fort De Russy area for a drink or two, and then return to the party.

The question he had raised as to why none of the Navy party at the Ala Wai Inn—with the exception of Lieutenant Brown and his wife—had appeared as witnesses for Thalia Massie at the Ala Moana trial might also be regarded as having a possible answer under these circumstances. If Thalia Massie had gone off in a huff, because—as she testified at the trial—she was "bored" with the party, this might well be the explanation for the unwillingness of her friends at the party to testify under oath as to the circumstances under which she left. It would also explain the reason why Tommy Massie, her husband, also failed to testify in support of her story.

As to the final critical question whether Tommy Massie believed at the time he killed Joseph Kahahawai that the Hawaiian boy was actually guilty of attacking and raping his wife, Kelley had no positive solution. At the Massie-Fortescue trial Kelley had taken the position that Massie was not temporarily insane; but the deeper issue—whether or not he believed his victim had raped his wife—was carefully avoided by both sides.

Only one point bore directly on the veracity of Massie's story, and that was Massie's positive statement that his wife was pregnant and that an abortion had to be performed at the Kapiolani Maternity Home. "There couldn't be any doubt about it," he testified. Yet the report of the attending physician, Dr. Paul Withington, showed a "negative diagnosis" after the curettement was performed. As Kelley remarked to newspapermen at the time, "Either Massie knew about that report, or he was a damned indifferent husband."

Summing it all up, Kelley became convinced that—as the Pinkerton Report set forth—"the testimony at the trial of the defendants makes it impossible to escape the conviction that the kidnaping and assault was not caused by those accused, with the attendant circumstances alleged by Mrs. Massie."

He was equally certain that Thalia Massie had not told a complete story of the events, and since she had left the jurisdiction of the Territorial courts, there was no way of getting at the undisclosed parts of her story. Again quoting the Pinkerton Report:

> We can only assume that the reason Mrs. Massie did not give to the authorities, immediately after the alleged assault, the same details of information she was able to furnish by her testimony at the trial, is because she did not possess it at the time she was questioned by those she came in contact with immediately after the alleged offense.[18]

This referred to her identification of the license number; her claim that she identified the car (although Chief Inspector McIntosh denied this); and her identification of the suspects.

The Pinkerton Report continued:

> No more satisfactory is Mrs. Massie's account of the time she left the Ala Wai Inn. That she was last seen by certain associates at 11:30 P.M. proved nothing as to the time she left the inn. No one, however, can be found who saw her leave the inn and thereby fix the time.[19]

As to the alibi of the five accused boys, the report states:

> Our investigation embraced a careful examination into the alibi of the accused and we failed to discover any important circumstances disproving in any manner any portion of the statements they made immediately upon their arrest, their examination by the police and prosecution subsequently, and their testimony at the trial. In other words, the movements of the accused on the night of the alleged assault remain precisely as they were originally accounted for.[20]

The report concluded that it was "doubtful at this late date if investigations of this alleged assault will disclose the identity of those who physically assaulted Mrs. Massie" and added: "Theories as to the possible manner in which this occurred may be stated, but without definite proof in support thereof, it obviously is unwise to state theories."[21]

Kelley's own investigator, Cornealous Gibbs, had gotten considerably further than the Pinkerton operatives in the effort to identify those who had beaten Thalia Massie, and also in establishing a theory as to what actually happened. But as Kelley pointed out in a final news conference:

"A theory is no damned good unless it can be supported with evidence and testimony in a trial."

Kelley had fought vigorously against Attorney General Harry Hewitt's early effort to "bury the case." His desire to "put Thalia Massie on the stand in effigy" by using the transcript of her testimony at the earlier trial was thwarted not only by political pressure but by failure of his investigators to provide evidence that could be used to support his own theory of the case.

The intensive effort to trace the only other tangible possibility—the involvement of "Sammy" and his three friends—had run into a blank wall of vague recollections, negative intimations by "Sammy's" friends, and "Sammy's" own insistence that he knew nothing about the affair.

Thus the only results from the delayed investigation that might have provided a clue to what happened on the Ala Moana that Saturday night in September were lost in the fading traces of time. Jack Kelley finally became convinced he could not retry the case. He appeared in Judge Charles Skinner Davis' court on February 13, 1933, and moved for a *nolle prosequi*—"no prosecution"—in the case of the Territory vs. Ben Ahakuelo, Horace Ida, Henry Chang and David Takai. He said the prosecution had no means of identifying Thalia Massie's assailants and no witness to establish a complaint.

He gave the following statement to newspapermen:

The evidence adduced at the trial of these defendants was such that it was not surprising that a verdict of conviction was not obtained. It is doubtful at this late date that an investigation will disclose the identity of those who physically assaulted Mrs. Massie. The testimony of Mrs. Massie, in view of her lack of knowledge of important details when first interviewed immediately after the assault, must give rise to grave doubts as to the accuracy of any of her statements.[22]

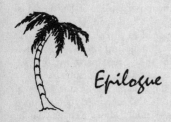

Epilogue

Clarence Darrow had asked, in his last words to the jury: "What has befallen this family? . . . What is behind this? Will fate ever have taken its toll of this family, and leave them to go in peace?"

There was something deeply prophetic in the old man's words; perhaps it was the inexorable "force of nature," as he called it, marching down the passageway of time. It may well be, as Darrow phrased it, that "there are so many ways to measure goodness and badness" that there can be neither blame nor justification for what happened in the Massie case.

The tragedy of this failure of justice affected not only the people involved directly in the Massie case; it lay deep within our society —then and today—far deeper than for those few unfortunate people who were caught in the meshes of that law and justice which offered one thing to four white people who were set free, and another to five "native boys" trapped in its web.

Late in the year of the Massie-Fortescue trial—on December 5, 1932—the investigation by the Governor of Hawaii, Lawrence Judd, was completed. The Pinkerton Report was never made public; but one statement summarized its results:

It would seem, in view of the evidence . . . there was no opportunity for the accused to commit the kidnaping and rape of Mrs. Massie either at the time alleged by her, or at any other time within this period. For such to have been possible, it would be necessary for many witnesses to have wilfully made false statements and to have perjured themselves at the trial of the accused.[1]

But what of the others caught in those meshes of law and justice? What happened to those who were trapped, and those who were freed? It is known what happened to Joseph Kahahawai: He was killed. Ben Ahakuelo is still in Honolulu, living on the windward side of Oahu, a member of the rural fire department. Ida became a storekeeper; the others moved into various pursuits.

Jones was married a year after the trial to Rose Anne Berry of New Bedford, Mass. Lord remained in the Navy and then dropped out of sight. But what of the others—Tommy Massie, Thalia Massie, and her mother, the gray-haired lady who, according to Jack Kelley, "pointed the finger of doom at Joseph Kahahawai?"

Except for the published reports in which Thalia Massie spoke of the "deal" she had made with the Territorial Government when she left Hawaii, little was heard of this ill-fated girl, except for casual reports of those who had seen her in New York or Philadelphia or Washington, until October 1933, a year and a half after the trial ended. Then a report from Washington, D.C., announced that she was going to Reno, Nevada to divorce Tommy Massie.

In January 1934 she appeared in Reno, and six weeks later she obtained the divorce on grounds of "extreme cruelty." She told newspapermen, "Tommy insisted we get a divorce. It was the terrible publicity of the trial!"

The divorce was granted February 22, 1934; and a month later she took a Mediterranean cruise aboard the SS *Roma*. As the liner neared Genoa, she went to the bridge one evening, slashed her wrist, and jumped or fell to the deck below. She was taken ashore, badly hurt. The ship's physician, Dr. Emilio Borrelli, said she had "hallucinations—she believes someone is trying to kill her."

Young Massie was at sea, on the battleship *Oklahoma*. He radioed his sympathy. "I am terribly grieved. Hope you will get in touch with me if I can possibly be of help. Fondly, Tommy."

Thalia Massie at Reno, Nevada, as she arrived to obtain a divorce from Lt. Massie. The divorce was granted February 22, 1934.

Thalia Massie did not reply to the message. She told an Associated Press reporter: "He has ceased to exist for me."

The unhappy girl finally returned to New York on the SS *President Van Buren* in May 1934. She went immediately to her family home at Sayville, Long Island, a gray Victorian mansion where she had grown up as a girl, and which was known as "the Fortescue place" until a few years ago, when it was torn down to make way for a housing development.

It was nearly twenty years later that the people of Hawaii again heard about Thalia Massie. Then it was from Los Angeles. She had "gone berserk" one night, according to the newspaper reports, and attacked her landlady, who was pregnant. The landlady, Mrs. Alfred Hugueny, sued her for ten thousand dollars.

This was in 1951—and Hawaii had still not achieved statehood. That came in 1959, after bitter debates in Congress over the ability of the "natives" to govern themselves.

Two years later Thalia Massie—at the age of forty-two—was a student at the University of Arizona. She met a twenty-one-year-old fellow student, Robert Uptigrove, and they eloped to Mexico and were married.

This lasted two years; then they were divorced and she went to Palm Beach, Florida, where her mother lived.

Tommy Massie had married again, in Seattle, Washington, on March 15, 1937. His bride was Florence Storms of Chewallah, Washington; and in 1940 he left the Navy and settled in San Diego, where he was last reported living quietly with his wife.

On July 2, 1962—more than thirty years after that terrible night in Honolulu on September 12, 1931—Thalia Massie went to bed in her apartment at West Palm Beach, near the home in Palm Beach where her mother, Mrs. Fortescue, lived. She never woke up. The coroner's report said she had died from "an accidental overdose of barbiturates."

The tragic story of this girl, "pursued, shamed and hounded from one end of the country to the other," as Darrow had said in his address to the jury, thus came to an end; and so ended "the Massie case."

A Personal Note

The intention was expressed at the beginning of this book to avoid any assessment of blame or responsibility for the tragic events that grew out of the attack on Thalia Massie. As far as possible, the writer has tried to observe this rule. There is one point, however, on which some comment seems necessary; and this concerns the role of Clarence Darrow in the Massie case.

The old man came down to the Islands believing his personal presence and his known tolerance and understanding of human suffering would help smooth over any racial problems that might exist. When he left the Islands two months later the racial issues were more deeply graven than ever.

There were many who blamed Clarence Darrow for the outcome of the Massie-Fortescue trial, which in itself was a paradox. He had always hated injustice and arrogance; he had nearly always aligned himself with the downtrodden people of his day, the unprotected victims of a hostile society. Yet in Honolulu he found himself ranged on the other side, fighting for those things he despised: arrogance and ruthlessness of economic overlords, the failure of man-made justice to protect the weak and disenfranchised. Why?

It is necessary for the writer at this point to indulge in some personal recollections. Clarence Darrow was well known to my family for three generations. His sister and my grandmother, Adelle Williams, were among the first half dozen coeds at Allegheny College in western Pennsylvania. As a young man, Darrow had spent summers at my grandfather's farm near Meadville. It was natural that he should visit my father while he was in Honolulu; and on several occasions I was present in the evenings when he came to my father's home.*

On one of these occasions, after the trial was over and before he left for the mainland, he unburdened himself of some thoughts

---

* Editor's note: The author's father, the late George Williams Wright, was editor of the Japanese-English newspaper, the *Hawaii Hochi*.

about the "race problem" in Hawaii. He seemed puzzled and troubled; and it was at this time that he made the comment about his hope of "healing racial wounds" in the Islands.

He had previously expressed to newspaper reporters covering the trial his frustration at being unable to understand the intricate mentality of the "Oriental." But the stolid reticence of the Hawaiian was even more puzzling.

"What is it about these people I do not understand?" he asked.

"You met all the issues," my father said, "except one—the only one that really had to be met. That was the racial issue."

He spoke of the background of Hawaii, covered in the early chapters of this book; the growing disenchantment of the Hawaiian people with the small clique of *kamaaina haoles* that had gained control of the Islands; the political ferment and discontent; and finally, the refusal of the *haole* elite to accept the decision of their own laws and courts in the case of the Ala Moana defendants. The Hawaiians and other "racial groups" in Honolulu, including the Portuguese, who were regarded as "white" but not *haole,* were not bitter against Darrow, or even against the Massie-Fortescue group, or the Navy. What they resented was a concept of justice that would throw five boys of mixed Hawaiian and other racial origins into prison, as hoodlums and gangsters—even though there had been no real proof of their guilt; and at the same time it would allow four mainland *haoles* to go free, after they admitted killing Joseph Kahahawai.

It was as simple as that.

Darrow sat for some time, pondering the matter. Finally he sighed, and in a rumbling voice that seemed to come out of the depths of his chest, he said:

"I suppose that's the reason for the verdict. I tried to keep the race question out of it—I'd like to see them all go free. It's bad enough just being in this world, without being hounded and persecuted by law."

This philosophy of the law was inherent in Clarence Darrow's thinking, born of old and bitter experiences: the Chicago Haymarket Square riots and the Pullman strike, in which he defended Eugene Debs; the fight for the lives of Moyer, Heywood and Pettibone, accused of murdering ex-Governor Steunenberg of Idaho in labor wars in the West; the Los Angeles *Times* bombing in which he defended the McNamara brothers. These things had stamped indelible marks on the old man's conscience; and now, at the twilight of his career, he still felt the fierce fire of the legal crusader. But the Massie case was not a crusade. It was, in a way, a fundamental miscarriage of justice; and Darrow was on the other side!

One morning after he had walked from his hotel on Bishop Street to the courthouse, with several newspaper reporters, he turned as we stood with him in the corridor, his gray eyes twinkling and his face fixed in that enigmatic "Wizard-of-Oz" look that was familiar to all of us.

"Do you boys know," he said, "that I have one thing on Jack Kelley and all the rest of the other lawyers. I've been practicing law for nearly fifty years" . . . He paused, his eyes still twinkling. "In all that time I have never prosecuted a human being."

This was true. Clarence Darrow had never held a position as Public Prosecutor or in the District Attorney's office. The nearest he ever came was when he was corporation counsel for the old Chicago & Northwestern before the turn of the century—and before the Pullman strike in Chicago. He had not even been a judge. He had practiced in the courts what he believed in his heart: that the law is a means of saving people as well as condemning them.

He had taken the Massie-Fortescue case because, as he said, he was "a practicing lawyer"—even though he had retired; "and they paid me to take the case."

These matters are mentioned because they concern, in a way, the ultimate results of the Massie-Fortescue trial. During the last days of that trial, in Darrow's closing words to the jury, he had said, "I would be sorry to leave this beautiful land with the thought that I had compared any class against another class . . . I never knew what it was in my life to have any prejudice against any race on earth."

Then, as if to apologize for his position, in the trial he said: "These islands, halfway between Asia, the Mother of all, and

307

America, the newest of nations, inhabited by a kindly people who live their lives in peace . . . this beautiful spot found by people who came here from the East and from the West, and other points! I have never known the Eastern people well, but the oldest race of the entire world has its place in the world, just the same . . . I have no feeling against them, or the four or five men who committed the crime against Mrs. Massie . . . no feelings on account of race."

And he added, almost as an afterthought:

"My feelings were well known and understood by my clients when I took this case. I'll not say one thing when I think something else."

Whether this expression of his feelings—the rambling, stumbling effort of a tired old man to get himself back on record—was known to his clients is not of any particular importance. Anyone who had known Darrow must have believed what he said. But in the course of his conduct of the Massie-Fortescue trial, he had avoided and evaded the one issue in the case that might have helped heal the "racial wounds." He had listened to the *haole* elite, the Dillinghams, the Castles, the Cookes, who did not like to admit the existence of a "racial issue," probably because they had helped create it. He had followed the theory of this narrow-minded segment of Honoluluans, whose views were expressed by one of the myopic editors of the local newspapers: "We in Hawaii *know* there is no race issue!"

The delusion that if the racial issue could be ignored, it would cease to exist, was the major blunder of the Massie case. The blunder was not primarily Darrow's, nor could it be assessed against any individuals—even the *malihini haoles* and their coalition with local fellow travelers of the *haole* elite, who preferred to view the whole affair as a "sex problem."

The fault lay at the very roots of Hawaii's social and political system. There is probably no use belaboring the matter. The Massie-Fortescue trial solved nothing. The Ala Moana trial left four Hawaiian boys with a stain that could not be legally erased, and the *nolle prosequi* in the retrial left Thalia Massie without a shred of hope of ever legally vindicating herself.

The fact that the sentences of the four defendants in the second trial were reduced from ten years to one hour was hardly a triumph for Clarence Darrow. It certainly was not a triumph for justice. It freed four white people but left Hawaii in a turmoil of racial bitterness and hatred that lasted for a generation. And it confirmed among many non-*haoles* of Hawaii what they had long suspected—that dark-skinned people would be sacrificed to the "white man's law," even lynch law; but the white people themselves would go free.

As David Kama had expressed it, standing over the grave of Joseph Kahahawai: "There is one law for the Hawaiians and another for the white people."

This may have been an exaggeration, but the effort of the *haole* elite of Hawaii to apply this doctrine was not an exaggeration. If any blame for the miserable muddle of the Massie case is to be assessed, it must belong—not to Clarence Darrow, or the Navy, or even the Southern gentlemen in Congress—but to the *haole* elite themselves. And since it is an ill wind that blows no one any good, it may be interesting to note what has happened to the *haole* elite—the Big Five—since the Massie case. On April 20, 1966, the man who might be regarded as having inherited the purple mantle of the Big Five, Malcolm MacNaughton, president of Castle & Cooke, Ltd., was quoted in the Honolulu *Advertiser* as having said in a speech:

> Hawaii is no longer the sleepy, easy-going, semi-tropical resort that it was 20 years ago. Things have changed . . . These developments came as a complete shock to the community at large.[2]

MacNaughton went on to note that "even after the turn of the century, the Castle & Cooke stockholder list grew only as marriages occurred or deaths saw shares passed on to a growing list of children and grandchildren. With this tight ownership went very close control." He also pointed out that under this "tight ownership and control" the large agencies and mercantile firms in the Territory —such as Castle & Cooke—had dominated not only the economic life but "much of the political life in the Islands."

During the period preceding the outbreak of World War II,

signalized by the attack on Pearl Harbor, "everyone was so busy . . . no thought was given to business or social changes that might be in the making, or that might develop—but develop they did!"

As the head man of Castle & Cooke remarked, "things have changed." Honolulu is now a bustling mid-ocean metropolis, with great new hotels and new industries sprouting up everywhere. Dozens of airplanes fly in and out of Honolulu International Airport every week, carrying most of the people formerly transported on the slow, sleepy voyages of the old *Matsonia*, the *Lurline* and the *Malolo*. Perhaps the most significant change is one that is seldom mentioned: the Big Five no longer rules Hawaii.

It is doubtful if the Massie case can be given credit for this change, or even the larger part of it. Change is a natural consequence of economic development and political progress. The passing of the old *haole* elite did not happen as a result of any single event, or series of events. Yet as one looks back over the past third of a century, it becomes evident that the first mortal blow against the "establishment" in Paradise was struck by the Massie-Fortescue trial and the events that followed. The Massie case, like the Dreyfus case, has a place in history that may not be well known or understood among the *malihinis* of today, but it will never be forgotten by the dwindling *kamaainas* of Hawaii.

Glossary

Hawaiian words and phrases used in this book:

aloha: (ah-low-ha) hello, good-bye, love.
haole: (how-lee) a white person; originally a stranger.
hapai: (hah-pye) carry.
hapa-haole: (hah-pah how-lee) half-white.
hapa-pake: (hah-pah pah-kay) half-Chinese.
kanaka: (kah-nah-kah) a Hawaiian or Polynesian.
kamaiina: (kah-mah-ina, as in "dinah") an old-timer.
lanai: (lah-nye) porch, or verandah.
luau: (loo-ow) Hawaiian feast.
makai: (mye-kye) toward the sea.
malihini: (mah-lee-hee-nee) newcomer.
mauka: (mow-kah) toward the mountains.
okolehao: (o-ko-lee-how) a Hawaiian liquor.
pali: (pah-lee) cliff; the Nuuanu Pali.
panini: (pah-nee-nee) cactus.
pilau: (pee-low) stinks.
pau: (pah-oo, or pow) finished, or, used as verb, stop.
wahine: (wah-heenie) woman.
waikiki: toward Waikiki; south.

Notes

A Night on the Ala Moana

1. Honolulu Police files, 1931: Ala Moana Case.
2. Report of Pinkerton Detective Agency to Governor Lawrence Judd of Hawaii, dated Oct. 5, 1932 (Archives of Hawaii), p. 186.
3. Pinkerton Report, p. 186-87.
4. Pinkerton Report, p. 210.
5. Honolulu Police files, 1931; Pinkerton Report, p. 98.
6. Honolulu Police files, 1931; Pinkerton Report, p. 111.
7. Transcript of trial, *Territory* v. *Ahakuelo et al.*, City and County Attorney's office, Honolulu, Hawaii, 1931 files.
8. Honolulu Police files, 1931; Pinkerton Report, p. 214.
9. Honolulu Police files, 1931; Pinkerton Report, p. 246.
10. Honolulu Police files, 1931; Pinkerton Report, p. 214.
11. Honolulu Police files, 1931.
12. Honolulu Police files, 1931.
13. Honolulu Police files, 1931; Pinkerton Report, p. 82.
14. Pinkerton Report, p. 3.
15. Pinkerton Report, p. 4.

Arrest of the Suspects

1. Pinkerton Report, p. 9.
2. Honolulu *Star-Bulletin*, Sept. 15, 1931.
3. Pinkerton Report, p. 82.
4. Pinkerton Report, p. 81.
5. Pinkerton Report, p. 51.

6. Pinkerton Report, p. 42.
7. Pinkerton Report, p. 42.
8. Honolulu Police files, 1931; Pinkerton Report, pp. 18, 162-63.
9. Honolulu Police files, 1931; Pinkerton Report, pp. 18, 162.

HE INVESTIGATION

1. County Attorney's files, Honolulu, 1931; Pinkerton Report, p. 89.
2. Honolulu Police files, 1931; Pinkerton Report, p. 168.
3. Pinkerton Report, p. 93.
4. Pinkerton Report, p. 93.
5. Transcript of trial, *Territory* v. *Ahakuelo et al.*
6. Pinkerton Report, p. 59.
7. Honololu Police files, 1931; Pinkerton Report, pp. 162-63.

POLITICS IN PARADISE

1. Honolulu *Advertiser*, Sept. 14, 1931.
2. Honolulu *Advertiser*, Sept. 14, 1931.
3. Honolulu *Advertiser*, Sept. 15, 1931.
4. *Hawaii: Restless Rampart*, by Joseph Barber, Jr. (Bobbs, Merrill), 1941, p. 25.
5. *Hawaii: Restless Rampart*, p. 23.
6. "A Memorandum," by W. F. Dillingham, printed May 17, 1932, p. 4 (Archives of Hawaii, File, Houston, V. K., Misc. Ala Moana Papers).

THE ALIBI WITNESSES

1. Honolulu Police files, 1931; Pinkerton Report, p. 195.
2. Honolulu Police files, 1931; Pinkerton Report, p. 196.
3. Honolulu Police files, 1931; Pinkerton Report, p. 246.
4. "A Memorandum," by W. F. Dillingham, p. 4.

THE MYSTERY WITNESSES

1. County Attorney's files, *Territory* v. *Ahakuelo et al.*; Pinkerton Report, p. 123.
2. County Attorney's files, 1931; Pinkerton Report, p. 134.
3. County Attorney's files, 1931; Pinkerton Report, p. 143.
4. Honolulu Police files, 1931; Pinkerton Report, p. 22.
5. County Attorney's files, 1931; Pinkerton Report, p. 168.
6. County Attorney's files, 1931; Pinkerton Report, p. 24.
7. County Attorney's files, 1931; Pinkerton Report, p. 25.
8. County Attorney's files, 1931; Pinkerton Report, p. 41.
9. "A Memorandum," by W. F. Dillingham, p. 4.
10. Records of the Queen's Hospital, September, 1931.
11. Pinkerton Report, p. 61.
12. Honolulu *Advertiser*, Oct. 15, 1931.

THE ALA MOANA TRIAL

1. Honolulu *Star-Bulletin*, Nov. 18, 1931.
2. Honolulu *Advertiser*, Nov. 19, 1931.

3. Transcript of trial, *Territory* v. *Ahakuelo et al.*
4. Pinkerton Report, pp. 172-73.
5. Transcript of trial, *Territory* v. *Ahakuelo et al.*
6. Pinkerton Report, p. 32.
7. Pinkerton Report, p. 167.
8. Transcript of trial, *Territory* v. *Ahakuelo et al.*
9. Transcript of trial, *Territory* v. *Ahakuelo et al.*
10. Pinkerton Report, p. 158.
11. Pinkerton Report, p. 106.
12. Pinkerton Report, p. 167.
13. Transcript of trial, *Territory* v. *Ahakuelo et al.*
14. Transcript of trial, *Territory* v. *Ahakuelo et al.*
15. Transcript of trial, *Territory* v. *Ahakuelo et al.*
16. Pinkerton Report, p. 70.
17. Pinkerton Report, p. 70.
18. Pinkerton Report, p. 71.
19. Transcript of trial, *Territory* v. *Ahakuelo et al.*
20. Transcript of trial, *Territory* v. *Ahakuelo et al.*
21. Transcript of trial, *Territory* v. *Ahakuelo et al.*

THE BITTER FRUIT

1. Honolulu Police files, 1931; Pinkerton Report, p. 207.
2. Transcript of trial, *Territory* v. *Ahakuelo et al.*
3. Pinkerton Report, p. 235.
4. Pinkerton Report, p. 215.
5. Pinkerton Report, pp. 217-18.
6. Pinkerton Report, p. 218.
7. Honolulu *Advertiser*, Dec. 3, 1931.
8. "A Memorandum," by W. F. Dillingham, p. 5.
9. "A Memorandum," by W. F. Dillingham, p. 5.

THE KILLING OF JOSEPH KAHAHAWAI

1. Territory's Exhibit 1, *Territory* v. *Grace Fortescue et al.*
2. Honolulu *Advertiser*, Jan. 9, 1932.
3. Honolulu *Advertiser*, Jan. 11, 1932.
4. Honolulu *Star-Bulletin*, Jan. 9, 1932.
5. New York *American*, Jan. 11, 1932.
6. Document No. 78, 72nd Congress, First Session, dated April 4, 1932: "Report on Crime in Hawaii," quoting a Report by the Department of the Interior to the Senate Committee on Insular Affairs.
7. "A Memorandum," by W. F. Dillingham, pp. 5-6.
8. New York *American*, Jan. 12, 1932.
9. *Hawaii Hochi Sha*, Jan. 12, 1932.

THE ARRIVAL OF CLARENCE DARROW

1. File, Houston, V. K., Misc. Ala Moana Papers (Archives of Hawaii).
2. "A Memorandum," by W. F. Dillingham, pp. 6-7.

NOTES

3. *Hawaii Pono*, by L. A. Fuchs (Harcourt, Brace, 1961), p. 66.
4. File, Houston, V. K., Misc. Ala Moana Papers (Archives of Hawaii).
5. Document No. 78, 72nd Congress, First Session, dated April 4, 1932: Report by Assistant Attorney General Seth Richardson.
6. Honolulu *Advertiser*, March 25, 1932.

THE MASSIE-FORTESCUE TRIAL

1. Transcript of trial, *Territory* v. *Fortescue et al.* (published in Honolulu *Advertiser*).
2. Honolulu *Advertiser*, April 12, 1932.
3. Records of Kapiolani Maternity Hospital, Honolulu, October, 1931.

THE VERDICT — AND THE PENALTY

1. "A Memorandum," by W. F. Dillingham, p. 7.
2. File, Judd, L. A., Misc. Ala Moana Papers (Archives of Hawaii)
3. File, Houston, V. K., Misc. Ala Moana Papers (Archives of Hawaii).
4. File, Houston, V. K., Misc. Ala Moana Papers (Archives of Hawaii).
5. Honolulu *Advertiser*, May 5, 1932.

THE FINALE

1. Honolulu *Advertiser*, May 5, 1932.
2. Honolulu *Star-Bulletin*, May 3, 1932.
3. Honolulu *Star-Bulletin*, May 4, 1932.
4. *Hawaii Hochi Sha*, May 10, 1932.
5. San Francisco *Examiner*, May 13, 1932.
6. New York *Times*, Feb. 14, 1933.
7. Pinkerton Report, p. 267.
8. Pinkerton Report, p. 268.
9. File, Houston, V. K., Misc. Ala Moana Papers (Archives of Hawaii).
10. "A Memorandum," by W. F. Dillingham, p. 8.
11. "A Memorandum," by W. F. Dillingham, p. 8.
12. *Hawaii Hochi Sha*, May 20, 1932.
13. Pinkerton Report, p. 46.
14. Pinkerton Report, p. 67.
15. Pinkerton Report, p. 277.
16. Pinkerton Report, p. 263.
17. Transcript of trial, *Territory* v. *Ahakuelo et al.*; Pinkerton Report, p. 129.
18. Letter from Arthur Rossetter, vice-president of Pinkerton Detective Agency, to Governor Lawrence Judd, dated Oct. 5, 1932 (Archives of Hawaii).
19. Letter from Rossetter to Judd, Oct. 5, 1932.
20. Letter from Rossetter to Judd, Oct. 5, 1932.
21. Letter from Rossetter to Judd, Oct. 5, 1932.
22. Honolulu *Advertiser*, Feb. 14, 1933.

EPILOGUE

1. Pinkerton Report, p. 261.
2. Honolulu *Advertiser*, April 20, 1966.

The Author and His Book

THEON WRIGHT *was born in Oroville, California, on June 24, 1904. He begun his career in 1921 as a cub reporter on the Honolulu* Star-Bulletin *while he was still in high school on the Hawaiian island of Oahu. He spent the years before World War II as a reporter for the Newark* Ledger, *the New York* Evening Graphic, *the Honolulu* Advertiser *and the United Press Association (for which he became manager of the Los Angeles bureau). Among the news events he has covered are the Hindenburg disaster, the Lindbergh kidnaping trial and the Massie case in Honolulu.*

After World War II, during which he served as an officer in the Special Warfare and Psychological Warfare branch of U.S. Army Intelligence, Mr. Wright went into public relations and business management work, at one time serving as assistant to the Chairman of the Board of Trans World Airlines.

A member of the Circumnavigators Club and a member and past president of the Adventurers Club, Theon Wright has written many books on adventure, mystery and crime. His latest best-seller is The Voyage of the Herman *(Hawthorn, 1966).*

RAPE IN PARADISE *was set into type by the Spartan Division of Argus-Greenwood, Inc. Mahony & Roese printed it by offset lithography and American Book-Stratford Press, Inc., did the binding. The text type is Caledonia, a linotype face designed by W. A. Dwiggins, and the display type is Mistral.*

A HAWTHORN BOOK

TALES OF THE PACIFIC

JACK LONDON

Stories of Hawaii by Jack London
Thirteen yarns drawn from the famous author's love affair with Hawaii Nei.
$4.95   ISBN 0-935180-08-7

The Mutiny of the "Elsinore," by Jack London
Based on a voyage around Cape Horn in a windjammer from New York to Seattle in 1913, this romance between the lone passenger and the captain's daughter reveals London at his most fertile and fluent best. The lovers are forced to outface a rioting band of seagoing gangsters in the South Pacific.
$4.95   ISBN 0-935180-40-0

Captain David Grief by Jack London
Captain David Grief, South Sea tycoon, came to the Pacific at the age of twenty, and two decades later he protected a vast trading empire. Eight long tales of daring and adventure by the famous American storyteller who did some of his best writing in that region.
$3.95   ISBN 0-935180-34-6

South Sea Tales by Jack London
Fiction from the violent days of the early century, set among the atolls of French Oceania and the high islands of Samoa, Fiji, Pitcairn, and "the terrible Solomons."
$4.95   ISBN 0-935180-14-1

HAWAII

A Hawaiian Reader
Thirty-seven selections from the literature of the past hundred years including such writers as Mark Twain, Robert Louis Stevenson and James Jones.
$4.95   ISBN 0-935180-07-9

The Spell of Hawaii
A companion volume to *A Hawaiian Reader.* Twenty-four selections from the exotic literary heritage of the islands.
$4.95   ISBN 0-935180-13-3

Kona by Marjorie Sinclair
The best woman novelist of post-war Hawaii dramatizes the conflict between a daughter of Old Hawaii and her straitlaced Yankee husband. Nor is the drama resolved in their children.
$3.95   ISBN 0-935180-20-6

The Golden Cloak by Antoinette Withington
The romantic story of Hawaii's monarchs and their friends, from Kamehameha the Great, founder of the dynasty, to Liliuokalani, last queen to rule in America's only royal palace.
$3.95   ISBN 0-935180-26-5

Teller of Tales by Eric Knudsen
Son of a pioneer family of Kauai, the author spent most of his life on the Garden Island as a rancher, hunter of wild cattle, lawyer, and legislator. Here are sixty campfire yarns of gods and goddesses, ghosts and heroes, cowboy adventures and legendary feats aong the valleys and peaks of the island.
$4.95   ISBN 0-935180-33-8

The Wild Wind a novel by Marjorie Sinclair
On the Hana Coast of Maui, Lucia Gray, great-granddaughter of a New England missionary, seeks solitude but embarks on an interracial marriage with a Hawaiian cowboy. Then she faces some of the mysteries of the Polynesia of old.
$ 4.95   ISBN 0-935180-3-3

Myths and Legends of Hawaii by Dr. W.D. Westervelt
A broadly inclusive, one-volume collection of folklore by a leading authority. Completely edited and reset format for today's readers of the great prehistoric tales of Maui, Hina, Pele and her fiery family, and a dozen other heroic beings, human or ghostly.
$3.95   ISBN 0-935180-43-5

Claus Spreckles, The Sugar King in Hawai by Jacob Adler
Sugar was the main economic game in Hawaii a century ago, and the boldest player was Claus Spreckels, a California tycoon who built a second empire in the Islands by ruthless and often dubious means.
$3.95   ISBN 0-935180-76-1

Remember Pearl Harbor by Blake Clark
An up-to-date edition of the first full-length account of the effect of the December 7, 1941 "blitz" that precipitated America's entrance into World War II and is still remembered vividly by military and civilian survivors of the airborne Japanese holocaust.
$3.95   ISBN 0-935180-49-4

Russian Flag Over Hawaii: The Mission of Jeffery Tolamy, a novel by Darwin Teilhet

A vigorous adventure novel in which a young American struggles to unshackle the grip held by Russian filibusters on the Kingdom of Kauai. Kamehameha the Great and many other historical figures play their roles in a colorful love story.

$3.95   ISBN 0-935180-28-1

The Betrayal of Liliuokalani: Last Queen of Hawaii 1838-1917 by Helena G. Allen

A woman caught in the turbulent maelstrom of cultures in conflict. Treating Liliuokalani's life with authority, accuracy and details, *Betrayal* also is a tremendously informative concerning the entire period of missionary activity and foreign encroachment in the islands.

$6.95   ISBN 0-935180-89-3

Rape in Paradise by Theon Wright

The sensational "*Massie Case*" of the 1930's shattered the tranquil image that mainland U.S.A. had of Hawaii. One woman shouted "Rape!" and the island erupted with such turmoil that for twenty years it was deemed unprepared for statehood. A fascinating case study of race relations and military-civilian relations.

$4.95   ISBN 0-935180-88-5

Hawaii's Story by Hawaii's Queen by Lydia Liliuokalani

The Hawaiian kingdom's last monarch wrote her biography in 1897, the year before the annexation of the Hawaiian islands by the United States. Her story covers six decades of island history told from the viewpoint of a major historical figure.

$6.95   ISBN 0-935180-85-0

The Legends and Myths of Hawaii by David Kalakaua

Political and historical traditions and stories of the pre-Cook period capture the romance of old Polynesia. A rich collection of Hawaiian lore originally presented in 1888 by Hawaii's "merrie monarch."

$6.95   ISBN 0-935180-86-9

Mark Twain in Hawaii: Roughing It in the Sandwich Islands

The noted humorist's account of his 1866 trip to Hawaii at a time when the islands were more for the native than the tourists. The writings first appeared in their present form in Twain's important book. *Roughing It* includes an introductory essay from *Mad About Islands* by A. Grove Day.

$4.95   ISBN 0-935180-93-1

SOUTH SEAS

Best South Sea Stories
Fifteen writers capture all the romance and exotic adventure of the legendary South Pacific including James A. Michener, James Norman Hall, W. Somerset Maugham, and Herman Melville.
$4.95   ISBN 0-935180-12-5

Love in the South Seas by Bengt Danielsson
The noted Swedish anthropologist who served as a member of the famed *Kon-Tiki* expedition here reveals the sex and family life of the Polynesians, based on early accounts as well as his own observations during many years in the South Seas.
$3.95   ISBN 0-935180-25-7

The Trembling of a Leaf by W. Somerset Maugham
Stories of Hawaii and the South Seas, including "Red," the author's most successful story, and "Rain," his most notorious one.
$4.95   ISBN 0-935180-21-4

Rogues of the South Seas by A. Grove Day
Eight true episodes featuring violent figures from Pacific history, such as the German filibuster who attempted to conquer the Hawaiian Islands for the Russian Czar; "Emma, Queen of a Coconut Empire"; and "The Brothers Rorique: Pirates De Luxe." Forward by James A. Michener.
$3.95   ISBN 0-935180-24-9

Horror in Paradise: Grim and Uncanny Tales from Hawaii and the South Seas, edited by A. Grove Day and Bacil F. Kirtley
Thirty-four writers narrate "true" episodes of sorcery and the supernatural, as well as gory events on sea and atoll.
$4.95   ISBN 0-935180-23-0

The Blue of Capricorn by Eugene Burdick
Stories and sketches from Polynesia, Micronesia, and Melanesia by the co-author of *The Ugly American* and *The Ninth Wave*. Burdick's last book explores an ocean world rich in paradox and drama, a modern world of polyglot islanders and primitive savages.
$3.95   ISBN 0-935180-36-2

The Book of Puka Puka by Robert Dean Frisbie
Lone trader on a South Sea atoll, "Ropati" tells charmingly of his first years on Puka-Puka, where he was destined to rear five half-Polynesian children. Special foreword by A. Grove Day.
$3.95   ISBN 0-935180-27-3

Manga Reva by Robert Lee Eskridge
A wandering American painter voyaged to the distant
Gambier Group in the South Pacific and, charmed by the
life of the people of "The Forgotten Islands" of French
Oceania, collected many stories from their past—includ-
ing the supernatural. Special introduction by Julius
Scammon Rodman.
$3.95   ISBN 0-935180-35-4

The Lure of Tahiti selected and edited by A. Grove Day
Fifteen stories and other choice extracts from the rich
literature of "the most romantic island in the world."
Authors include Jack London, James A. Michener, James
Norman Hall, W. Somerset Maugham, Paul Gauguin,
Pierre Loti, Herman Melville, William Bligh, and James
Cook.
$3.95   ISBN 0-935180-31-1

In Search of Paradise by Paul L. Briand, Jr.
A joint biography of Charles Nordhoff and James Norman
Hall, the celebrated collaborators of *Mutiny on the "Bounty"* and a dozen other classics of South Pacific literature.
This book, going back to the time when both men flew
combat missions on the Western Front in World War I,
reveals that the lives of "Nordhoff and Hall" were almost
as fascinating as their fiction.
$4.95   ISBN 0-935180-48-6

The Fatal Impact: Captain Cook in the South Pacific
by Alan Moorehead
A superb narrative by an outstanding historian of the
exploration of the world's greatest ocean—adventure,
courage, endurance, and high purpose with unintended
but inevitable results for the original inhabitants of the
islands.
$3.95   ISBN 0-935180-77-X

The Forgotten One by James Norman Hall
Six "true tales of the South Seas," some of the best stories
by the co-author of *Mutiny on the "Bounty."* Most of these
selections portray "forgotten ones"—men who sought
refuge on out-of-the-world islands of the Pacific.
$3.95   ISBN 0-935180-45-1

Home from the Sea: Robert Louis Stevenson in Samoa,
by Richard Bermann
Impressions of the final years of R.L.S. in his mansion,
Vailima, in Western Samoa, still writing books, caring for
family and friends, and advising Polynesian chieftains in
the local civil wars.
$3.95   ISBN 0-935180-75-3

Coronado's Quest: The Discovery of the American Southwest by A. Grove Day
The story of the expedition that first entered the American Southwest in 1540. A pageant of exploration with a cast of dashing men and women — not only Hispanic adventurers and valiant Indians of a dozen tribes, but gray-robed friars like Marcos des Niza — as well as Esteban, the black Moorish slave who was slain among the Zuni pueblos he had discovered.
$3.95   ISBN 0-935180-37-0

A Dream of Islands: Voyages of Self-Discovery in the South Seas by A. Gavan Daws
The South Seas . . . the islands of Tahiti, Hawaii, Samoa, the Marquesas . . . the most seductive places on earth, where physically beautiful brown-skinned men and women move through a living dream of great erotic power. *A Dream of Islands* tells the stories of five famous Westerners who found their fate in the islands: John Williams, Herman Melville, Walter Murray Gibson, Robert Louis Stevenson, Paul Gauguin.
$4.95   ISBN 0-935180-71-2

How to Order

Send check or money order with an additional $2.00 for the first book and $1.00 thereafter to cover mailing and handling to:
Mutual Publishing
2055 North King Street, Suite 202, Honolulu, HI 96819

For airmail delivery add $2.00 per book.

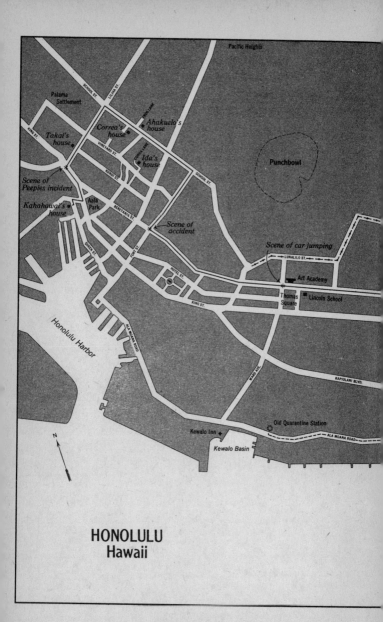

Pacific Heights

Palama Settlement

Correa's house

Ahakuelo's house

Takai's house

Ida's house

Punchbowl

Scene of Peeples incident

Kahahawai's house

Aala Park

Scene of accident

Scene of car jumping

LUNALILO ST.

Art Academy

Thomas Square

Lincoln School

KING ST.

Honolulu Harbor

ALA MOANA ROAD

WARD AVE.

KAPIOLANI BLVD.

N

Old Quarantine Station

Kewalo Inn

ALA MOANA ROAD

Kewalo Basin

HONOLULU
Hawaii

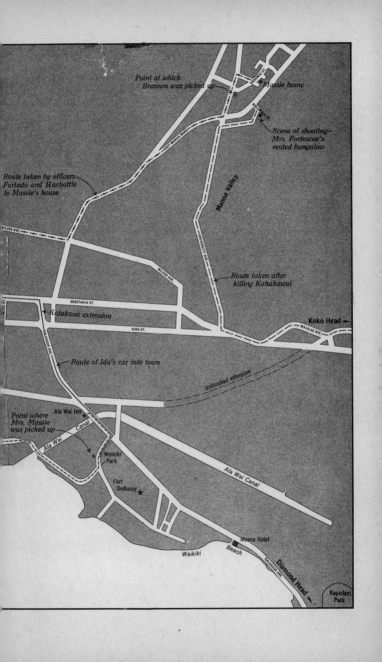

Point at which
Branson was picked up

Massie home

Scene of shooting—
Mrs. Fortescue's
rented bungalow

Route taken by officers
Furtado and Harbottle
to Massie's house

EAST MANOA ROAD

Manoa Valley

UNIVERSITY AVE.

Route taken after
killing Kahahawai.

WILDER AVE.

WILDER AVE.

BERETANIA ST.

Kalakaua extension

KING ST.

WAIALAE AVE.

Koko Head →

Route of Ida's car into town

Unfinished extension

Ala Wai Inn

Point where
Mrs. Massie
was picked up

Ala Wai
Canal

Ala Wai

★ Waikiki
Park

Ala Wai Canal

Fort
DeRussy ★

Moana Hotel

Waikiki   Beach

KALAKAUA AVE.

Diamond Head

Kapiolani
Park